W9-ADD-293

How Things Got Better

How Things Got Better

Speech, Writing, Printing, and Cultural Change

HENRY J. PERKINSON

BERGIN & GARVEY
Westport, Connecticut • London

Library of Congress Cataloging-in-Publication Data

Perkinson, Henry J.
    How things got better : speech, writing, printing, and cultural
change / Henry J. Perkinson.
        p. cm.
    Includes bibliographical references and index.
    ISBN 0–89789–431–6
    1. Communication and culture. 2. Social Darwinism. I. Title.
P94.6.P47   1995
302.2—dc20   94–38492

British Library Cataloguing in Publication Data is available.

Library of Congress Catalog Card Number: 94–38492
ISBN: 0–89789–431–6

First published in 1995

Bergin & Garvey, 88 Post Road West, Westport, CT 06881
An imprint of Greenwood Publishing Group, Inc.

Printed in the United States of America

The paper used in this book complies with the
Permanent Paper Standard issued by the National
Information Standards Organization (Z39.48–1984).

10 9 8 7 6 5 4 3 2

For Audrey

*The first work of grace is simply to enable us to
begin to understand what is wrong.*

Simon Tugwell

Contents

Introduction

How things got better is a snappy title. But what does it mean? What things am I talking about? And what do I mean by *better*?

The things I have in mind are those things that human beings create. This includes a lot, but it doesn't include everything. It doesn't include trees and animals and plants, or birds in the air, or fish in the sea. It doesn't include the natural world, the physical world. In short, when I talk about things getting better, I am talking about our social, political, and economic arrangements as well as institutions like schools, governments, businesses, and factories, churches, and families; and I am talking about our knowledge, for we create our knowledge, too. We can call these human creations culture.

How does culture get better? By *better* I mean what most people mean when they talk about things getting better: "Today is a better day." "These are better cookies." "He played better." "Little Tommy is behaving better." In most cases, people talk about something getting better by comparing it to some other something experienced in the past. Improvement, in other words, is measured historically. "This is better than that" means that some present something has fewer defects, faults, inadequacies, mistakes, errors, and limitations than some past something. "Today is a better day than yesterday." "These are better cookies than those you baked last week." "He played better than the last time." "Little Tommy is behaving better than he did before." So, by getting better I mean the diminution of those agreed-upon errors, mistakes, limitations, and inadequacies that always inhere in the culture that we fallible human beings create. When this happens, the life chances of those living in that culture improve.

How do things get better? How does culture improve? If we look at the world that human beings did not create—the world of nature—we can see, or it has been customary to see, a hierarchy of creation: from the single-celled microorganism to the human being. The complex organisms are, or have been said to be, better than the less complex organisms—have more life chances. Moreover, since the nineteenth century, most people have believed that the more complex organisms descended from the less complex. The species evolved: At each stage of evolution, species became more complex, less limited (i.e., a better species). This evolution took place, we think, as Darwin said it did: through a process called natural selection. Organisms had offspring which differed, or varied, slightly from their parents. Nature selected among those offspring those that were not fit and eliminated them. Over long periods of time, the species evolved through natural selection.

I suggest that cultural evolution is also Darwinian. The culture that we human beings create (our offspring, as it were) is always subject to further modification or refinement. With cultural evolution, however, selection is done not by nature, but by human beings. Critical selection replaces natural selection. Culture evolves or is created through the procedure of critical selection. We criticize the existing culture and then we modify it in light of the criticisms. Thus, all culture evolves through the modification or refinement of existing culture.

If I am correct about this and culture does improve through the procedure of critical selection, then whatever enhances or facilitates criticism will facilitate improvement. And this, I suggest, is precisely where the media come in: Media facilitate criticism. Media facilitate criticism by encoding culture, by making it objective. This objectification of culture helps people to perceive its inadequacies, its limitations, its faults—and once they uncover them, people do try to eliminate those faults. Insofar as those inadequacies or faults are eliminated, the culture improves. I do not claim that progress is inevitable. Things do not always get better. But they do, sometimes. In this book, I try to explain how this happens.

The media of most importance in the history of culture have been speech, writing, printing, and television. Historians have long noted the rapid changes in culture that came with the emergence of each of these media. These rapid cultural changes took place, I suggest, because the media encoded the existing culture of the times, objectified it or some aspect of it, and thereby facilitated criticism. Criticism uncovered inadequacies, weaknesses, limitations, and errors. This led to modifications and refinements of the existing culture.

When I say that media facilitate cultural improvement, I do not mean that the media are the agents of such improvement. Media have no agency. They neither determine nor cause cultural change. Human beings are the agents of cultural progress. I can sum up my argument in three propositions:

1. Cultural progress is possible and has taken place in Western civilization.

2. Such progress as occured came about through rational human action.

3. All media of communication—speech, writing, printing, and yes, television— have facilitated this cultural progress.

One last point: After bringing about dramatic changes in Western culture, each of these dominant media of communication became, in time, instruments to conserve culture against change. That is, in time, speech, writing, and print all became media to socialize people to the existing arrangements, to get them to subscribe to, accept, and even revere the traditional institutions as well as the customary policies and procedures and the reigning values, beliefs, and understandings.

Yet although media of communication do seem to wind up as preservers of the status quo, as means for preventing improvement, it is clear that they have helped to improve culture. Our culture is not perfect, but these dominant media of communication have helped us make our culture more practical and more rational. What follows is an attempt to explain how this happened.

How Things Got Better

Part One

How Speech Made Things Better

Chapter One

The Beginnings of Humanity

We do not, and simply cannot, know when language began. True, we can speculate and guess, but we can never corroborate our speculations and guesses. This is why, as long ago as 1865, the scientifically oriented Society of Linguistics of Paris included an article in its by-laws prohibiting discussion about the origin of language.[1] Yet the speculations continue until the present. Gordon Hewes has compiled a massive bibliography on the subject.[2] The New York Academy of Sciences recently held a symposium on the topic with over seventy-five contributors.[3] Moreover, the speculations get better. We have weeded out some of the bad guesses. Currently, scholars have abandoned the "bow-wow" theory, which held that language originated when humans created onomatopoeic words to imitate the sounds of nature—words like sneeze, splash, and bow-wow. Nor do scholars any longer accept the "yo-heave-ho" theory, which claimed that language evolved from the grunts and groans evoked by physical labor; or the "sing-song" theory, which placed the origin of speech in the love songs and chants of early humans; or the "ha-ha" theory, which has language evolving out of laughter.[4]

Most of the recent speculations about the origins of language have come about as the result of a number of ongoing experiments in teaching language to chimpanzees. Allen and Beatrice Gardner taught sign language to a chimp named Washoe, who, within four years, had a vocabulary of 130 words. Another researcher, David Premack, taught another chimp, Sarah, to use plastic disks as a medium for conversation. Sarah acquired a vocabulary of 120 words in two years.[5]

Even more impressive than what they were trained to do is the evidence of what chimps did voluntarily after training; they invented names for objects whose names they had not been taught—one invented the name *water-bird* for a duck, another used the label *open-eat-drink* to refer to a refrigerator, and a brazil nut was called a *rock-berry*, and an orange an *orange-apple*.

Recently, Irene Pepperberg has taught a parrot a vocabulary of forty English words. Alex the parrot can vocally identify some fifty different objects and can request them individually or refuse them if offered to him. He can also ask to be moved to different parts of the room.[6]

These experiments have generated interest in the origin of language, and new theories have appeared. One theory with considerable support is that all language originated in gestures.[7] Others have proposed that language is innate; according to this theory, we have a bioprogram for language.[8] The most widely held theory is that language is simply a continuation of the hypothesis-testing conduct that all organisms employ in adapting to the environment.[9] I subscribe to this last mentioned theory. My intention here, however, is not to add to the debates about the origins of language but to talk about the various functions of language in the evolution of culture.

Following Karl Buhler, I will concentrate on the main functions of language he identified: the expressive function, the signaling function, and the descriptive function.[10] To these, following Karl Popper, I will add the argumentative function.[11] In addition to these four functions, I will follow the work of Rosenstock-Huessy and briefly discuss other functions of language he identifies, such as the command function and the narrative function.[12]

My thesis is that language contributed to the evolution of culture by enabling human beings first to encode the existing, or pre-existing, culture, which enabled them, second, to criticize that culture. Criticism resulted in the uncovering of inadequacies, which led to the revision or modification of the existing culture. In short, through language, things got better.

THE EXPRESSIVE FUNCTION OF LANGUAGE

All language has an expressive function: It reveals, or purports to reveal, an inner state. In the course of evolution this was the original function of language. Organisms—plants as well as animals—can express their inner states in their overt behavior. If we look at a plant, we can tell that it needs water, sunlight, or repotting. Its outward appearance—its behavior, its color, its posture—expresses some inner state. Animals, too, express their inner states through skin coloration, sounds, body movements, posture, scents, and gestures. All of this I take to be language.

Human beings share this expressive function of language. We sometimes say to someone "You look happy"; or "you look hungry"; or "you sound tired," "sad," or "frightened." In such cases, we are taking that person's behavior—his or her facial expression, skin color, body movements, or the sound of his or her voice—as an expression of some inner state. Sounds and gestures, movements, scents, posture, and changes in coloration are but some of the ways we express our inner states, our feelings of pain and hunger, our fears, and our pleasures.

Being able to express inner states and being able to understand such expressions when others make them is necessary for our survival. Whenever we confront a snarling animal—such as a large dog—we take the sounds being emitted and the facial expressions as expressions of animosity toward us, and we try to avoid contact. We are able to find our way around other species—avoiding some, fondling others—only because of the existence of expressive language. Without expressive language, the newborn would not survive. By cries, shrieks, squeals, grunts, and other sounds, babies of all species express their inner state of hunger. This is not done by sound alone: When voiceless young cormorants are begging, they close their bills to express their need for food, and they open them for water.

Probably the most widely recognized example of how the expressive function of language increases survival is its use in biological reproduction. The urine odor of female dogs, for example, varies yearly according to their readiness to mate. A male dog can distinguish each variation to the extent that he can calculate the exact day when a female will be ready for mating, and dogs for miles around will congregate in her home area and wait for her that day. Many fish produce a phosphorescent light to express readiness to mate, whereas many birds evince vivid display behavior to express their desire to mate.

Once we recognize body movement, sounds and odors as language, we can readily see that every action of every organism is a form of self-expression. All behavior and all actions are expressions of inner states. But expressive language is not always understood. We do not always understand what the actions or the behaviors of others mean; we are not sure what inner states are being expressed. Is that animal hungry or lonely? Is that person happy or sad? Yet some expressions are more revealing than others: Expressions of anger, for example, or fear are usually clearly understood by other organisms, especially by organisms from the same species. Those expressions that more effectively reveal inner states become signals.

THE SIGNALING FUNCTION OF LANGUAGE

When some instance of self-expression leads to a specific reaction in another, then we can say it was taken as a signal. The emphasis here is on the reaction: The gesture, sound, or posture evokes, triggers, or releases behavior in others. The signaling function of language thus presupposes the expressive function and so is on a higher level. All animals, even microscopic ones, possess the signaling function of language. And plants, too, may have it. This is understandable because the emergence of the signaling function increased the life chances of organisms. For unless other organisms, especially members of one's species, respond to expressions of anger, hunger, fear, distress, then such expressions of inner states would not guarantee survival. And in a dangerous world responses to the life threatening expressions of other organisms have to be automatic and immediate, as do responses to calls of distress or fear. Through evolution, then the signaling function of language emerged in all species: Only those organisms would survive that could and did signal and respond to signals. Here are some examples of what I have called the signaling function of language:

Dolphins have a distress signal. When they hear it, all dolphins within hearing range become silent and search for the animal sending it. When they reach the distressed animal, they push it to the surface to breathe. The combined effort will keep a sick dolphin breathing for days, even weeks, and even dolphins that are complete strangers to each other will cooperate to do this without ceasing until the sick or injured animal gets better or dies.

Male singing birds mark out their territory with their song, flying from point to point to advertise their limits and to warn other males to keep out. Not only does this keep out males, it attracts females. Only a song that is exactly right for the species will attract females of that species. Any male whose song is not perfect fails to breed.

Most female moths give off a pheromone that brings males to them. With their feathered antennae, many male moths can smell a female from a distance of two miles.

The hyena's laughter is not laughter at all. It is an eating signal, calling the pack to a food find or a prey that has been killed.

Kangaroos signal alarm and danger by thumping their tails on the ground. This thumping can be heard for some distance, and all within earshot will scatter.

Some birds open their wings to reveal different colors or special markings when they are about to take flight. This signal provokes a whole flock of birds to take off at the same time.

Ants use gestures to indicate the kinds of duties they want their co-workers to perform.

Because the signal repertoire of animals is necessary for survival, these signals are part of their innate language. They exist as part of their biological make-up. Perhaps the most highly developed signaling functions of language yet discovered among animals are those of bees and primates. Bees signal by dancing. When a bee discovers an unusually good quality of food (nectar), it flies back to the hive and by a waggle dance signals both the direction and the distance of the find. It repeats the dance until enough bees respond to secure the nectar.

The signals used by primates include gestures as well as sounds. Mountain gorrillas, for example, use chest beating as an alarm signal. A gorilla will signal friendliness by folding its arms across its chest. Sound signals come in the form of grunts, screams, roars, and shrieks. Anthropologists have distinguished about twenty-two different sound signals that mountain gorillas use.

The rhesus monkey not only uses a shrill bark as an alarm signal but seems to have six different sounds for different kinds of predators and different locations of predators—a different call for a perched eagle than for a flying eagle, for example; and a different call for a snake. Each call elicits a different response from those who hear it: They climb trees to avoid snakes or hide in bushes to escape eagles. The monkey uses variations in tone to produce different signals. The same call can be used to express and signal fright and, with a slightly different tone, loneliness, if the animal is lost.

Among primates, chimpanzees have the largest repertoire of signals. They can use facial expressions to reveal a wide range of feelings, such as agressiveness, threat, attack, fear, hunger, pain, and so on. Simultaneously, they will produce various sounds. A low-pitched "ho" will be used to greet another chimpanzee, and occasionally friends will fling their arms around each other when they meet.

Contact signals are prominent among chimpanzees. If they are nervous, they will reach out and touch each other for reassurance. The first one reaches out palm up and the other accepts the palm with its palm down. A dominant male will touch the back of another male to give it confidence. A chimpanzee will pat a branch as an invitation to sit down. If a chimpanzee wants to sample another's food it will hold out its hand, palm up.

Until recently, it was thought that animals could perform only the expressive and signaling functions of language and not the descriptive function, which presupposes the first two and thus is on a higher level. We had assumed that only human beings possessed the descriptive function. But the aforementioned experiments with chimpanzees have demonstrated that, under controlled conditions, animals can learn the descriptive function of language. Even so, human beings have taught animals this function.

For human beings the descriptive function is normally and initially performed through speech. It was the evolution of human speech that first permitted the emergence of the descriptive function of language. The first human speech was not descriptive, however; it was nothing more than a modification of the signal function.

THE ORIGINS OF HUMAN SPEECH

Most anthropologists use speech as one of the criteria for distinguishing humans (*homo sapiens*) from their ancestors. Earlier humanoids could communicate: Through grunts, snorts, shrieks, cries, barks, and whistles, they could both express and signal. But they could not speak.

We have no way of knowing exactly when speech evolved, but we can assume that it did evolve because it had survival value: Being able to speak increased life chances.[13] Because survival value is always relative to the environment, human speech must have evolved when part of the population was being persistently forced into new ecological niches to which it was not fully adapted. This points to the great periods of glaciation, when ice slid down from the polar zones to cover the north temperate regions.

There were four different ice ages. The approximate dates of the middle, or coldest, part of each of these periods were 600,000; 400,000; 150,000; and 35,000 B.C. During the first two ice ages, *homo sapiens* had not yet evolved. *Homo habilis*, an ancestor, had evolved, but lived in Africa and so did not inhabit the north temperate zone where the glaciation took place. By the third ice age, a more recent ancestor had evolved, called *homo erectus*, who had migrated into the north temperate zone. However, *homo erectus* did not have a brain of the size and structure assumed necessary for the complete development of speech. The fossilized skulls of *homo erectus* indicate a lack of Broca's area, located in the frontal lobes.[14] In addition, the supralaryngeal tract necessary for human speech is also missing.[15]

Yet *homo erectus* did have a culture that distinguished him from the primates. He lived in caves, where he is known to have had fires; charred bones indicate that cooking had begun. He hunted large game animals of considerable variety: deer, horses, wild pigs, bison, elephants, rhinoceros, baboons, and other monkeys. He butchered them with stone hand-axes and stone choppers. Lacking speech, he learned and taught these skills for making fires and for constructing and using tools through signals and imitation—just as chimpanzees learn and teach the trick of peeling a vine stem and inserting it into ant hills to get ants.

So human speech must have emerged during the fourth ice age, which began about 70,000 B.C. The fossil record reveals that by this time, *homo sapiens* had evolved with a brain that had grown to more or less its present proportions. This fourth glaciation subjected humans to severe environmental pressures that endangered their survival. The great ice sheets changed the weather drastically, causing huge migrations of both animals and humans in search of food and warmth. Under these ecological conditions, the social order that humans had created must have undergone severe strain.

For eons humans had lived together in bands of roving hunters. Like animals, each band had lived with complete indifference toward other bands, as long as territory was respected. But now the scarcity of food led some bands to attack others in order to steal their food. There must have been frequent wars among the bands as well as revolutions and counterrevolutions within, when leaders failed to protect members of the tribe or failed to secure them sufficient food. It was a time of war, anarchy and chaos. In brief, Hobbes's description of the life of earliest times of human life was correct: The period of the fourth glaciation was "a time of continual strife, a time when every man was enemy to every man, a time when the life of man was solitary, poor, nasty, brutish and short."

It was out of these conditions that human speech arose. Through speech human beings created peace and political order. So the origin of speech was a political act. Once again, Hobbes was correct: The political state emerged as a way to overcome war, chaos, and anarchy. What Hobbes did not recognize, of course, was the crucial role of speech in the creation of the polity.

HUMAN SPEECH AND THE POLITY

Political organization had existed before the evolution of human speech. We know that primates do have political organization, so early humanoids must have had a similar polity: a polity consisting of roving bands under the leadership of a dominant male, or sometimes a fraternity of dominant males, responsible for control, defense, and leadership. This was, and is a polity based on power and fear: Dominant males must assert their prerogatives at all times to prevent insubordination and mutiny.

In this form of political organization, the leader rules through signals—signs that elicit automatic responses from followers. But because of the breakdown of political life brought about by the vast ecological changes during the last ice age, the old signals must have become less and less effective. Under the new conditions, those who *did* respond to the signals of the leader did not always survive, whereas those who did *not* respond did sometimes survive. Through these new contingencies of survival, then, the responses previously elicited by signals were extinguished. The result was the breakdown of political order—a time of anarchy and continual war.

Then, through speech, *homo sapiens* created a new political order. Here's how it happened.

Most scholars do agree that the imperative is the oldest form of human speech.[16] These first words, imperatives, were simply modifications of the calls used by primates and early humanoids to signal (signals like *Stop! Come! Help! Danger!*). But the imperative is not a signal. It does not elicit an immediate innate response from others. With the emergence of human speech, that language which had previously functioned as a signal (*Stop! Come! Move!*) is now encoded in words. This encoding of a command in words establishes a distance between the listener and the command, a distance that allows the listerer to appraise the command and to criticize it. In human speech, there is what Jacob Bronowski called a "delay" between the receipt of a message and the sending out of a message.[17] He regarded this as the central formative feature in the evolution of human language.[18] With the imperative, unlike the signal, we see this delay. The imperative is a command, an order. With an order, unlike a signal, the listener is not programmed to respond: He or she decides to obey. The act of obedience is the act of an agent; it is not a conditioned response.

With the imperative, those who would be leaders issue commands, but they address the listener as a "thou"—as an agent, as someone who can accept or reject their authority or the authority of the command. The listener decides whether or not the speaker is one to be obeyed. At any rate, with the beginning of human speech, language now takes on a new function, a command function. Listeners do not respond automatically, as happens with signals. There is a delay: There is a decision to obey or not to obey.

The imperative does not describe—it prescribes or proscribes. As Rosenstock-Huessy puts it, the imperative does not state a fact, it stages an act. The speaker who uses descriptive language accepts the world as it is; not so the the speaker who uses the imperative. The imperative changes the world. This is why the imperative evolved before the descriptive function of language. The political and social arrangements became intolerable during the last ice age. Humans had to change them. Through the imperative they created a new political order.

Through human speech, through the command function of language, *homo sapiens* created new political arrangements that had never exised before. It was a political order of authoritative leaders and obedient followers. Humans no longer lived in a natural polity based solely on power and fear. They now lived in a human polity. Things got better.

The first form of human speech, imperative speech, provoked the emergence of narrative speech. Commands or imperatives wake up the listener, who responds as an "I." The leader commands, "Move forward!" The listener responds, "I have moved forward." Narrative speech reveals an emerging self-consciousness, something new in the history of the species. Species other than *homo sapiens* are conscious: They experience feelings of pain and pleasure—at least those with central nervous systems do. But only *homo sapiens* seems capable of self-consciousness, capable of reflection on the self as an "I" who obeys a command addressed to a "thou." Through speech—narrative speech—human beings acquire an identity, what Julian Jaynes calls an "analogue I"—an I about which one can talk, can narrate.[19]

So human speech, first in the form of the imperative and the narrative, transformed people into self-conscious participants in a political process. The commands to act and the decisions to obey created a kind of trust between the speaker and the listener—a social contract—that marked the beginnings of a new, human, political order. No group of animals has ever engaged in a social contract; none has a polity based on trust.

Human speech made possible the new human polity based on a social contract, and human speech preserved it—through the naming function of language. With the naming function, we have the first instance of the descriptive use of language. The naming function of speech rose logically from the narrative function, which, as we saw, revealed the emergence of self-consciousness, an analogue I. To maintain identity and individuality, the analogue I had to have a name. The bestowal of a name tells the public who the person is. (His name is Sam.) But a name also calls forth the person; it tells him what he must be. (*Sam* means honest and industrious.) No animals name one another. Humans not only give their offspring names, they always do this in a serious ceremony in which they invoke the spirit to sanctify the act.

But in addition to conferring an identity and an individuality on its holder and in addition to introducing that person to his or her future, the bestowal of a name also initiates the person into the polity. Naming is always a political act. With the naming function, *homo sapiens* indicated that someone could not become a member of the polity as heretofore—by simply being born into it. Now one had to be initiated into the polity and take on responsibility for maintaining and preserving it. The bestowal of a name certified that the person was a legitimate member of the polity, with all the rights and duties ascribed thereto.

One of the consequences of naming was the institution of burial. Burial first arose as a solution to the political problem of succession of leaders. For once a trusted leader died, the people did not know whom they could trust. Burial ceremonies solved this. Such burial ceremonies of the leaders were always simultaneously inauguration ceremonies, in which the successor—through elaborate ritual—took the name of the now dead leader. Originally, then, only leaders were buried (or cremated), and burial was a political act. Burial is an essential part of human culture. No animals bury their dead. All human communities do.

With burial, human life begins. When an animal dies, its life is over. But a human being has a name, an identity, and there are narratives about his or her deeds and actions. As long as his or her name is recalled and deeds narrated the human being lives. Burial ceremonies create a human brotherhood—a brotherhood across the generations, a brotherhood unknown in the animal kingdom.

So, with the advent of human speech, things got better. With speech, language took on new functions. Through the command, the narrative, and the naming functions, *homo sapiens* created a new polity, a polity based on trust, not fear and intimidation; a polity founded on a social contract. In this new world they themselves had created, human beings attained self-consciousness; they acquired names and, therefore an individual identity and a worth to one another that had never existed before. For human speech created not only a new polity, a human polity, it also created a new society, a human society.

SPEECH AND SOCIAL ORDER

Early in evolutionary history, the sexes had become differentiated. Families emerged and, in some species, role differentiation between the sexes appeared. So society, a social order, did exist prior to *homo sapiens*. But what is distinctive about human society is that it is based on kinship. And kinship, as Levi-Strauss and others have pointed out, is not possible without speech.[20]

Animals—and earlier humanoids—have always had relationships: mates and offspring. But with speech, these relationships were given names: wife, husband, son, daughter, mother, father, brother, sister; as well as aunt, uncle, niece, nephew, etc. To apply these names in some uniform way, there had to be criteria and regulations. When did a female become a wife? When did a male become a husband?

The proper use of these names gave rise to another ceremony: marriage. If the marriage ceremony is essentially the bestowal of the names husband and wife on a man and a woman, why did *homo sapiens* invent such a ceremony? Once again, we see human culture evolving through humankind's efforts to eliminate, or overcome, the inadequacies recognized in the then existing arrangements. The marriage ceremony was invented as a means of securing peace, a way of terminating the continual strife common among most primitives and among early humanoids caused by the ceaseless eforts to capture one another's mates. Whereas the endless battles to steal and secure mates had been the basis for the old political order based on the power and strength of the dominant males, such goings-on were not appropriate for the new human polity. Marriage, sanctified by a ceremonious ritual, proscribed attempts at mate stealing; one was now a husband or a wife—excluded from sexual competition.

Moreover, the marriage ceremony was not simply the bestowal of the names husband and wife on a man and woman, it was a cermony in which this man and that woman accepted those names. Thus, the ceremony included the promissory function of language: "I will be, or I promise to be, a faithful, loyal, obedient, husband or wife." It is only by going through such a ceremony that one acquired the legitimate name of *husband* and *wife*, and only then could the offspring be called legitimate sons or daughters. With marriage, the family became the foundation of social order. People now began to perceive one another in new ways—not simply as males and females, but as kin: The offspring of those who were called husband and wife were called sons and daughters, and they called one another brother and sister and addressed their parents as mother and father.

In human society, people, throughout their lifetimes, progress through many different kinship roles: from son or daughter to husband or wife, then father or mother, and finally, grandfather or grandmother; along the way one also can become a brother or sister, aunt or uncle, cousin, nephew or niece, not to mention son-in-law, daughter-in-law, brother-in-law, sister-in-law . . . and on and on through a complex web of relationships. This complex web of kinship established social order and harmony. For each of these roles carried rights and privileges which guaranteed credit and trust among people. The names of kin command respect and enforce manners. (Do I not recall my father saying to me, "Don't hit her. She's your sister!") This respect, these rights, these privileges had never existed before. So with the human family, created through speech, things got better. People had a share in life never possible before.

Kinship gives rise to rules prohibiting incest. The rules vary greatly among different groups, but no human group is without them. The rules divide all members of the society into two categories—possible spouses and prohibited spouses. The rules of incest ensure that every community will practise some form of exogamy. As Levi-Strauss writes, "The prohibition of incest is less a rule prohibiting marriage with the mother, sister, or daughter, than a rule obliging the mother, sister, or daughter to be given to others."[21] These exchanges among families continually create new social alliances among people, rejuvenating society as well as reducing the continual strife common among animals and earlier humanoids.

So with human speech, things got better. The human family and kinship structures created by the naming and promissory funtions of language secured social peace, social stability, and social continuity.

Yet there is more to be told: human speech also created human knowledge.

SPEECH AND KNOWLEDGE

All organisms—from the lowly paramecium to *homo sapiens*—create their own knowledge. They do this by trying to solve problems through trial-and-error elimination.

Consider the lowly paramecium. When this primitive animal collides with an obstacle, it first reverses and then swims forward in another direction. We might say that through the collision, it "learned" that the way straight ahead is barred and, as a result, modified its behavior. The paramecium adapts to the environment through trial-and-error elimination. But why does this happen? The jolt to the paramecium, I suggest, leads it to modify its behavior because it, like all animals, has a sense of order. The paramecium "expects" regularity; it does not "anticipate" the jolt. But for this very reason, the collision serves as a refutation of the paramecium's "hypothesis" that it can continue on its path. Moreover, its reaction to the discovery of its error (reversing itself and then swimming forward in another direction) also indicates that the paramecium anticipates regularities, because this reaction depends on the implicit assumption that the object that gave it a jolt will continue to remain at the same point, for otherwise a change of course might bring it into collision with the same obstacle.[22]

All organisms have this sense of order, this expectation of regularities. It is this sense of order that enables them to advance their knowledge to learn to adapt to the environment. To survive, every animal must find out what the objects in its environment mean to it. And the organisms must take the appropriate action: locating the object, pursuing it, or fleeing from it. Acquiring this knowledge is a procedure of trial-and-error elimination: The animal tries one hypothesis or conjecture; if and when it is discovered to be erroneous, the animal modifies its behavior, eliminating the error by trying another hypothesis. Animals can do this only because they have a sense of order, an expectation of regularities. If animals did not sense that stationary objects will remain stationary, that moving objects will continue in a straight course, they could never locate objects, pursue them, or avoid them. For the same reason, the hunted animal deviates from a regular course—it zigs and zags to make its position less predictable.

What is different among species are the means or methods by which they can detect errors or recognize "refutations" of their "hypotheses." The paramecium has to wait until it bumps into things. But higher animals have evolved specialized senses—sight, hearing, taste, smell, and touch—through which they can detect and anticipate errors. The senses give due warning for avoidance or pursuit. By looking, listening, tasting, and smelling, animals avoid objects, pursue prey, and flee predators.

Because all species must continually solve problems of survival, early humans must have had a vast store of knowledge. They could classify objects: insects—edible or not; wood—usable or not; carnivores—threatening or not; fruits—ripe or not. They could make judgments about size, weight, direction, speed, and so on. They knew the specific qualities of mud, frozen ground, snow, ice, the varieties of stones, and the various plants. They knew how to make structures: tents, huts, corrals, pits, nets, fireplaces, and drainage ditches.[23] They knew how to hunt, how to secure food, clothing, and shelter. And as we have just seen, they knew how to maintain the social contract that guaranteed political order; they knew how to maintain the social order by respecting the institution of marriage and the rules prohibiting incest.

All of this knowledge was practical knowledge—skills that helped solve the problems of survival. And we must be clear that early humans, like animals, had *only* practical knowledge—one might call it kinesthetic knowledge: It was subjective knowledge, encoded in the nervous system as part of the repertoire of human behavior. Humans acquired all these skills through trial-and-error elimination and transmitted them to the young via signals and imitation. But until descriptive language evolved humans could not describe these skills, discuss them, criticize them.

They could only perform them.

Animals have the same kind of subjective, practical, kinesthetic knowledge. To a bird, for example, a cat is a potential predator: an amorphous complex of limited size, shape, and rough outline associated with a pattern of position and measurement in the environment. When the bird sees this sensory input, this triggers the pattern of flight behavior. But once they had created descriptive language, humans could know a cat in a way simply not possible for a bird: "This cat is black and white." "It has a round face." "It looks hungry." "That cat is sleeping." Birds and other animals cannot have this kind of knowledge because it is possible only through descriptive language.

The earlier humanoids, just like birds and other animals, had perceived objects and actions solely in relation to their own immediate problem situations: For them, like the animals, the world consisted of objects to be eaten, avoided, or attacked; every niche in the environment was a safe place, a warm place, or a dangerous place. But with the emergence of descriptive language, a human was able to discriminate an object as an object: "This is a tree." "That is a rock." Perceptions changed. Now, for the first time humans could perceive an object or an action apart frrom the amorphous complex of environmental and temporal characteristics with which the object is associated in the environmental problem situations the perceiver faces.[24]

The descriptive function of language, as we saw, first emerged as names—originally names for people and names for kin relationships. Next came names for objects and actions. Names for man-made objects (axe, spear, fire) and names for natural objects (tree, fruit, lion) were probably first spoken in rituals. In rituals, objects were spoken to, addressed as persons. Only after they had been spoken to, given a name, could they be spoken about. The names for actions also were first spoken in rituals as commands or evocations (*Cook! Kneel! Pray!* became *cooking, kneeling, praying*). The evolution of descriptive language is repeated ontogenetically in children who at the age of two or three—when descriptive language first emerges—discover that every object has a name, a name that carries no implications of the various ad hoc functions, activities, or relationships of the object with other objects. The child now uses words like *cookie* or *car* as the descriptive names of objects, not as commands or requests related to some problem situation.[25]

Descriptive language enabled humans to create a new world—a world of knowledge. By naming and describing objects and actions humans created Information, a kind of knowledge that, as Jacob Bronowski points out, simply did not exist for the earlier humanoids.[26] And *homo sapiens* could transmit this kind of knowledge to the young with greater facility than earlier humanoids could ever transmit practical knowledge through signals and imitation. With descriptive language adults could say, "Don't eat that apple. It is not ripe; it is too green."

Now humans could create verbal maps of the territory where they hunted. They could name every place that contained a certain kind of food, describe how to get there from here, and tell others what to look out for. They could name the animals and distinguish the young from the old and male from the female (the calf from the steer, the colt from the horse, the cow from the bull). Moreover, with descriptive language, hunters could cooperate and work as a team, each with assigned roles, much more efficiently than was possible by using signals. So, with descriptive language human beings' practical skills improved and their life chances improved. Things got better.

Perhaps the most astonishing consequence of the evolution of descriptive language was that knowledge now became objective. Information—the new kind of knowledge made possible by descriptive language—is not part of a person's nervous system. It is not kinesthetic knowledge; it is exosomatic. Knowledge now can exist apart from the knower, encoded in language.

Once knowledge became objective, it could advance and grow much more rapidly. Now humans could encode their practical knowledge, converting it into information: "This is how to make an axe." "Deer come to the lake to drink every morning." They could describe the problem situations they confronted: "How can I kill that lion?" "How can I destroy my enemies?" "How can I protect my family?" They could describe the actions they had taken in the past and those planned for the future. Most important, they could now criticize that knowledge as they never could before when it was subjective, practical knowledge. They could develop the argumentative function of language.

THE ARGUMENTATIVE FUNCTION

As long as knowledge was kinesthetic, subjective, a part of the knower, it was difficult to criticize it. One had no distance from it. But once knowledge was encoded in language, once it became objective, humans could approach it critically. They could now discover mistakes in the description of the problem situations and uncover inadequacies in the actions taken. Descriptive language and argumentative language helped humans become better problem solvers than before. Through language they could engage in indirect problem solving—describing the problem situation, proposing solutions and then criticizing them. This was a much safer way of conducting trial-and-error elimination and a more effective way of surviving. With the descriptive and argumentative functions of language, things got better. Human knowledge improved.

Earlier humanoids (*homo erectus*), as we saw, had created a culture. This culture had not changed for thousands of years. Tens of thousands of generations had maintained patterns of technological traditions without discernable change.[27] But during the last ice age *homo sapiens* through the medium of language began to break out of this monotony.

We know that during the Aurigmacian period in Europe, which lasted until perhaps 25,000 B.C., the tool kits used by *homo sapiens* underwent improvement, including, for the first time, the appearance of blade tools as well as tools to make other tools. It is also important to note that whereas the tools of the earlier traditions had lasted relatively unchanged for literally millions of years, from this time on the styles and traditions persisted for much shorter spans of time and were more localized.[28] Both of these characteristics indicate that the styles and traditions of tools were now subject to continual criticism and were then modified in light of the criticism. During this period, we also find dramatic improvement in weapons: spears, spear throwers, and harpoons. In addition, for the first time, there are indications of the use of pottery and cookware.

I am suggesting, as have many anthropologists,[29] that human speech, especially the descriptive and argumentative functions, made possible this technological improvement, this improvement in tools and weapons and utensils. Humans could now describe their artifacts and thereby criticize them. "This axe is heavy." "This blade is dull." Once again, through language, things got better. With better weapons and tools, *homo sapiens* became a better hunter—the best hunter of all species. Descriptive and argumentative language enabled humans to create a new world, a world of information. *Homo sapiens* didn't just have better skills, better tools, better practical knowledge than their ancestors. They had more. They had a whole new world of knowledge. First, they had knowledge or information about their own culture, about what they had created: their polity and their society. They had information about hunting and killing, about weapons, tools, nets, and traps. They had information about the relations of child to parent, man to woman, leader to follower, tribe to tribe. All this information was encoded in language. So it was objective knowledge. It could be criticized and then modified in light of the criticism. A second kind of knowledge now possible was knowledge about the natural physical world, a world humans had not created but a world they lived in together with all other species. Those species that had evolved earlier than *homo sapiens*, including earlier humanoids, did not have knowledge about the natural physical world. They only knew, and know, how to function more or less successfully in that world. Theirs was, and is, solely practical, subjective, kinesthetic knowledge. It was only with the evolution of descriptive language that humans could create a world of objective knowledge about the natural world. Now humans could know that flowers bloom, that butterflies emerge from cocoons. They could know that there are earthquakes, epidemics, eclipses, and many other goings-on in the universe. They could know these things and these goings-on only because they could name them, describe them. Animals cannot, and earlier humanoids did not, have such knowledge.

Yet humans could now do more than describe. They could argue, which means that they could explain. They could explain those goings-on in the physical universe and explain why things were as they were in their polity and their society. Humans explained such things by telling stories about them, stories that made things coherent or understandable.[30]

Humans created stories because of that sense of order, that expectation of regularities that I have suggested is innate in all animals. After having created new arrangements by means of language—political arrangements and social arrangements—and after having created a new world of information—information about the all they had created, their culture, as well as information about the physical universe they inhabited—after having done all this, humans then proceeded to impose order on that world of information by presenting arguments in the form of stories that would explain why the world was the way it was.

Earlier, in their sacred rituals humans had spoken to objects; they had evoked and commanded events. By naming them, humans had brought them into existence. The initial naming of objects and actions was always a ritual ceremony in which a spirit or god was evoked to sanctify the proceedings. Thus objects and activities not only had names, they had gods. There was a god of cooking, a god of hunting, as well as a god of the hearth, a god of the fire. And humans often invoked the appropriate god before they hunted, or cooked, or engaged in any specific activity, or before they used an axe, lit a fire, drank a drink. So when humans set out to impose order on the world of information they had created, the only order they could impose was the order they were familiar with, the order of their own daily existence. By naming objects and events, humans had brought them into existence as beings, as persons. By invoking a god or spirit to sanctify this act of naming, they had created a spiritual being who could control events or influence objects. Accordingly, early *homo sapiens'* explanations of the goings-on in the universe were animistic. They explained physical phenomena as the acts of personified or anthropomorphized objects and happenings: The sun and moon were alive, as were rivers, mountains, trees and brooks—all were manifestations of intelligence. Stones, too, and salt, grain, and wood—all had human-like personalities. Some happenings were said to be the acts of gods. Rain, for example, or snow, or thunder and lightning, or calamities and catastrophies like sickness and accidents—all were attributed to gods, who behaved as they did because they were pleased or angry.

Early *homo sapiens* also made up stories to explain the origins of the polity and the society. Humans had created these through the medium of speech. But now they were explained as the work of the gods. Usually these stories had some god or gods giving humans a list of rules and commandments to follow. Sometimes the gods appointed one person as leader or ruler.

Because the world of early *homo sapiens* was peopled with animate objects and gods that human beings could neither control nor command, humans had to cooperate with all that existed. They had to accommodate to a physical universe wherein all objects had minds and personalities of their own. They had to propitiate the gods who directed the course of events—or pacify or cajole them. This brought forth new ceremonies and rituals—religious ceremonies—and new roles—priests and shamans.

Humans have always been the victim of their own stories. When early *homo sapiens* conjectured that most of what was going on, or had gone on, was the acts of animated objects, or happenings that gods had ordained, they concealed the human origin of culture. In the myths and stories humans created to explain and order things they hid from themselves the fact that they, through speech, had created their culture and their world of knowledge. Now, because humans took these things to be the creations of the gods, the polity and the society became secure—arrangements to be preserved and conserved, not criticized and improved. And their knowledge, too, became sacred lore—something to be preserved and passed on, intact, from generation to generation. Thus, the medium of speech, after having wrought the most profound revolution since life began—the creation of human culture—now calcified that culture into what we call an oral culture: traditional, conservative, unchanging.

Only when humans could achieve some distance from their stories and myths would they be able to criticize them, to uncover their inadequacies and then modify those myths in the light of their criticisms. This happened when human beings developed the new medium of writing. With writing, things got even better.

Part Two
Writing and the Origins of Civilization

Chapter Two

Proto-Writing

Speech made man human; writing civilized him. Civilized humans live in a world entirely different from the world of tribal humans. Tribal humans interacted with their world through speech alone. Their oral culture necessarily limited the quality and quantity of their interactions. Their gods were immanent spirits that animated all that exists, making the world of objects a numinous world: Every stone, every tree, every stream was an agent with a mind and will of its own. In a world such as this humans could not impose their will on other things; they could only try to live in harmony with them—through compliance, or sometimes through cunning and trickery or cajolery and entreaty. Human beings had no projects other than survival.

If their interactions with things were limited and circumscribed, so were their interactions with other human beings—limited primarily to their kin. The network of relationships they were born into determined who they were—their position and status in the tribe. They were safe and secure within the tribe, but not beyond its perimeters. There was little or no specialization of tasks, so tribal humans had no opportunities for advancement or growth. As to their relations to the past and future, tribal humans relied solely on memory: their own memory of those who had come before them, and the memory of those who followed them. Writing, when it emerged, encoded the culture that humans had created through speech. This better enabled them to criticize it and then modify it in the light of that criticism. Writing allowed humans to create a new world, a civilized world, where they had new and different kinds of interactions with other human beings, new interactions with objects in the world, new interactions with the past and the future, and new interactions with the spiritual world they had created.

THE EXPRESSIVE AND SIGNALING FUNCTIONS OF
PROTO-WRITING

No one knows who invented writing, or even when it began. Most scholars do credit the Sumerians with inventing it sometime in the fourth millenium B.C. But much, much earlier than this human beings had invented what can be called proto-writing. The earliest proto-writing served an expressive function. For writing, it appears, evolved through the same stages of development as human speech: first the expressive function, then the signaling function, next the descriptive function, and, finally, the argumentative function. Here I want to talk about the first three functions of proto-writing. Indeed, there is no proto-writing that functions argumentatively. The argumentative function of writing had to await the invention of the phonetic alphabet.

Anthropologists have found examples of expressive proto-writing in caves that go back to before the upper paleolithic period. The earliest instances are imprints of hands in black and red paint. We know that these were deliberate expressions because some of them are negative imprints made by blowing paint against the wall where the hand was placed.[1] Other caves contain tracings of animals. Later, in the upper paleolithic period, we find signs intentionally incised, or painted, on objects or on rock walls; and graphic, or sculptured, reproductions of the forms of human beings. During this period humans made those truly remarkable and now widely known cave paintings found in France and Spain. John Pfeiffer has suggested that this paleolithic cave art was more than simply expressive proto-writing. According to him, it served a mnemonic function, or what I call a signaling function. Hidden deep in the recesses of caves, these paintings, he suggests, played a role in the initiation ceremonies of young boys. Most of the paintings depict scenes of hunting or are about hunting. At that time, the lore of hunting was vital for survival; it had to be preserved. The paintings helped the elders remember and elicited or triggered their memories—those memories of the hunting lore that were to be transmitted to the young.

Of course, these paintings may simply have been expressive proto-writing, as I have suggested. We cannot tell. But we do know that sometime after they started to talk, humans did begin to use written signs as signals.

Written signals appeared when a written expression—a mark, a tracing, an incision—became a symbol, a sign that stood for something or for someone, a sign that was recognized clearly and its significance understood immediately. Written signals brought no changes in the culture. The first written signals actually helped to solidify and conserve the existing social and political arrangements. Proto-writing, for example, helped make the family more secure. Oral humans lived in tribes, in which the family was the basis of social order. New families were created by the ceremony of marriage, in which, as we saw, a man and a woman accepted the names of husband and wife. The need for some tangible evidence that people were married gave rise to one form of proto-writing: a tattoo, a mark, an incision, a ring, a dress, or a headdress—something more or less permanent to attest to the fact that they were now identifiable as husband and wife.

In addition to contributing to the permanence of the basic social institution of marriage, proto-writing helped make the political institutions more secure. The tribal polity of an oral culture is based on the social contract between the people and their leader. When the leader died, a new contract had to be renewed with a new leader. This inauguration ceremony gave rise to proto-writing—a headdress, a costume, a tatoo, an emblem, or an insignia—something tangible, something more or less permanent that was conferred on the new leader to signal that he truly was the leader. Proto-writing thus made the polity more permanent by creating the office of leader. The office transcended the leader; it perdured beyond the lifetime of any particular leader. But the office existed only by virtue of the fact that there was some tangible sign, mark, or insignia that the people could confer on a new leader, extending to him the power and the force of the office.

Not only the leader, but the followers, too, had to engage in the social contract. For the followers, this took place through an initiation ceremony. Those undergoing initiation received some permanent, tangible evidence—in the form of a tattoo, an incision, or a costume—that signaled that they were now truly members of the tribal polity.

A final example of signal proto-writing is the totem. Each tribe and clan had its own name, its own identity. Often this was the name of the animal that helped the tribe survive. For in the beginning, paleolithic humans survived simply by following animals that were larger, more powerful, and swifter than they. Those animals could break through the underbrush and create paths impossible for humans to make. They could track and kill prey that humans could not take on. Humans survived by foraging on the remains of their prey. So human beings must have held those animals in awe and must have idenfified themselves as their followers.[2]

In time, of course, once they began to speak, humans were able to improve their weapons so that they became more proficient hunters, able now to track and kill the very animals they had once held in awe. But they sill remained followers of the animals. Often, tribes of hunters specialized: They followed bison, or they followed elk, or they followed reindeer. From them, and through them, the tribe secured its food, its clothes, its weapons, its artifacts. Understandably, then, members of the tribe carved figures or drew pictures of those animals they followed and upon whom their lives depended. These carvings and pictures became totems and emblems—signs that stood for the tribe itself. This emblematic proto-writing created a group identity ("I'm a member of the elk tribe") that had not existed before, a fraternity that helped bind together the members of the tribe, making their social and political arrangements more permanent.

THE DESCRIPTIVE FUNCTION OF PROTO-WRITING

So far, I have suggested that proto-writing, which at first served only expressive and signaling functions, exercised a conservative force on human culture by preserving the existing political and social arrangements, helping to make them more permanent and secure. But when people began to use proto-writing to serve a descriptive function, it helped make things better. Most importantly descriptive writing destroyed animism.

When humans first began to speak, they named things. This created a world that had never existed before—an objective world of information, a world of objects and events. Then humans tried to explain the going-on in that world by telling stories or myths. As they understood and explained, there were immanent spirits that animated all that exists, making the world of objects a numinous world. But then sometime after they had named the objects in their world, and somtime after they had composed stories to explain their actions, humans began to count some of these things and some of these goings-on. Counting destroyed that numinous world.

Possessing, like all animals, a biological clock that distinguishes sleep time from wake time—night from day—it seems reasonable to assume that humans first began counting that which they could already distinguish: days and nights. These early attempts at counting brought recognition of a new kind of regularity: recurrence. Humans discovered that some things would be again as they had been before and were now: the day and the night, the phases of the moon, the seasons—all had a recognizable regularity, recognizable, however, only by counting. Human beings counted the days that measured the phases of the moon and also counted the days that measured the bodily processes of women: the number of days between menstruation, how many days pregnancy lasted, how long a new mother could give milk. These processes, too, revealed a temporal regularity manifest in the proto-writing of numerical notation. For as humans counted they made notations—marks or incisions on a stick, bone, or stone—that, in time, disclosed these regularities. For once these various passages of time were encoded in proto-descriptive writing, these different goings-on could be explained, interpreted, and ordered. Humans could construct calendars for these events.

Through careful, painstaking analysis with a magnifying glass and microscope, Alexander Marshack has discovered notations on some of the mobilary art work from the paleolithic caves. He suggests that some of these objects served as lunar calendars. Paleolithic hunters used these calendars to foretell when the moon would shine brightly, and when not—information of vital importance to man the hunter and man the hunted. Over time, through trial-and-error elimination, humans improved their calendars, which enabled them to make more accurate predictions about periods of light and periods of darkness, periods of cold, warm periods, and hot periods. Marshack has also suggested that the so-called Mother Goddess statues found in profusion in paleolithic caves were female clendars used to instruct young girls in the physiological changes taking place in their bodies and used also by pregnant women and mothers to measure the length of pregnancy and the length of lactation.[3]

Once they began counting, humans created a totally new world. For the unexpected and truly remarkable consequence of counting was the change it brought about in the cosmology of human beings. The first cosmology had been the product of human speech. Through speech humans had created a numinous world, a world in which everything was alive, every object an agent who acted through intelligence and choice—rocks, trees, rivers, and mountains were all animate.

Counting denuminized that world. Numerical notation encoded the world that humans had counted, encoded it quantitatively. First, they made cuts and incisions, then they gave these cuts names—"one," "two," "three," . . . —and devised signs for each number. When objects or events were encoded as quantities, humans could manipulate them. They could add quantities and subtract them; they could establish identities betwen quantities (equal to) and recognize that this quantity is greater than (or less than) that. As a result, humans achieved a distance from this world never possible before. Now they could, and did criticize the explanations they had earlier created about the goings-on in the world.

When they discovered the mathematical regularities objects displayed in their actions, when they uncovered the necessary mathematical relationships that existed among these objects, humans realized that they could predict the behavior of these objects. Such understanding contradicted the belief that those objects were alive, that they possessed intelligence and will, that they acted with purpose and intent of their own. In the face of this contradiction humans now began to denuminize their world. The things they counted ceased being animate beings and became objects—inanimate objects that had identifiable characteristics and describable traits, objects that followed regular patterns in what they did or in what could be done to them.

The agency that humans had earlier imputed to those objects did not, however, totally disappear. It became transcendent. No longer immanent in the objects themselves, these agencies now became spirits or gods that lived beyond this physical world in another world, heaven. In spite of their distance, however, these gods determined and controlled the goings-on of objects in this world. Thus, there was a god of the river, a sun god, a moon god, an earth god, and on and on—a god for everything that existed, a god that controlled from a distance.

This denuminization of the world must have taken place over a long period of time. Humans did not forget the time when the world was alive, when it was animated by spirits. They created stories and myths to explain what had happened—myths that recount how the gods had once dwelt on earth and then, later, ascended into heaven. In accord with this denuminization of the world, the animal totems of the tribes and clans became symbols for some transcendent god. But because the gods had intelligence and will, like humans, we find that the images and statuary used to depict the gods gradually, over time, became more anthropomorphic—they became part human, part animal, and, in some cases, finally emerged as fully human figures.[4]

When they began counting, human beings wound up creating three worlds, where earlier there had been one. In place of the monolithic numinous world created by the earliest human speakers, where all objects were animate—like humans—there now emerged (1) an inanimate world of physical objects, a world that could be counted and measured; (2) a world of human beings, who—unlike the occupants of the first world—were intelligent agents capable of choice; and (3) a world of the gods, who, like humans, were intelligent agents and who could—from a distance—control, guide, direct, determine all that happens in the first two worlds.

Before descriptive proto-writing (in the form of counting and numerical notation) came along human beings had had an "I-thou" relationship with the rest of the universe. Writing created an "I-it" relationship with the objects of the physical world, retaining an "I-thou" relationship with the gods who now resided in heaven. Through writing, then, humans became conscious of their own uniqueness—different both from physical objects and from the gods, and somewhere in between them in the chain of being. Moreover, humans now came to believe that they were on earth to serve the gods by doing what the gods told them to do. So, for the first time in their history humans had a project beyond survival. By punctiliously serving their gods, humans would preserve the civilization they had so laboriously created.

As the numinous world of the earliest human beings gradually gave way, it was replaced by the magical world of proto-literate humans. For writing not only caused the spirits to retreat from this world and become gods who ordained whatever happened in this world, writing also now became the medium of communication between gods and humans. Humans communicated with the gods primarily through oral prayers and songs, but the gods communicated to them through signs. Just as the gods could control the goings-on in the world from their distant heaven, so they could, through signs, communicate with humans from a distance. And so it came to pass that in the world in which humans now lived, anything could be a sign of something else—a storm, a leaf, a stick, a summer rain, a bolt of lightning: Each could be a sign that a god was angry or pleased; it could be a warning from the gods or a threat, a message. The world had become magical. Nothing was what it appeared to be. Everything was, or could be, a sign. Every object, every event could have a hidden message, could contain a message from the gods.

The need to know the will of the gods gave rise to the art of divination and to the office of priest-diviner. The priests, people thought, could better divine the messages from the gods, could better tell humans what the gods wanted them to do. And well they could, simply because the priests monopolized the art of mathematics, through which they created calendars that enabled them to predict the monthly, seasonal, and annual changes in nature that are so relevant to the preservation of civilization.

The office of priest now stood just beneath the office of political leader and shared some of its powers. The priests usually served as advisors to the political leaders, who now, as a result of such sage counsel, more effectively controlled and directed the people of the tribe. The political leader told the people what the gods wanted them to do, what tasks to perform.

The emergence of the offices of political leader and priest created permanent social hierarchies and social inequalities that had not existed before. Yet without hierarchy and inequality, civilization could not have come into being.[5] For so long as humans had lived in a numinous world, as one agent among many others, they had no special place in the world, no task, no project, no mission. In the magical world they now lived in, however, humans had their orders—orders from on high, orders from the gods, communicated to them through their leaders.

The retreat of the spirits from the physical world had made that world less enchanted, had turned it into a world of objects—objects that humans could manipulate, control, and use to serve their own purposes. But make no mistake about it: Those purposes were dictated to humans by the gods—via priests and political leaders. Human beings, thus directed and organized, had a new power, a new freedom. In consequence, things got better. Life chances improved. For their new understanding of the world gave human beings the power and strength to survive the ecological crisis that befell them when the last ice age ended.

THE BEGINNINGS OF CIVILIZATION

During the last glacial period, different tribes of paleolithic humans spread out to Greece, and then to the near East, through Siberia to the new world and also to China and Japan. Then, about 13,000 years ago, a global warming trend caused the mile-high glaciers that had covered most of the Northern hemisphere to begin to break away toward Greenland. As the climate became more mild, the flora changed from grassy plains to forests of evergreens and birches. The loss of grazing lands produced an ecological catastrophe. The giant elk, the bison, the woolly rhinoceros, and the woolly mammoth, all disappeared, while horses, cattle, musk oxen and antelope sharply decreased.[6] Humans could no longer survive through hunting alone. Once again, human beings entered a time of anarchy, war, and decadence as they struggled to survive under new ecological conditions.

Some continued to follow the ever-dwindling herds of animals as they traveled in search of food. Many of these followers must have died. Some increased their efforts to gather food: nuts, berries, roots—anything edible. But they could not do this in the winter, so many of these perished, too. Some turned to fishing and digging for crustaceans. But this, too, was difficult during the winter months. Some began efforts to produce food by planting crops.

As early as 13,000 B.C., people in what is now Turkey, Syria, and Iraq were harvesting wild wheat and domesticating some of the animals native to the area. In time, they also domesticated the cereal grains by weeding and digging the soil with sticks and antlers after using fire to clear the land and fertilize it. This slash-and-burn agriculture made the farmers into nomads, who periodically had to move on in search of new lands to farm. They, too, had difficulty in securing enough of a harvest to last through winter. Moreover, various natural disasters—drought, flood, blight—could annihilate their crops and the herds of animals they had domesticated. They also lived in constant danger of having their crops plundered and pillaged by outsiders. Yet many managed to survive—indeed as Hugh Thomas notes nomadic farming lasted in Russia until well into the nineteenth century A.D.[7]

In only a few regions did permanent settlements appear, and these did not usually last—except for those that appeared between the ninth and seventh millenium B.C. along the great rivers: the Nile, the Tigris, the Euphrates, the Indus, and the Yellow. As early as 9000 B.C. we find evidence of settled life in villages along the Tigris and Euphrates in South Mesopotamia (now Iraq). Here civilization began.[8] Writing made it possible.

In all these early settlements on the rivers, farming depended on the flood that came every spring. In all cases (except for the Nile, where it was not necessary), the people built vast irrigation networks to hold the flood water and direct it to the farmlands. This hydraulic agriculture was possible only because the people knew when the rivers would flood, when the tides would rise and fall. This knowledge came from the priests, who used calendars—written calendars—to make accurate and dependable predictions. The early lunar calendars had been continually refined and improved and, in time, were supplemented by calendars based on the sun.[9] In this magical world they had created, people viewed the flooding of the rivers as the work of the gods. The priests used the calendars to divine when the gods would cause the rivers to flood, and then they informed the political leaders what the gods had ordained. The political leaders could then tell the people what to do.[10] Clearly, the gods had saved the people. The Sumerians, for example, the first people to establish city states in Mesopotamia, believed that the god Enki filled the Tigris and Euphrates with sparkling water and stocked them with fish. Moreover,

> The plough and yoke he directed,
> The great prince Enki.
> Opened the holy furrows,
> Made grain grow in the perennial field.[11]

The other early river civilizations also credited their escape from the hazardous struggle for survival to the beneficience of the gods—not to their written calendars.

The intensive agriculture practiced in the river settlements resulted in high productivity of the cereal grains that originally grew wild in those areas. Moreover, these foodstuffs could be stored for long periods of time, which enabled people to survive the winters and even endure periods of drought, blight, and other natural calamities. The population increased, but so did the crops.[12] In time, there emerged a system of distribution that created the wealth necessary for civilization.

When people settled down in the river valleys and did what the gods told them to do the ground brought forth large crops of grain, which were, of course, the property of the gods. The farmers, therefore, brought the grain to the gods—to the temples, where the priests fed some of it to the gods.[13] The rest they stored and then redistributed to the people as the gods ordained.[14] For the first time in history, human beings had something vital to their survival that they could accumulate in large quantities. Moreover, the accumulated grain became something that could be exchanged for other goods not available in the river communities, and so they were able to trade grain for wood, stone, and metal.

PROTO-WRITING AND THE NEW ECONOMIC ARRANGEMENTS

The grain brought to the temple was stored in jars sealed with clay, and then the jars' contents were identified by means of a seal that could be rolled around the edge of a jar of any size. The cylindrical seal consisted of a picture or pictograph and a numerical weight or measure. The priests could then transpose the symbols and numbers to clay tablets or to parchment, which served as records of the commodities received stored, and distributed. Now it became possible to know from a distance—by consulting the inventory records—what was in the storage area, and to know what exchanges had taken place—by consulting the account records.

By encoding these commodities in writing, people did, in time, come to recognize how cumbersome and inadequate their traditional patterns of reciprocal trading were. So instead of actually physically exchanging commodities, people could use their written records in the exchange transaction. They could exchange goods at a distance. In addition to records of inventory and accounts, descriptive proto-writing also enabled people to create bills of lading, orders, receipts, bills of sale, contracts, letters of credit, and coins[15]—all of which made trade more complex, more abstract, and more distant from the commodities.

The development of complex trade created a class of merchants and traders who worked under the aegis of the temple. The division of labor did not stop there. For because they no longer lived in a numinous world in which all objects were alive, humans could now construe almost anything as a commodity—something to be measured or weighed, something to be counted and assigned a quantitative value; almost anything could be traded and exchanged, bought and sold—even human beings. Now, for the first time, some human beings bought and sold other human beings as commodities. Slaves, however, were never great in number in Mesopotamia and seemed to be used as private servants. But forced labor did come into being both in Egypt and Mesopotamia. There, humans were treated as commodities, hired for their labor power, and used to build dams, irrigation canals, roads, temples, colossal statuary, and other edifices, all of which became marks of civilization.

Once they began to view the world quantitatively, people realized that the value of any commodity could be enhanced by refining it, processing it, transforming it into a useful or artistic object. Not everyone could do this, of course. It required special talents and abilities possessed by only a few. Prior to the emergence of civilization, production had been a household matter, with each family of the tribe engaged in essentially similar tasks. There had been no division of labor—except for the offices of political leader and priest. But now some people were liberated from farming to become specialists—craftsmen and artisans, who worked on the wood and stone materials the civilized communities secured in exchange for their grain. These specialists initially, for at least part of their time, worked for the temple: stone masons, sculptors, brick makers, carpenters, potters, metal workers, leather workers, and basket weavers.[16] The temple also employed men as fishermen and herdsmen, and women as wool cleaners, spinsters, cooks, brewsters, and keepers of pigs. Supervisory personnel also emerged to guide, direct, and keep account of all this work: architects, astronomers, engineers, and accountants. These were all specialists in mathematics, which was the most developed descriptive language humans had yet developed.

These new economic arrangements destroyed the traditional basis of society. Under tribalism, that base had been the kinship network. But now one's occupation, not one's relatives, determined one's place in the social order. This civilized social order was hierarchical—a hierarchy based on function. True, all members of the city or city-state served the gods, but they performed different functions—functions arranged in a hierarchy from the king and the priests at the top, to the slaves at the bottom. The large group of freemen in the middle was also hierarchically ordered: At the top were the mathematical specialists, then the traders, artisans, and craftsmen, down to the herdsmen and farmers.

As tribalism gave way to civilization, things got better. The life chances of most people improved. There was more freedom, more opportunities to grow and develop. For the first time, great numbers of people were freed from the necessity of working solely to secure food. They had the opportunities to learn and ply a skill or talent in an occupation, a craft, a trade, an art. And the material culture improved, too. The specialists improved the artifacts of the traditional culture. Once they began fabricating objects not for themselves but for someone else—a god, a king, or an unknown customer—these artisans and craftsmen were able to attain a distance that enabled them to be more critical. So they could and did uncover mistakes in the practices and inadequacies in the artifacts, and then they could and did refine those practices and modify those artifacts in light of what their criticisms had uncovered.

The wooden, stone, and bone tools, weapons, and utensils were now replaced by metal ones. Clay pots molded by hand gave way to highly artistic pottery fashioned on potters' wheels. Wheeled vehicles took over the hauling jobs once performed by sledges. Animal-drawn plows, together with yokes and harnesses, took the place of hoes and digging sticks. To rafts and canoes were now added sailboats. Woven fabrics supplemented materials made from the hides of animals.

Art, too, improved. Now, for the first time, humans erected monumental temples, palaces, tombs, colossal statuary made of stone or metal; they fabricated exquisite jewelry, seals, paintings, wall sculptures, furniture, carpets, tapestries, and musical instruments—string, percussion, and wind. Writing—proto-writing—had helped humans to become wealthy. Of course, not all members of the community shared in this wealth, but theoretically they did insofar as it, and they, all belonged to the gods. So all—from the lowest to the highest—shared membership in the wealth of the civilization.[17] But wealth brought problems. The insatiable quest for more led communities to become militaristic—to protect their own wealth and to appropriate that of others. This resulted in the development of nation-states. And, once again, writing played a significant role in this development.

PROTO-WRITING AND THE POLITY

When the early river settlements began to accumulate wealth, they became the targets for the nomadic bands who tried to steal and plunder their stored food. To protect themselves, these communities selected someone as military leader and equipped him with troops. Those military leaders who successfully defended the community retained and maintained their power by becoming lords or princes. In return for the protection he gave people, the prince demanded support for his work—taxes, military personnel, and corvee services.[18] Competition and rivalry among the settlements brought more militarism—wars and conquests—that led, ultimately, to centralized nation-states under one leader, a king. Writing—proto-writing—helped bring this about. Every military leader possessed and wore, or carried, insignia and emblems that embodied his authority as leader. But when they fought, each military leader set out to destroy the emblems and insignia of the other leader. And every leader lived in fear of the destruction of his own. For the destruction of his emblems and insignia symbolized the problem every leader faced continually: his vulnerability. The solution hit upon was to declare that the insignia and emblems were holy and sacred, conferred by the gods. In Mesopotamia, for example, the coronation ceremony of the king consisted of his receiving the emblem of royalty that had been placed before the altar of the god, in imitation of the actual insignia, which were believed to lie on a table before the throne of the god Anu in heaven.[19] In Egypt, the kings became gods themselves, adorned with the insignia and emblems of sacred royalty. This proto-writing in the form of insignia and emblems functioned to protect the political leader now that he had become so vulnerable. Proto-writing ensured political stability by making the office of king sacred, thereby establishing the office as permanent and its occupant as legitimate.

Although all property theoretically was the private property of the gods, the king now confiscated much of it. He built palaces for himself and for his governors and troops, constructed tombs and obelisks and statues, erected temples for priests and those who worked for them, and completed and maintained waterworks, dams, roads, and highways. Under the king, the polity became centralized and bureaucratic. Writing made this possible, because through writing the king could rule from a distance: He could transmit his orders to his administrators and receive back reports from them. Now, from a distance, the ruler could ascertain what was wrong and correct it. Some of these pronouncements from the king became something like what we call law. In the tribal past, the political leaders, or an assembly of elders, had resolved all disputes among members of the tribe. The written pronouncements from the king destroyed tribal justice and made things better.

Written pronouncements are both more abstract and impersonal than oral commands or decisions. They provide justice from a distance—not just a spatial distance, but a temporal distance, too, relating the past to the future. Written pronouncements liberated people from the immediate and contemporaneous judgments of the elders, released them from claims of family and kin. In place of the coercive bonds of family privilege and family duty, we have the beginnings of the idea of justice. And because the pronouncements of the king allegedly came from the gods, justice from the outset was rooted in divine, not human, will.

Chapter Three

Alphabetic Writing

Proto-writing had permitted human beings to encode the traditional culture they had earlier created through the medium of speech. This facilitated criticism of that culture and led to its modification and improvement. Proto-writing had helped make things better: It had destroyed animism and replaced it with a magical world— a world in which gods in a distant heaven communicated orders and commands to humans through various signs and signals. Proto-writing had also destroyed tribalism by enabling people to interact at a distance. This had brought into being large, complex hierarchical social networks and centralized bureaucratic political empires along with a palace-centered redistributive economy.

As contacts with others expanded, the opportunities for growth increased, and life chances improved. As the number and quality of their social interactions advanced people became less fearful and less suspicious of strangers. They became more tolerant. Living in the first cities, humans became more civil. Life in an urban environment made humans more urbane.

Yet although human beings had improved their culture and bettered the quality of their life, they were not free. They still lived under the rigid controls of the gods, the dictates of their political leaders, and the constraints of a social hierarchy. In time, they were liberated by a new kind of writing—argumentative writing. Argumentative writing became possible only after the invention of the alphabet. The Greeks invented the alphabet. So it is in Greece that we first find argumentative writing, which is why freedom begins there.

The earliest Greeks, the Mycenaeans, established a civilization similar to those set up in Mesopotamia and Egypt: an oriental despotism with a centralized, bureaucratic polity, a redistributive economy, and a hierarchical social order based on occupations in service to the state. The Dorian invasions of the thirteenth and twelfth centuries B.C. destroyed this civilization, scattering Greeks and Dorians all over the Mediterranean and Aegean. This began what are called the dark ages of Greece. Culture retrogressed: The political, social and economic arrangements of the Mycenaean civilization disappeared and tribalism returned—although vestiges of the earlier civilization remained.

Most of what we know about the dark ages we gather from the epic poems of Homer.[1] Traveling bands, or *aidoi*, composed these oral epics sometime between the twelfth and eighth centuries B.C. Here we see a two-class society made up of nobles, who were the descendents of the earlier nobility of Mycenaea, and their clients, the tenant farmers. The government in each colony was in the hands of the nobility, one of whom was usually a king or chief. He sometimes consulted a council of nobles. There was also an assembly of the people, but they neither initiated nor ratified decisions, existing solely to give public support for decisions made by the king or council.

Although the Greeks had retrogressed to tribalism and now had political, economic, and social arangements much more primitive than those of the civilizations surrounding them, it was they who invented the alphabet sometime in the eighth century B.C. The alphabet enabled them to carry out the argumentative function of language in writing. Through argumentative writing, they broke through the stage of oriental despotism that characterized all the other civilizations of the middle east. Within the next 300 years, the Greeks transformed their political, social, and economic arangements: They created the first democratic polity, the first market economy, and the first free society. Furthermore, they invented science, philosophy, and literature. All this they accomplished through the medium of argumentative writing.

THE PHONETIC ALPHABET

The invention of the alphabet was a stroke of luck. For one of the casualities of the Dorian invasion had been the complete disappearance of the Mycenaean system of writing, leaving the Greeks during the dark ages with no system of writing at all. So when they invented the alphabet, it was not by modifying a writing system they were already familiar with; it was by modifying the system of another culture (which is probably easier to do). Moreover, the improvements they made of the Phoenician syllabary actually created an entirely new system of writing, one different from all that had existed before. All previous systems had been syllabic; that is, each written sign stood for a word or for a spoken syllable. The Sumerians had first invented the syllabary writing system sometime around 3100 B.C. Over the next millenium, the main principles of syllabic writing spread to Egypt, China, and India.[2]

Although syllabic writing is based on a common-sense empirical analysis of speech, it contains insuperable difficulties as a medium for performing the descriptive and especially the argumentative function of language. The attempt to have a sign for every syllable led to a great number of signs, more signs than anyone could remember without long training. Some later cultures that adopted the syllabic system attempted to reduce the number of signs by grouping syllables under a common sign. The Phoenicians, for example, used a sign for a set of syllables that began with the same sound—thus, they used one sign for the syllables *ba, be, bi, bo, bu*. By such a stratagem, they reduced the number of signs to something under thirty. But this economy increased the ambiguity of the written signs, because each sign could stand for any one of several different sounds and thus forced the reader to infer what the correct syllable was.

Syllabic writing thus created a dilemma by throwing up two related, unsolvable problems: On the one hand, if the system reduced ambiguity by providing a sign for every syllable, the number of signs required was too great for most people to remember; on the other hand, if the system reduced the number of signs by some stratagem, then the signs became increasingly ambiguous. Moreover, the reduced syllabaries, like those of the Phoenicians were not flexible enough to capture all spoken language. The Phoenician syllabary, for example, could index only syllables beginning with a consonant.

Possibly because they were unencumbered by any system of writing, the illiterate Greeks resolved this dilemma. The abandoned the syllabary system or the logic of the syllabary and created an alphabet. Because the Greeks adopted the symbol system used by the Phoenicians, it looks as if they simply refined the earlier system by introducing signs for vowels. But as Havelock points out, the Greeks actually abandoned the empirical approach characteristic of all syllabic systems.

Instead of trying to create a separate sign for each spoken syllable or set of syllables, the Greeks created a sign for each phoneme. Phonemes are the minimal acoustic constituents distinctive from each other out of which a given tongue is constructed.[3] But some phonemes, the consonants, do not exist by themselves in spoken language. In spoken language, consonants always appear with one or more vowels. Vowels are vibrations of a column of air in the larynx or nasal cavity which are modified by the vocal chords. Consonants are the controls, restrictions, and releases (the stops and starts) imposed on these vibrations (the vowels) by the interactions of the tongue, teeth, palate, lips, and nose. The number of vowels (vibrations) possible is limited in any language, as are the consonants (stops and starts). The Greek system of writing, therefore, provided a complete coverage of all possible phonemes while keeping the required letter signs under a total of thirty. A combination of two to five of these, forming dipthongs and double consonants, could "identify with precision any linguistic noises that the mouth could choose to make."[4]

Prior to the invention of the alphabet, learning to write and read remained a technical accomplishment that required years of training, so writing had been the province of a small elite, called scribes. Havelock calls this "craft literacy." The limitations of the pre-alphabet system of writing forced scribes to resort to formulaic writing—using sets of phonemes and sentences to reduce the ambiguity of the written marks. The earliest written records in the various syllabaries are all in simplified, standardized statements—in form and content. So although people could use a syllabary for the expressive and the signaling functions of language, its power to describe was severely limited, and performing the argumentative function was practically impossible.

Oppenheim tells us that the ancient Mesopotamian cuneiform writing—of which we have a great number of samples because the Mesopotamians wrote on clay—contains no polemics, no arguments, no criticisms. "What is written on clay typically either records past transactions or formulates traditionally determined relations; hardly ever is it intended to refute divergent opinions or to discuss the relative merit of alternate possibilities."[5] This does not mean that the Mesopotamians were not critical, but only that they did not—because they could not—use the medium of syllabic writing for this purpose. It also means that without written criticism, the Mesopotamians, and all the other prealphabetic cultures, had no opportunity to construct a tradition of criticism. Without a critical tradition, it is impossible for a culture to improve continually. Cultures without a critical tradition become static—as did those of Mesopotamia and Egypt.

WRITING AND THE ORIGIN OF HISTORY

The Greeks were the first to encode their culture in writing and the first, therefore, to achieve a distance from their culture. They were the first, consequently, to criticize their culture in writing and to have those written criticisms read—or listened to—by the population at large.

Unlike the syllabaries, which as we saw, admirably served and supported the social, political, and economic arrangements of the oriental despotisms, the alphabet subverted and corroded the tribal arrangements of the Greeks. Perhaps even more important, the alphabet facilitated criticism of the magical world humankind had lived in for thousands and thousands of years. The alphabet helped the Greeks create a rational world.

The world described by the oral epics of Homer was a magical world, a world in which events and actions were determined by the gods. In the *Iliad*, for example, it is the gods who provoke the quarrels among men that start the war. It is a god who leads the armies into battle, who speaks to each soldier at turning points, who urges the soldiers on and who defeats them.

Writing—alphabetic writing—preserved these oral epics of Homer, but at the same time alphabetic writing helped destroy the magical world they described. As a result, in the very act of creating an authorized version of Homer, writing made the content of the *Iliad* and the *Odyssey* less authoritative as a source of true understanding of the world humans lived in.

Before they were written down, the aidoi had recited these epics, adapting their recitations to their audiences—modifying or changing sections, deleting and adding passages. Once written down, however, the authorized version prevented such modifications and changes, but even more important: the authorized version could be read by all. (Actually, there appears to have been more than one written version because the tyrant Peisistratus in the second half of the sixth century B.C. appointed a committee to compile a correct final version of Homer's epics.[6]) Of course not everyone could read and write—indeed, it was not until the bottom half of the fifth century that the Greeks set up the schools that made widespread literacy possible. But even if not everyone could read the authorized versions of the epics, all could be read to. And this is what happened. Before literacy became widespread, Homer had become the educator of Greece. For those who did learn to read, however, it now became possible to scrutinize the content of the epics more carefully. Those critical endeavors brought about dramatic changes in the culture.

This happened because argumentative writing—made possible by the invention of the alphabet—created history. Oral cultures—and keep in mind that after the fall of Mycenae, the Greeks had only an oral culture—have no history, only myths. This is not to say that oral cultures do not recognize that the past is different from the present, but rather they have no awareness of past or previous accounts of the past. In oral cultures, myths recount—describe and explain—the doings and dealings of humans in the past: "long, long ago," or "once upon a time."

Myths are human creations and, therefore, must be inadequate, false, mistaken, erroneous—simply because human beings are fallible. But because human beings do seek order and coherence, they do modify or change their myths when they recognize these mistakes and contradictions. So people living in an oral culture, like the Greeks of the dark ages, did modify and change their myths in light of the inadequacies they discovered there. But in an oral culture, there is no record of the changes—no record of past mistakes, errors, rejected ideas, or outmoded explanations. The descriptions and explanations supplied by myths in an oral culture are always up to date—they always represent the latest state of the art as recognized by that culture. They are always coherent, always acceptable. Thus, oral cultures have no history of human beings' continual attempts to describe and explain the goings-on in the universe. Oral cultures have only a continuous present, an orthodox, conservative, yet up-to-date version of the past.

With writing, history begins. The distinction between history and myth is not that one is a false record of the past whereas the other is a true record. For history, like myth, is the creation of fallible humans—so it, like myth, will always be false, inadequate, erroneous, mistaken. What makes history different from myth is that with history we have records of some previous descriptions and explanations of the past. History was made possible by writing—alphabetic writing. Syllabic writing did not produce history—it produced only chronology—because syllabic writing was never refined enough to record myths.

Once the myths are written down, they can no longer be modified or changed when people discover their inadequacies. Once there was an authorized version of the *Iliad* and the *Odyssey*, then people had no recourse if and when they found the authorized version inadequate, except to create new stories, altogether, stories with a different content, stories that were not only alternatives to the stories of Homer but stories that at the same time implied or explicitly presented a criticism of the stories put forward by Homer. History begins—and myth ends—when people have a record of earlier (inadequate) records of the past.

The first written criticisms of Homer came from Hesiod, who was a real person whereas Homer himself may have been a legendary character who never existed. A sometime farmer and poet of the late eighth and early seventh centuries B.C., Hesiod composed, in writing, *Theogony*, a poem that criticizes Homer's explanation of how and why things happen as they do.[7] Hesiod did not set out to destroy the magical world of Homer, only to tidy up his cosmogony. But in less than 300 years, the critical tradition inaugurated by Hesiod destroyed the magical world described by Homer.

As Herodotus said, Homer and Hesiod stand at the beginning of Greek thought about the gods.[8] Homer had left the classification of the gods in a confusing state. In the *Theogony*, Hesiod tried to clear this up by cataloging the gods according to genealogy:[9]

First of all came Chaos, and after him came
Gaia (earth) of the broad breast
to be the unshakable foundation
of all the immortals who keep the crests
of snowy Olympus . . . (lines 116-118)

From Chaos was born Erebos, the dark
and black Night,
and from Night again Aither and Hemera,
the day was begotten,
for she lay in love with Erebos
and conceived and bore these two. (lines 123-126)[10]

Hesiod's attempt to bring order to the cosmos by his genealogy failed. The *Theogony* contained contradictions that were uncovered when it was critically scrutinized. Hesiod contended that the earth, the sky, and the sea were gods—Gaia, Ourama, and Pintos—who coupled, reproduced, and behaved generally like human beings. But once put into writing and made public these notions about the gods were critically reflected on and rejected. Here is the famous argument of Xenophanes (620?-520? B.C.):

Homer and Hesiod have ascribed to the gods
all the deeds that among men are a reproaach and disgrace:
thievery, adultery, and mortal deception. [. . .]

Ethopians imagine their gods as black and snub-nosed;
Thracians as blue-eyed and red-haired. [. . .]

But if oxen and horses and lions had hands,
or could draw and fashion works as men do,
horses would draw the gods shaped like horses,
and lions like lions, making the bodies of the gods
resemble their own forms.[11]

So, from the time of Xenophanes, the Greeks—some Greeks—rejected the notion that the gods had human forms and behaved as humans did. But if the order in the universe was not due to the acts of the gods, then how was it to be explained? The answer put forth by the first Greek philosophers was that order is immanent in the universe itself.

WRITING AND THE ORIGIN OF PHILOSOPHY

It begins with Thales of Miletus (fl.[flourished] 585 B.C.), who made the first philosophical speculations about the nature of things. With Thales, the world became more rational. As he saw it, everything in the universe was intelligible because everything had an essence, an *arche*. The *arche* was not a god, but it was eternal and immortal—and, therefore, divine. For Thales, the *arche* was water or moisture. This seems commonsensical because if we heat anything or crush it, it will exude moisture. Yet, Thales' theory was not based on observation. (How could water be the essence of fire?) His theory was a bold speculation, a conjecture, to explain the stability and order he perceived in the universe.

Although we have no written record of Thales' theory, he must have written it down, because it was criticized and modified by his pupil, Anaximander. Anaximander (fl. 570 B.C.) not only wrote his own theory down, he is probably the first Greek to write in prose. He argued that the *arche* could not be water or any other known element. For if one of those were primal, it would conquer the others, because air is cold, water is moist, and fire is hot: "therefore, if any one of them were infinite, the rest would have ceased to be by this time."[12] The essence of things, Anaximander concluded, must be neutral in this cosmic strife. Furthermore, Thales' theory fails to explain change. Anaximander set out to remedy this with an even bolder speculation: He conjectured that the *arche* was the boundless, the indefinite, the *aperion*. The *aperion*, he claimed, is the form of all opposites. Thus, fire and water, hot and cold, moist and dry are all in the *aperion* and come into being by a process of separating out. Although all things come to be and pass away, the *aperion*, the boundless, is eternal.

The third philosopher from Miletus was Anaximenes (fl. sixth century B.C.), who criticized Anaximander's theory because it did not really explain change. Anaximenes claimed that the *arche* is air: The soul is air, fire is rarified air; when condensed, air becomes first water and then, if further condensed, earth and, finally stone. For him all change is a process of rarefication or of condensation. With Anaximenes, apparent differences of kind or quality are, for the first time, reduced to differences in quantity: All differences among things are quantitative— they are made up of more, or less, air. Anaximenes never made any mathematical application of this principle, but Pythagoras (fl. 532 B.C.) did, demonstrating that all physical phenomena—sound, for example—can be described in the form of mathematical equations. Here we are at the beginnings of physical science, which is based on the assumption that all differences of quality are reducible to differences in quantity and only when so reduced can be regarded as scientifically described.

With the Milesian philosophers, a new era in the history of culture began. For the first time humans had created a rational world, a world in which "a single order underlies the chaos of our perceptions."[13] So by the Sixth century the Greeks had replaced the magical order with one that was rational. They did this by criticizing that magical world and then modifying and changing their conjectures in light ot the criticisms. So from the sixth century B.C. on, humans (or some humans) assumed that the universe is inherently orderly—that there are principles, rules, laws, a logic within the universe itself that can rationally explain whatever happens.

The abandonment of mythological explanations of the nature and origin of the universe followed hard upon the heels of the invention of alphabetic writing and was a consequence of that invention—or, more specifically, it was a consequence of the argumentative writing that the invention of the alphabet made possible. Now people could criticize the ideas and theories of their predecessors, the ideas that they had encoded in writing. And then they could come up with alternative theories, theories that were better because they were not open to the same criticisms. Human beings' understanding of the universe they inhabited got better through their own critical endeavors. And instead of myth, people now had history—the continuous record of previous inadequate conjectures about the nature and origin of the universe.

Anaximander had shown that water was not the essence, or *arche*, of the universe. But then, following him, Anaximenes had argued that the *arche* could not be boundless. Was it, as he claimed, air? No, announced Heraclitus (fl. 500 B.C.)—it was fire! The trouble with the Milesian philosophers, Heraclitus announced, was that they assumed that the universe was stable and only change had to be explained. But actually, the world is changing—continually. According to this boldest of all speculators, the appearances of things are not real. Change appears to us to be transitions of things into their opposites: life and death, being awake and being asleep, youth and old age. But, in truth, opposites are identical; it is only to humans that they appear as non-identical. All things are one; they are part of the everlasting fire, the process of the world.

But if this is so—if opposites are identical, if all things are one—then there can be no change, ever. This was the conclusion drawn by Parmenides (fl. 475 B.C.) who taught that the world is one, an undivided whole, without parts, homogeneous and motionless: Motion was impossible in such a world. There was no change: Change was an illusion.

The critical tradition of the pre-Socratic philosophers ends with Parmenides. The philosophers who follow were less concerned with arguing against predecessors than with pronouncing and preserving standardized theories. In place of arguments criticizing the theories of others, these later philosophers now put forward arguments to "prove' the correctness of their answers.

Here we arrive at Platonism. Platonism signals a return to an earlier anthropomorphic understanding of the universe. From Plato we learn that a divine mind, or divine intelligence, designed and created the universe. But there is a difference from the earlier anthropomorphism. Rationalism is not abandoned; it is simply changed. Instead of being embedded in the critical tradition of conjecture and refutation carried on by the pre-Socratics, rationalism now assumes the guise of justification. Thus, Plato demarcates knowledge from opinion and explains that knowledge (*scientia*) is that which can be justified or demonstrated to be true, whereas opinions are merely beliefs (*doxa*). The earlier, pre-Socratic, philosophers had made no such demarcation between knowledge and opinion; they viewed all knowledge as conjectural, and always open to criticism. With Plato justificatory rationality replaces critical rationality.

At this juncture, the argumentative function of writing—after having destroyed the magical world of the ancients—now became the defender and legitimatizer of "true," or "correct" understandings of the universe. Instead of being a medium through which humans pursue the truth, writing now became a medium through which some people pronounced, and others received, the truth. The Greeks, and others, following them, became people of the book—holding certain books to be depositories of true wisdom. When this happened, it curtailed further improvement in the understanding of the universe. With the advent of printing, many centuries later, our understanding improved—things got better.

WRITING AND THE ORIGINS OF DEMOCRACY

The rational, physical universe the Greeks created had its counterpart in their social and political arrangements. Just as they insisted that there is an intelligible order in the physical universe—an order concealed by the visible, physical world—so they came to insist that a hidden intelligible order lay behind the visible, social, and political arrangements. From the eighth century on, they engaged in the pursuit of that intelligible order—a quest for the just society.

Once again, it begins with Hesiod. His *Works and Days* contains sharp criticisms of the society of the late eighth century. Homer, earlier, had described the goings-on of the nobility, the *basileus*. Hesiod, a farmer, complains of the "crooked decisions" these nobles make. He accuses his brother, Perseus, of seizing the better share of their inheritance by bribing the nobles who decided such matters as family disputes about inheritances.

> Now once before we divided our inheritance,
> but you seized the greater part and made off with it,
> gratifying barons who eat bribes,
> who are willing to give out such a decision.[14]

The *Works and Days*, however, is not simply a complaint about the injustice Hesiod had experienced: It is a general indictment of an unjust society:

> But Zeus will destroy this generation of mortals also,

In the time when children, as they are born,
grow grey in the temples,
when the father no longer agrees with the children,
nor the children with their father,
when the guest is no longer at one with the host,
nor companion to companion,
when your brother is no longer your friend,
as he was in the old days.
Men will deprive their parents of all rights,
as they grow old,
and people will mock them, too,
babbling bitter words against them,
harshly, and without shame in the sight of the gods;
not even
to their aging parents will they give back
what once was given.
Strong of hand, one man shall seek
the city of another.
There will be no favor for the man
who keeps his oath, for the righteous
and the good man, rather men shall give their praise
to violence
and the doer of evil. Right will be in the arm.
Shame will
not be. The vile man will crowd his better out,
and attack him
with twisted accusations and swear an oath
to his story.
The spirit of Envy, with grim face
and screaming voice, who delights
in evil, will be the constant companion
of wretched humanity,
and at last Nemesis and Aidos, Decency and Respect,
shrouding
their bright forms in pale mantles, shall go
from the wide-wayed
earth back on their way to Olympus,
forsaking the whole race
of mortal men, and all that will be left by them
to mankind
will be wretched pain. And there shall be no defense
against evil.[15]

Hesiod entreats Perseus to listen to justice, the way (*Dikai*). Homer earlier had
spoken of *Dikai* as the actual decisions rulers made. These were "straight" or
"crooked" according to the extent to which they conformed to the customs, the
unwritten rules and precedents which justify decisions.[16] But for Hesiod, *Dikai* is
a goddess, the daughter of Zeus. He had introduced *Dikai* in the *Theogony* as the

goddess who was to reform the morality of the other gods and goddesses. Now, in the *Works and Days*, *Dikai* becomes the source of reform of human morality. When humans make "crooked decisions," they violate her and she brings retribution upon them. Those who do not do what is right affront the goddess, and so they suffer the punishment of the gods:

> If a man sees what is right and
> is willing to argue it,
> Zeus of the wide brow grants him prosperity,
> But when one, knowingly, tells lies and
> swears an oath on it,
> when he is so wild as to do incurable damage
> against justice,
> this man is left a diminished generation hereafter,
> but the generation of the true-sworn man
> grows strong.[17]

Humans alone, Hesiod explains, have been blessed with the goddess Justice— "as for fish and wild animals, and the flying birds, they feed on each other." But to human beings Zeus gave justice and "she in the end is proved the best thing they have." For without justice, people could never improve their society. With justice, things could get better: "there is an outcry when justice is dragged to perforce when bribe-bearing men pull her about and judge their cases with crooked decisions."[18]

Although his social criticism is clear, Hesiod had no concept, no idea of justice: He had only a notion that such a goddess existed and must be respected. We do not know if Hesiod ever secured redress from the crooked decisions that afflicted him, but we do know that over the next 200 years, the people of Greece attempted to create a more just, a more moral, a more rational society—a society in which fewer people would suffer evil at the hands of other people. I suggest that these efforts to improve society sprang from the written social criticisms of Hesiod. For, as Heraclitus wrote, Hesiod was the most popular teacher of Greece: "Of him people think he knew most."

The most victimized, or those most conscious of their victimization, were, like Hesiod himself, farmers. In *Works and Days*, Hesiod urged farmers to pursue wealth. But even those farmers who did become wealthy still suffered from powerlessness. The roots of the problem were political, not economic. If the farmers were to improve their lot, the political arrangements had to change. The earliest attempts to do something about political inequities took the form of migrations of settlers from the established communities. These migrants set up new colonies, *poleis*, with new political arrangements in which they, for the first time, had political power and could participate in decision-making. Meanwhile, in some of the older established communities (Corinth, Megara, Sicyon) political change was brought about by tyrants—usually these were members of the nobility who, for one reason or another, took up the cause of those clamoring for relief from the "crooked decisions" of the nobles. But tyranny offered no permanent solution, because even with a "good" tyrant, there was always the problem of succession. Finally, in the early sixth century, a more permanent solution came in the form of state constitutions, composed by lawgivers.

In Athens, which became the bellwether polis of Greece, the first Attic poet, Solon (640-558 B.C.), sharpened the criticisms of the political arrangements by his poems on the theme of justice. He accused the aristocracy of causing political strife because of its heedless pursuit of wealth. Solon, like Hesiod, did not object to the pursuit of wealth but rather, again like Hesiod, objected to the unfair way the aristocracy used its political power to attain wealth. "Wealth I do indeed desire," Solon wrote, "but ill-gotten wealth I will not have: punishment therefore surely cometh with time." The crooked acts of the aristocracy, he claims, have brought, and will continue to bring, punishment upon the community itself: "Like such a sudden wind is the justice of Zeus. He is not, like mortal man, quick to wrath for each offense; but no man who hath an evil heart ever escapeth his watchful eye, and surely, in the end, his justice is made manifest. One man payeth early, another late. If the guilty man himself escape and the fate of the gods not come upon him and overtake him not, it cometh full surely in aftertime: The innocent pay for his offense—his children, or his children's children in later generations."[19]

Solon's fame and popularity erupted dramatically in the late seventh century, when he composed a poem urging the Athenians to seize the island of Salamis from Megara. This led to the successful colonization of the island when some 500 Athenians settled and secured full political and economic freedom. Then in 594 B.C. Solon was made an Archon, or Magistrate, of Athens, which allowed him to create a more permanent solution in the form of a constitution whch destroyed the hegemony of the aristocracy.

Since the early seventh century, Athens had been ruled by magistrates or Archons who were selected by lot from among the nobility. Solon abolished the exclusive right of the nobility to hold these positions by making them elective offices decided by the assembly. Solon also enlarged the assembly to include the lower classes. In addition, he created a council of 400 to initiate and administer the laws. Membership in the council was based on wealth, not birth. All these political reforms helped make things better—at least for the middle classes, who now participated in political decision making. Athens became a more just society.

Yet more important than the actual political reforms he inaugurated, Solon gave Athens written law. Laws, of course, had existed in Greece before Solon, but these had been customary, traditional, unwritten laws. The nobles had resolved conflicts and made decisions in accordance with the traditional laws known to them and to them alone. The significant contribution of Solon and the other lawgivers was to write the laws down and make them public so all could consult them. Solon actually wrote the laws on wooden plaques, the so-called *Kyrbeis*, and put them on public display: "I wrote down laws alike for base and noble, fitting straight judgment to each."[20]

Written laws now became the basis for justice. For Hesiod, justice had been a goddess who rewarded humans when they made straight decisions and punished them when they made crooked ones. Solon recognized that the fear of divine retribution was not enough to prevent rulers from making crooked decisions. Laws, however—written laws—could help people protect themselves against crooked decisions and unjust practices. For written laws created an impersonal authority, something permanent, definite, and valid to which people could appeal in times of distress. Moreover, Solon arranged it so that anyone could initiate prosecution for a criminal offense. "That city is most just," Solon said, "where all citizens, whether they have suffered injury or not, equally pursue and punish justice."[21]

Once the laws were written down, justice became secularized. No longer a goddess, justice now became simply the characteristic of a good society, the creation of human beings. For the laws, people now realized, were not gifts from the gods, as the Greeks had earlier believed. The laws came from human beings. Human beings, therefore had to assume responsibility for the well-being of their society. "Our city will never perish by the decree of Zeus, or the will of the blessed immortal gods," Solon wrote, "but by the citizens themselves, who in their wildness wish to destroy this great city."[22] The laws would tame this wildness; the laws would establish good order (*eunomia*). "A law abiding spirit createth order and harmony and at the same time putteth chains on evil doers; it maketh rough things smooth; it checketh inordinate decrees, it dimmeth the glare of wanton pride and withereth the budding bloom of wild delusion; it maketh crooked judgments straight and softeneth arrogant behavior; it stoppeth acts of sedition and stoppeth the anger of bitter strife. Under the reign of laws, society and wisdom prevail ever among men."[23]

In the Greek language, the literal root of *eunomia* (good order) is *nomos* (law). Law is literally the basis for good order. Henceforth the Greeks used the term *nomos* to describe the written law, and *nomos*, as Heraclitus said, became "the soul of the city."[24]

Written laws transformed the Greeks into citizens, free citizens—the first free citizens in history. But freedom without equality is insufficient. People can only protect themselves if they have political equality. Solon's reforms did not go far enough. He had provided the Athenians with institutions for self-protection, but he had not allowed all people to use them. Power remained in the hands of the wealthy, who alone could hold political office and who, therefore, were the sole interpreters of the laws.

The reforms of Cleisthenes in 503 B.C. gave Athens political equality (*isonomia*). He opened political office equally to all citizens, which made all equal before the law. Athens had now become a democracy. Under democracy, things got better for all Athenian ciizens, as Euripides later declared: "Naught is more hostile to a city than a despot; where he is, there are in the first place no laws common to all, but one man is tyrant, in whose keeping and in his alone the law resides, and in that case equality is at an end. But when the laws are written down, rich and poor alike have equal justice, and it is open to the weaker to use the same language to the prosperous when he is reviled by him, and the weaker prevails over the stronger if he have justice on his side."[25]

A democratic polity is not without its problems, one of the most serious of which is the existence of factions who attempt to see to it that public decisions favor their particular group at the expense of the public interest. Cleisthenes tried to destroy all existing factions by abolishing the clans, which, at that time, were the source of all factions. In place of the clans, he made the demos, or local community, the basic political unit. Then he tied each deme to the central government by assigning each the responsibility to maintain the many written records necessary to a functioning democracy: records of representatives sent to the assembly and council, tax records, voting records, conscription records, records of public service and public works, and, most important of all, records of residence, which now that the clans no longer existed, provided proof of citizenship. A final democratic instrument that Cleisthenes devised—also made possible only because of the invention of writing—was the practice of ostracism: Each citizen could indicate who he most wished removed from the city by writing his name on a piece of pottery (a potsherd = *ostraken*). The candidate with the most votes against him was exiled for ten years.

So, with writing, the political arrangements got better. Writing had initially helped create a more democratic polity when poets like Hesiod and Solon described and held before the public the injustices common in the existing polity. Later, writing helped maintain the democratic polity through written laws and written records.

THE RETREAT FROM DEMOCRACY

In a democracy, words are weapons and the power to use language effectively becomes the paramount skill of citizens active in political life.[26] Those who claimed to teach such powerful skills in Greece in the fifth century B.C. were called Sophists. Mainly they taught rhetoric, although some of them conducted inquiries into the correct use of grammar.[27]

The invention of rhetoric was a direct consequence of the invention of writing. For writing not only encoded the content of culture, it also encoded the form of language itself—making it possible to analyze it critically, which never could be done before. So when the poems of Homer and Hesiod were written down and the language subjected to critical analysis, the Greeks discovered the principles of meter, rhythm, and harmony, as well as the use of repetition, rhyme, and antithesis. To Homer and Hesiod, such knowledge had been practical knowledge: They knew how to write poetry, but they could not explain it to others. But now, critical analysis made it possible to teach others how to use these techniques to compose poetry and prose as well. Thus, literary prose came into being with a view to emulating poetry—especially the persuasive power of poetry.[28] As a result, literary composition became less a matter of inspiration from the muses and more a matter of rational composition: the employment of rules and principles. Instead of seeking inspiration, would-be writers sought instruction in style from the Sophists.

But the Sophists did more than teach the techniques of rhetoric; they also taught a philosophy of culture. According to that philosophy, culture is not the creation of the gods, not a gift to humans from the gods. Rather, human beings create culture: The ideas, the theories, the laws, the political arrangements are all the creation of human beings. As Protagoras (481-411 B.C.), the most famous of the Sophists, said, "Man is the measure of all things." From this, their enemies drew the conclusion that the Sophists taught that there is no truth—only opinion; no justice—only convention; no goodness—only custom. Some of the Sophists themselves—but not all—also drew this conclusion.[29]

The most ardent opponents of the Sophists were Plato and his pupil, Aristotle. They both taught that truth, justice, and goodness existed. Moreover, they claimed that those who know what truth, justice, and goodness are are entitled to be the political leaders of the state. The intellectual and moral arguments of Plato and Aristotle against the Sophists (and the destruction of the written works of the Sophists by the disciples of Plato and Aristotle) branded the Sophists as enemies of Western civilization and expunged from the Western tradition for many centuries the notion that humans make their culture. In place of this notion, both Plato and Aristotle taught that there is a transcendent political order, an ideal known to a few. Accordingly, the intellectuals, the philosophers—those who really know truth, justice, and goodness—should run the affairs of the state.

What Plato did was to change the basic conception of what a just society is. Since the time of Solon, a just society for the Greeks had been construed as a society governed by laws. As Solon had put it, a just society exists "when the people obey the rulers, and the rulers obey the laws."[30] But now, following Plato, who insisted that a just society was one ruled by intellectuals, the most basic political question became "Who should rule?" A just society, therefore, came to be construed as one in which the right person, or the right group, rules. The spell of Plato over Western civilization is broad and deep, as witnessed by successive efforts in the West to determine who should rule: The intellectuals, the wealthy, the holy, those of certain blood lines, the workers, the majority—each of these at various times has been put forth as the key to the creation of a just society.

Plato's answer to his own question (that the intellectuals—those who know what truth, goodness, and justice are—should rule) was not the answer adopted by the Greeks and their successors in the West. Lofty as this ideal was, there was no guarantee that humans, even exceptional ones, could ever know what truth, justice, and goodness are. But, taking Plato's question as *the* basic political question, the Greeks decided that rulers should have "right opinion." According to Isocrates (466-338 B.C.), a contemporary of Plato, one acquired "right opinion" from the study of one's culture: the study of literature and history, which served to initiate one into the best that had been thought and said and done. This kind of education gave one what the Greeks called *paideia*, what the Romans later called *humanitas*, and what we call culture. Those who had culture and used the traditional wisdom as a guide in decision making were deemed the most fit to rule, according to this tradition.

We see that writing—after having helped the Greeks improve their political arrangements, after having helped them create a polity in which people were free and equal before the law—after doing all this, writing now became a medium to preserve the polity against change. For now, everyone defined a just state as Plato had: A just state is one ruled by the right people. And the right people, everyone agreed—following Isocrates—were those who had read the writings of their traditional culture. Only those who had been initirated into their culture, only those who were cultured, should rule. In truth, only they could be trusted to make political decisions in accord with the established cultural tradition. In consequence, once writing became a medium of conservation, a medium for preventing change, no significant political changes occurred in the West until the advent of a new medium for encoding culture. Printing, when it arrived, helped make things better.

WRITING AND THE ORIGIN OF THE MARKET ECONOMY

When the Mycenaean civilization collapsed in the thirteenth and twelfth centuries B.C. and writing disappeared, this marked the end of the palace-centered redristributive economic system in Greece. During the ensuing dark ages, the clans—under the leadership of the descendents of the Mycenaean aristocracy—laid claim to possession of the land, and each family household became the basic economic unit: Each household grew its own food, made its own clothing, and engaged in reciprocal trade through barter and the mutual exchange of gifts. Itinerant craftsmen supplemented the work of the household by making utensils, weapons, bridles, and tools on the spot. But as the epics of Homer make clear, the self-sustaining household was the center of economic activity during this period—recall Penelope's skill at the spindle and loom and Odysseus's ability to build ships and furniture.

The earliest Greek contacts with a foreign people came sometime in the ninth century B.C. with the Canaanites of the Levantine coast, a people known to the Greeks as Phoenicians. From the Phoenicians, the Greeks obtained silver, iron, tin, and lead in exchange for slaves. But most important, from the Phoenicians the Greeks received syllabic writing, which, as we saw, they modified into alphabetic writing. With this invention, the Greeks could develop the record-keeping instruments and skills necessary for engaging in trade at a distance. As a result during the eighth and seventh centuries, they established permanent trading ports in the distant near east as well as on the southern coast of Europe and the northern coast of Africa.

Intercourse with the more highly developed civilizations of the near east revealed to the Greeks the low level of their own arts and crafts. During the dark ages, the Greeks had retreated to a style of art characteristic of the earlier Mesolithic and Neolithic periods, a style that art historians have labeled geometric: art that uses straight, crooked, and curved lines and geometric figures. But the Greek geometric style was different from all other geometric art. During the dark ages the Greeks, not having any form of writing, used the geometric style to narrate and preserve stories of past glories and splendors in works of art. So what made Greek geometric art distinctive was that the Greeks used it to represent actual real events, depicting the doings of both animals and humans. The geometric style was, of course inadequate to represent reality: When artists portrayed horses and chariots, they depicted legs and chariot wheels side by side in the correct number, regardless of whether or not they were visible; they shaped the human body as a triangle, always facing front, whereas the legs could be twisted to show the direction of motion.

Contact with the more developed art of the near east brought the Greeks to a new understanding of how to do things. Their art acquired a new elegance and grace, becoming a new artistic style called the orientalizing style. The art of the countries of the near east was, and remained, decorative—probably because these oriental kingdoms had always had some form of (syllabic) writing as a medium to preserve their stories and, therefore, had little need for representational narrative art. The Greeks, however, adopted the artistic skills and technologies of those countries to create a truly magnificent representational art—using art to portray human beings and their works, which long thereafter remained the particular focus of Western art.

A number of Greek communities began to manufacture pottery of the highest artistic quality. At the same time, many of the peasant farmers switched from animal husbandry to arable farming. By the seventh century, the Greeks were actually engaged in trade throughout the near east and southern Europe, exchanging their pottery, grain, and slaves for luxury items of metal and textiles avidly sought by the aristocracy.

Long-distance trade brought increasing prosperity to the Greek communities. Most of them now built protective walls around their cities and constructed monumental temples. The most dramatic consequence of the increased prosperity was the growth in population: In the region of Attica, for example, the population quadrupled between 800 and 700 B.C.[31] The rapid population expansion brought serious political, social, and economic problems to the Greek polis, problems which, as we saw, centered on the conflict between the aristocracy and the rest of the people.

During the dark ages, the aristocracy had been a warrior class that protected the people (*demos*): The people were their clients; and in return, the clients provided the aristocracy with goods and military service. By the end of the eighth century, however, the importation of metal and know-how had completely changed military technology. The design and manufacture of armor and weapons had led to the creation of heavily-armed troops, called Hoplites, who replaced the individual champions of the earlier period. Most of these soldiers were farmers who could afford to buy the arms and weapons. In some states, one third of the independent farmers served as Hoplites.[32] These mass armies of heavily armed troops became the most effective military force in the Mediterranean and middle east for the next 500 years. Praised and honored in songs and poems, the Hoplite soldier took over the role of defender of the community. Here is the famous panegyric to the Hoplite by Tyrtaeus:

> This is excellence (*arete*), this is the finest possession of men
> the noblest prize that a young man can win.
> This is the common good for the city and all the people,
> when a man stands firm and remains unmoved in the front rank
> and forgets all thought of disgraceful flight,
> steeling his spirit and heart to endure,
> and with words encourages the man
> standing beside him.
> This is the man who is good in war.[33]

In Sparta, the Hoplites eliminated the aristocracy and Sparta became a land of equals—a total Hoplite state in which all citizens were soldiers and all citizens were forbidden to engage in farming, trade, or any productive activities. (The *perioki*—those whom the Spartans had conquered—did the farming, the manufacturing, and engaged in the other service activities necessary to the state.) The Spartans permitted no written records and discouraged all writing. Without writing, Sparta became a static society. Things did not get better there.

In other communities like Athens, the Hoplites remained subordinated to the aristocracy, unable to hold political office. To strengthen their position, the Athenian aristocracy now began to use their political power to secure the land owned by the clans. They were able to exploit the system of clan ownership, reducing their clients to debt bondage, forcing them to grow grain, which the aristocracy then exported in exchange for luxury items. Some of their clients they sold into slavery.[34] The greed of the aristocracy, Solon warned was going to destroy the city:

> The leaders of the people have an evil mind,
> they are ripe to suffer many griefs for their
> great arrogance; for they know not how to
> restrain their greed.[35]

In addition to the political reforms discussed earlier, Solon also initiated economic reforms in an attempt to avert the destruction of the city. He abolished all debts to the aristocracy and forbade debt slavery. He also brought home many of those Athenians who had been sold into slavery abroad. He returned the rights of the people to their own property. These economic reforms were secured and made permanent by the political changes that allowed all citizens to participate in the decision making of the polis.

Many of the poor people had hoped that Solon would redistribute the land. He did not; but he did lay the groundwork that enabled all Athenian citizens to share in the economic growth of the city. On the one hand, he encouraged the development of manufacturing, first by granting citizenship to all craftsmen who migrated to Athens with their entire households to practice their crafts; and second by decreeing that only those who had taught their sons a trade were entitled to support in their old age. On the other hand, to ensure an adequate food supply for these artisans and craftsmen and their families, he prohibited the export of agricultural products, except for olive oil.

Solon also introduced an official standard of weights and measures and issued the first Attic currency. With these last reforms, Solon created the necessary and sufficient conditions for the invention of a market economy—the first market economy in history. In a market economy, the political authority of the society gives up control of production and distribution. In contrast to the palace-centered economies of Egypt, Mesopotamia, and Mycenae, the impersonal mechanism of the market now allocated resources and commodities in Athens.[36] The market in Athens did not actually come into being until after Solon's death and after the Athenians began to mint their own coins, probably about 575 B.C.,[37] but it was the direct outcome of Solon's economic reforms.

The first market was the produce market, the *agora*, a place where farmers came to sell food retail to the landless craftsmen and merchants. Soon Athens also had a wholesale provisions market, where farmers could sell produce in bulk to traders for long-distance trade. Finally there appeared a money market, where money lenders and banks could buy, sell, and rent money.[38]

The market economy that first began in Athens in the Sixth century was one of the consequences of the invention of writing. For the market could not exist without money, and money, in all its functions, is possible only because of writing. The Greeks and other people early on had a kind of money insofar as they used some things as units of value for various types of transactions. Thus, oxen and other livestock were used in the transfer of property in marriage negotiations. The Greeks also used tripods as standards of personal wealth and employed iron nails and measured quantities of precious metal in buying and selling transactions. But none of these was suitable as a medium of exchange: They all lacked standardization or were too easily adulterated, too bulky to transport, or too time consuming to deal with. Coins were the first medium of exchange. The first coins were minted in Lydia between 625 and 600 B.C., although they probably were not used initially as a medium of exchange but simply as a unit of value to pay workers for service to the state. Coins were uniform weights of precious metal calibrated into an extensive system of fractions. Their invention facilitated retail transactions: Sellers and buyers no longer had to weigh out quantities of metal; they simply counted the coins. Each city stamped its official seal on one side of the coin and a design on the other. This guaranteed the weight and purity and protected against clipping or shaving the edges or back.

The emergence of a medium of exchange could only have taken place in a literate culture because only in a literate culture will people (1) believe that some markings on a piece of metal do encode a standard value, (2) accept such an artifact in exchange for some real good, and (3) recognize such an artifact as real income. I do not mean that the illiterate cannot engage in money transactions. Obviously, they can. But they can do this only because they live in a culture in which literacy exists: They understand what writing and reading are, even if they have not mastered these skills, and they know that standardized meanings and values can be truly encoded and decoded in regularized, commonly accepted, and widely understood transactions. Although illiterate cultures have created "money" to serve as a standard of value (e.g., wampum), no illiterate culture has created money to serve as a medium of exchange.

The second kind of market, the wholesale market, was also possible only because of writing. For a market to function, the buyers and sellers have to exchange information about the supply and demand conditions, which are always measured by price. Yet this information is meaningless without knowledge of prior transactions—knowledge of the past record of prices. Here, money serves not just as a medium of exchange but also as a unit of accounting. So an international wholesale market requires written records of supply and demand conditions over time, encoded in the unit of account.

The third kind of market that emerged in Greece, the money market, was possible only because of writing, simply because such a market functions through credit instruments: letters of credit, IOUs, drafts, and other negotiable paper. According to M.I. Finley, the money market was never too developed in Athens, especially not before the development of parchment in the late third century B.C.[39]

The market economy made things better for the Greeks. The retail market broadened choices. In a barter transaction, a seller of sheep who wants a cow is limited to trading with a person who has a cow and wants a sheep. When coins became a medium of exchange, the seller of sheep could sell sheep to anyone in the market who wanted sheep and could pay for them, and with this money the seller could buy cows from anyone who had cows to sell.[40]

The international wholesale market made thing better by transforming products into standardized commodities. Standardization is necessary for a regularly functioning market. Without standardized goods, buyers cannot bid for specific types of goods and prices cannot measure market conditions. Thus, cows, eggs, grain, and olive oil were graded into classes acceptable to trade. Standardization protects the buyer and the seller by ensuring a minimal quality control over commodities traded.

Just as the wholesale market improved and maintained the quality of commodities traded, so the money market improved financial transactions. That is, by encoding these transactions in writing, people were able to scrutinize them more critically. This led to the realization that money is capital, a factor of production, and should therefore, like any other factor of production, earn income (interest). Here, then, was a new way to become wealthy: through participating in the money market as an investor, lender, or speculator.

The entire market economy helped make things better by providing more opportunities for more people to become wealthy. In the market people could not only sell in order to buy, but they could buy in order to sell: They could buy cheap and sell dear. In the market, through the market, one could "make money." Indeed, the invention of money meant that riches could have no limit; each person could always strive for more. Moreover, money can buy anything, and there is nothing the person with money cannot become. Solon noted this in one of his poems:

> Money wins friendship, honor, place and power
> And sets man next to the proud tyrant's throne.
> All trodden paths and paths untrod before
> Are scaled by nimble riches, where the poor
> Can never hope to win the heart's desire.
> A man ill-formed by nature and ill-spoken,
> Money shall make him fair to eye and ear;
> Money shall earn him health and happiness,
> And only money can cloak iniquity.[41]

THE RETREAT FROM THE MARKET ECONOMY

Although it did create great wealth for Greece, the market economy also created new problems—problems hinted at in the last line of Solon's poem. Should money be able to buy anything? Should everything be marketable? Should people be able to buy and sell public offices? Or love? Or another human being? These moral criticisms of the market led, in time, to the proscription of certain kinds of market transactions: simony, prostitution, and slavery.

By the fifth century B.C., most of the intellectuals of Athens stood opposed to the pursuit of wealth, denouncing it as subversive of the moral and social order. In Sophocles' (496-406 B.C.) *Antigone*, he has Creon say: "Nothing so evil as money ever grew to be current among men. This lays cities low, this drives men from their homes, this trains and warps honest souls till they set themselves to works of shame; this still teaches folk to practice villanies, and to know every godless deed." Plato, writing a little bit later held that it is impossible to be good in a high degree and rich in a high degree at the same time. He condemned the tendency of those who traded in the market to make "gains without limit," and in the *Laws*, he prohibited interest on loans. Aristotle, Plato's pupil, called all interest "usury" and condemned it as unnatural; retail trade, too, he regarded as unnatural.[42] The pursuit of money, he claimed led people "to turn every quality of art into a means of getting wealth." For Aristotle, the unnaturalness of the retail and the money markets lay in the fact that in the market one uses goods and money for the purpose of making money—not for their real purposes: The real purpose of money he says, is as a medium of exchange; the real purpose of goods is for the well-being of the people—a shoe is for wearing, not for making money.[43]

This condemnation of the economic arrangements of Greece by its philosophers, playwrights, and poets did not seem to dissuade people from believing that material wealth brings happiness. The markets of Greece continued to flourish and grow, especially in Athens, which Pericles (c.495-429 B.C.) said "draws the produce of the world into our harbor so that to the Athenian, the fruits of other countries are as familiar a luxury as those of his own."[44] And when, in the next century, the conquests of Alexander extended Hellenistic civilization so that it stretched from the Indus river to the Nile, it became, in Rostovtzeff's words, "one great market, controlled by the Greek or Hellenized merchant and the Greek manufacturer.[45]

If the retreat of the intellectuals from the economic realm had little or no effect on Greece, it did have a serious impact on Rome, who conquered Greece, but was, in turn, conquered by the Greek poets, playwrights, and philosophers.

The source of wealth for Rome throughout its history—from the Republic through the Empire—was not trade, but conquest. Originally, this came in the form of loot and tribute; later, when the Empire had expanded to include most of Europe and the near east and there were no more lands to conquer and exploit, wealth came to Rome in the form of taxes. The state redistributed the income to the upper classes in grants of land and contracts to build public works: roads, aqueducts, temples, amphitheaters, mausoleums, and public baths. The rest of the population—citizens, slaves, and freemen—worked for the rich or maintained their own workshops and factories. There were retail markets, but the state, and sometimes rich individuals, interfered with their operation by supplying free food to the poor, or food at below market prices.

The upper classes of Rome despised the market and loathed those who did become wealthy through it. The Roman upper classes, who received their wealth from the state and their social values from the Greek intellectuals, regarded those who made money in the market as vulgar, lacking culture. Here is Petronius's vicious satire of Trimalchio, a freed slave who had become a millionaire:

> I shipped a cargo of wine, bacon, beans, perfume and slaves. And then fortune came through nicely in the nick of time: sold her gold and clothes off her back and put a hundred gold coins in the palm of my hand. That was the yeast of my wealth. Besides, when the gods want something done, it gets done in a jiffy. On that one voyage alone, I cleared about five hundred thousand. Right away I bought up all my old master's property. I built a house, I went into slave-trading and cattle-buying. Everything I touched just grew and grew like a honeycomb. Once I was worth more than all the people in my home town put together I picked up my winnings and pulled out. I retired from trade and started lending money to ex-slaves. To tell the truth, I was tempted to quit for keeps, but on the advice of an astrologer, who'd just come to town, I decided to keep my hand in. . . .
>
> Meanwhile, with Mercury's help, I built this house. As you know, it used to be a shack; now its a shrine. It has four dining rooms, twenty bedrooms, two marble porticoes, an upstairs dining room, the master bedroom where I sleep, the nest of that viper there, a fine porter's lodge, and guestrooms enough for all of my guests. In fact, when Scaurus came down here from Rome, he wouldn't put up anywhere else, though his father has lots of friends down on the shore who would have been glad to have him. And there are lots of other things I'll show you in a bit. But take my word for it: money makes the man. No money and you're nobody. But big money, big man. That's how it was with yours truly: from mouse to millionaire.[46]

Cicero's criticism of economic activities is more straightforward. Following Aristotle, he divides occupations into the "liberal" and the "vulgar." He condemns the "odious occupations of the collector of customs" and the "menial work of the unskilled laborer," and "equally contemptible," he adds, is the business of the retail trade. The work of the mechanic is "degrading," whereas the least reputable of all trades—as Terence also said—are "fishmongers, butchers, cooks, and sausage makers." Moreover, "business on a small scale is despicable, large scale trade is only less despicable."[47] As Cicero viewed it, agriculture, (large estate farming) and service to the state are the only occupations fit for a gentleman.

The argument presented by the Latin writers—by Petronius, Seneca, Horace and Cicero—and subscribed to by the Roman upper classes was that only those with culture merited having wealth. Here's Seneca:

We still remember Calvisius Sabinus, the millionaire. He had the fortune of a freedman—and the brains: I never saw such tasteless wealth. His memory was so bad that he'd forget Ulysses' name one minute, Achille's the next, and Priam's the next, men we know as well as our tutors.[48]

In casting culture—literary culture—as the criterion for wealth, these ancients were simply extending arguments to the economic realm that were already familiar in the political and intellectual realms. In all three of these realms, as we have seen, writing had come to play a conservative role. According to the arguments, only those who had a broad and deep knowledge of the written tradition—a broad and deep knowledge of the traditional culture—were fit to rule; only they could know the truth about the nature of things; only they deserved or merited wealth. Recall that writing had originally improved things in all three realms first by destroying the existing arrangements and then by creating new arrangements. Now, finally, writing had become the medium for preserving those new arrangements, thereby becoming the medium for preventing change.

WRITING AND THE OPEN SOCIETY

In this chapter, I have argued that argumentative writing first arose among the Greeks because this function of writing became possible only after the invention of the alphabet. Argumentative writing destroyed the magical world all civilizations had lived in until this time and replaced it with a rational world: In a rational world, people explain all that happens by reference to laws, rules, and principles, not by reference to some transcendent spirit or god. I have also suggested that writing destroyed Greek tribalism and replaced it with a democratic polity in which all people, or most of them, were free and equal before the law. Finally, I have suggested that argumentative writing facilitated the growth of the market economy.

My thesis, once again, is that argumentative writing helped make things better. It remains only to pull together the three major contributions of Greece to Western civilization and display the common thread that unites them. Rationality, democracy, and the market all share the notion that things get better in the intellectual realm, in the political realm, and in the economic realm when we subject them to criticism.

In the intellectual realm, when we criticize theories and ideas, we uncover their weaknesses and inadequacies—often in the form of contradictions. Then, because human beings seek cognitive order, this uncovery leads to improvement—it sets afoot intellectual efforts to refine, modify, or change the theories in light of the criticisms. The Greek invention of the alphabet enabled people to encode their theories in writing. This allowed them to attain some distance from the theories and thus subject them to more careful critical scrutiny. The pre-Platonic Greek philosophers inaugurated this critical tradition in writing. They created critical rationalism—the practice of consciously and deliberately improving our theories through criticism. As a result, things got better; our theories improved, and people came to understand better the universe they inhabited.

In the social and political realms, improvements also come about through criticism. That is, things get better when those adversely affected by some law, practice, policy, or procedure can complain, criticize, or challenge what hurts them. This leads to change. And when the ensuing refinements, modifications, or changes diminish the evils complained about, then we say improvement has taken place. When a society has regular, institutionalized procedures through which people can protect themselves by both voicing their criticisms and complaints and securing a response, we call this a democracy. The Greeks, under the leadership first of Solon and then Cleisthenes, did create the first democracy, a polity that had institutionalized arrangements that all citizens could use to protect themselves against laws, policies, and practices that adversely affected them.

In the economic realm, the quality of our goods and services gets better when we subject them to criticism. The market is a mechanism for the expression of such criticism, and criticism takes the form of price. The value or worth of any good or service is simply the price it will bring in the market. Buyers display their criticisms through the prices they are willing to pay for a given good. ("That's not worth it; I won't buy it.") They criticize commodities by reducing the price they are willing to pay for them. Sellers can then respond to the criticisms displayed by buyers by improving their goods. Or, instead of improving the quality of their goods, they may improve the quantity—making the purchase a better buy by giving buyers more for their money. The Greeks created the first market economy, in which we find retail markets, wholesale markets, and money markets. Through the market, the quality of goods and services improved, the economic transactions became more efficient and productive, and the Greeks became more wealthy.

Rationalism, democracy, and the market are all characteristics of what may be called an open society. By an open society, I mean one wherein people can improve things through criticism. It is a society in which criticism is encouraged and critics are protected. I do not claim that the ancient Greeks created a full-fledged open society. The murder of Socrates, if nothing else, reveals how little they understood what they were doing. Had they realized that criticism is the spring of cultural progress, they would have encouraged and protected him. Greek society certainly was not completely rational, or thoroughly democratic, and it did not have a complete market economy.[4][9] But the Greeks did begin to move Western civilization toward an open society. They were the first to institutionalize criticism in their political, economic, and intellectual arrangements.

THE GREAT RETREAT

The journey toward and open society, however, was short lived, probably because an open society creates a strain on people: An open society has no certainty, no security, no stability. When everything is open to criticism, everything is liable to change: theories and ideas, laws and procedures, the prices of goods and sevices.

To many, an open society appeared chaotic and disordered. It was not, of course, disordered, for there is an order to an open society, but the order is abstract. That is, rationalism, democracy, and the market are not mechanisms that provide answers to the intellectual, political, and economic problems that people confront: Rationalism—critical rationalism—does not tell us which of our theories is true; democracy does not tell us which of our proposals is good; the market does not tell us what a fair price is. On the contrary, the market, democracy, and critical rationalism are all human inventions for ascertaining what is unfair, bad, or false. Rationalism is simply a set of abstract procedural rules (called logic) that help us weed out false theories: The rationalist rejects as false those theories that lead to contradictions. Democracy is simply a set of abstract procedural rules through which we weed out bad policies and bad decisions. Bad policies and bad decisions are those that cannot survive critical discussion and debate. The market is a set of abstract procedures through which we weed out unfair prices: The trader in the market rejects a price as unfair when he or she can purchase the same goods elsewhere at a lower price.

Although people can weed out false theories, bad decisions, and unfair prices by following the abstract rules and procedures of rationalism, democracy, and the market, what remain are not true theories, good policies, or fair prices. What remain are theories, policies, or prices that we can tentatively accept or hold onto only until additional criticism uncovers what is wrong with them.

In an open society, individuals must each assume responsibility for the theories they accept, the policies they subscribe to, and the prices they pay for goods and services. There is no authority to tell them what to think, what to accept, what to pay. In an open society, the individual is faced with competing theories, competing proposals and demands, and competing goods and services. In the open society, there is no cooperation among thinkers to proclaim an agreed-upon truth, no cooperation among citizens to subscribe to an agreed-upon common good, no cooperation among merchants and traders to sell at an agreed-upon fair price. Instead thinkers compete with one another by criticizing each other's theories; citizens and groups of citizens compete by criticizing each other's demands and proposals; and merchants and traders compete by lowering their prices.

Perhaps most difficult of all, in an open society people have to give up subjective certainty. For in an open society one's subjective feelings are irrelevant—how one feels about them has no bearing on what theories are accepted, what policies are decided on, what prices are charged. The open society is an objective world, not a subjective one. The impersonal workings of the institutional arrangements human beings have created determine these matters: The procedures of research and scholarship determine what theories are false, the democratic process determines what policies are bad, and the procedures of the market determine what prices are unfair. In an open society, regardless of what anyone may feel or believe, a theory is false if someone refutes it; a policy is bad if it causes pain or suffering to someone or some group; a price of a commodity is unfair if others sell it for less.

It comes as no surprise then that many Greeks experienced what Gilbert Murray called a failure of nerve, what Dodds called a fear of freedom, what Popper called the strain of civilization, and what I will call the great retreat.[50] The intellectuals led the retreat, and the commanders were Plato and Aristotle. They, of course, did not construe their undertaking as a retreat but rather as a crusade to make things better—an effort to create a more ordered society, a more coherent world view, a more stable polity, a more moral economy.

Casting themselves as the defenders of truth, goodness, and justice, these intellectuals declared that human beings *could* know truth, *could* pass good laws, *could* determine a fair price. At least they thought some people could do this: Those people who were the best and brightest, those who had studied and had absorbed their written culture.

I am not claiming that the intellectuals who led the great retreat ignored or completely discarded rationalism, democracy, and the market. What they did was modify these inventions to accomodate and legitimize their own claims that human beings could know truth, pass good laws, and determine a fair price. Thus they reconstrued rationalism as justificatory rationalism: A theory, they said, was true if one could justify it, if one could present arguments or reasons to confirm it. They rejected democracy because, they said, it did not lead to a just society. Justice, as Plato argued in the *Republic*, is an ideal knowable only to a select few, who had to be especially educated and trained to become rulers of the state. A just society, the intellectuals insisted, was a meritocracy. And although they did not reject the market economy, these intellectuals viewed it as an unnatural activity, and therefore one to be subordinated to the wisdom and prudence of those who ruled the state.

For almost two thousand years after Plato and Aristotle, Western culture did not change significantly.

There were no new political arrangements: The empire perdured, first as the Alexandrian Hellenistic Empire, then as the Roman Empire, and finally as the Holy Roman Empire. Throughout this time, people deemed a just society as one in which the rulers were good and noble men.

The economic arrangements did not improve during this period. The market never completely disappeared, but it was constrained and limited by the political rulers—secular and religious leaders—who imposed their ideas of a fair price on all economic transactions.

No new theoretical understandings appeared. The ideas of the Greeks, especially those of Plato and Aristotle, were accepted as true; and when Christianity triumphed the ideas of these "pagan" philosophers were used to justify the revealed truths of religion.

Argumentative writing, invented by the Greeks sometime in the ninth century B.C., had helped humans improve Western culture over a period of some five hundred years. Then, for the next two thousand years, argumentative writing prevented further cultural improvement. With the invention of printing, which appeared in the West in the late fifteenth century, things once again began to get better.

Part Three

Printing and the Origins of
Rational Civilization

Chapter Four

Printing and the Open Society

Print created the modern world—the world of science, the world of the modern state, the world of capitalism—and it created the open society. As we saw in previous chapters, the media that had emerged earlier in history—the medium of speech and the medium of writing—had helped improve things by encoding the existing culture so people could criticize it and then modify it in light of the criticism. Printing did this, too, but it did more. In George Sarton's words, "printing made it possible for the first time to publish hundreds of copies that were alike and yet may be scattered everywhere."[1] By duplicating, reproducing, and disseminating culture to all who could read, printing enlarged the number of critics who could participate in the critical dialogue through which human beings improve their culture. By creating a larger community of critics, printing accelerated the progress of culture: Within two hundred years of the advent of the printing press, the existing political, social, and economic arrangements, as well as the existing intellectual milieu, gave way to better ones.

For a long time prior to printing, the culture of Western civilization had remained unchanged. During the medieval period, the improvements that writing had brought about became immunized against criticism because people viewed that which had been encoded in written manuscripts as something sacred and authoritative: the Holy Bible and the writings of the Church Fathers, for example, as well as the writings of such secular authorities as Aristotle, Galen and Ptolemy. The theories, the proposals—the answers—contained in these writings had become so authoritative that knowledge had not advanced, the political arrangements had not gotten better, and the economic conditions had not improved since antiquity.

THE PRINTING PRESS AND THE MODERN WORLD

Historians usually credit Johann Gutenberg with the invention of the first printing press, which he constructed sometime in the middle of the fifteenth century.
On the surface, this transition from script to print lacked dramatic significance.
Scribes were not put out of work; they still continued to copy manuscripts by
hand. In fact, nearly as many manuscript "books" survive from the second half of
the fifteenth century as from the first half. Indeed, for over a century, scribes continued to cater to the luxury trade, turning out deluxe volumes for those who could
afford them. Moreover, the physical appearance of the early printed book followed
the manuscript tradition, and the first printers fashioned their type after the letters
used in written manuscripts. What was obviously different, of course, was that all
the letters of the alphabet were cast from molds which produced vowels, consonants, and ligatures of a uniformity that could not have been achieved by the most
skilled calligraphers. This standardization created what Elizabeth Eisenstein has
called "typographical fixity."[2]

Typographical fixity did bring about a dramatic change. By making it possible
to construct hundreds of copies that were exactly alike and that could be scattered
everywhere, the printing press accomplished in less than two hundred years what
the scribes had tried to do for almost two thousand years: recover and preserve the
cultural heritage of Western civilization.

It is true that the bookshops of ancient Rome, the Alexandrian library, and even
certain medieval monasteries all contained large collections of ancient texts. But
these were incomplete, isolated, and transitory collections. Without multiple, standardized copies of these texts, the culture of the past was continually in danger of
being lost. Even the rise of lay stationers in university towns in the twelfth and
thirteenth centuries, who employed teams of scribes to copy manuscripts, did not
markedly change the number, the dissemination, or the preservation of the available manuscripts.

Scholars in every field continued to have only limited access to diverse and
incomplete collections of texts from the past. Moreover, what the scribes copied
by hand often contained mistakes and errors, which perdured—or were made
worse—in subsequent copying. Consider the case of medical literature. Prior to
the printing of Galen's *Anatomical Procedures* in 1530, the hand-copied manuscripts of Galen's works had scrambled anatomical data, confused the nomencla-
ture, and corrupted pictures and diagrams. Some important Galenic texts had almost disappeared. In addition to corrupted and drifting texts, manuscripts sometimes migrated or were misplaced or destroyed. Furthermore, there was no uniform method of cataloging them: Manuscripts lacked title pages, and this prevented the development of any rational scheme for storing and retrieving texts.[3]

The printing press changed all this. Typographical fixity prevented the continual
decay and drift of ancient texts and stopped the loss of manuscripts. Once they
were encoded in print, the works from the past became permanently preserved,
correct and correctable, and easily retrievable. Retrieval became easier still when

printed books were given title pages and their pages were numbered. Sometime in the sixteenth century indexes appeared, which further facilitated the retrieval of encoded infomation, for now the only essential feat of memory was to remember the order of the alphabet.[4]

Before the coming of the printing press, there had been several abortive classical revivals. These unsuccessful attempts to recover the culture of antiquity had all foundered on the technical inability of scribes and scriptoria to reproduce ancient texts in sufficient numbers. But the classical revival initiated by Italian literati and artists in the late fourteenth century did succeed spectacularly—so spectacularly that historians have called this period between the fourteenth and sixteenth centuries the Renaissance. The printing press enabled this revival to succeed whereas earlier ones had failed. It was the printing press that made Petrarch's prediction come true: "The slumber of forgetfulness will not last forever," he had promised. "After the darkness has been dispelled, our grandsons will be able to walk back into the pure radiance of the past." Printing did not cause the Renaissance, since the classical revival begun by Petrarch's generation was already under way by the time the printing press appeared. Printing simply preserved and made permanent that revival. Ever since then, the works of antiquity have been with us continually.[5]

Printing did more than simply recover and preserve the works of antiquity. Now, tor the first time, people could distinguish between themselves and the ancients—or, more correctly, between the culture of the ancients and their own culture. People are modern precisely because they can distance their culture from ancient culture, and they can do this because the civilization of the past is encoded in print, thus becoming a phenomenon complete in itself, detached from the contemporary world. Moderns have a new temporal consciousness, a new understanding of themselves and their relation to the past. Print did not create this new understanding; human beings created it. But they created it because print had enabled them to discover what was wrong with their earlier understandings. Once all the existing manuscripts were encoded in print, people could readily see that ancient civilizations were over, done with, finished. They became critical of all previous constructions of antiquity that had failed to distinguish it correctly and replaced them with a new temporal consciousness.

This new modern temporal consciousness of ancient culture was further enhanced by distinctions printers made in published texts that scribes had never made in hand-copied manuscripts. Printers were in the business of selling large quantities of many different books. Their products had to be clearly labeled and accurately described so that they could merchandise them successfully. Thus, printers and printer-booksellers, largely for economic reasons, clearly and accurately identified the author of each book published—usually by means of a title page—because it was in their interests to do so. Not being subject to such economic pressures, scribes had paid little attention to identifying clearly and accurately the authors of the texts they copied. According to Goldschmidt, a title like *Sermones*

Bonaventure found in a medieval codex might have any one of the following meanings:[6]

a. Sermons *composed* by St. Bonaventure of Fidenza.
b. Sermons composed by *some other writer* called Bonaventure.
c. Sermons *copied* by a friar called Bonaventure.
d. Sermons copied by an unnamed friar who *belonged to a house* called after St. Bonaventure.
e. Sermons *preached* by some friar called Bonaventure (but not composed by him).
f. A volume of sermons which once *belonged to a friar* called Bonaventure.
g. A volume of sermons which once *belonged to a house* called Bonaventure.
h. A volume of sermons by various authors, of which the first (or the one deemed most important) was by some Bonaventure and which consequently was *shelved* in a library under *Bonaventure.*

This variety of possibilities dampened any consciousness of who wrote what and when, whereas the bio-bibliographical procedures introduced by printing brought about a temporal consciousness never before possible. Readers could now clearly identify the ancient authors and what each had written. For the first time, people perceived the works of antiquity from a fixed distance. For in the very act of recovering the culture of antiquity, the people of the Renaissance discovered themselves: They were moderns, not ancients.

What did it mean to be modern? Historians since Burckhardt have described the Renaissance man as *l'uomo universale*—the polymath, the virtuoso of many talents, skills, and interests. The emergence of such a character is clearly a consequence of printing, which made available a storehouse of ideas and information not accessible before. Printing liquified knowledge and sent it coursing among the readers of books: Printing dispelled ignorance. Now anyone who could read could learn the arts, crafts, sciences, and technologies described and explained in print—described in words, pictures, diagrams, charts, and tables. Leon Battista Alberti (1404-1472), the prototypical universal man, writing about himself in the third person said that "to him, letters, in which he delighted so greatly, seemed sometimes like flowering and richly fragrant buds, so that hunger or sleep could scarcely distract him from his books."

During the age of the scribe, many forms of knowledge had become esoteric, passed on by a select few who instructed all initiates in the secrets of the trade. Printing destroyed this secrecy; it overcame the isolation of trades and techniques, the separation of the liberal arts from the mechanical ones: printing decompartmentalized. Printing destroyed the guild system, opened closed shops, and encouraged a freer trade in ideas that led to new syntheses and unexpected syncretions. Instrument makers, for example, could now profit more from disclosing trade secrets in books than they could by concealing them, as they had during the medieval period. In the case of lensmaking—which had existed since the thirteenth century—the publication of trade secrets gave rise to the telescope, the microscope, and the science of optics.

PRINTING AND THE OPEN SOCIETY

The early impact of printing was twofold: It restored or recovered ancient wisdom, and it made public that knowledge and those skills that the guilds and crafts had long held secret. This double information explosion created a more open society, in sharp contrast with the closed society of the medieval period. In this open society, wherein the printing press disclosed knowledge and information and scattered it everywhere, people discovered that they were free to enact the self they chose to be—they could become individuals: "Thou man, masterful molder and sculptor of thyself," as Pico della Mirandola put it in *The Dignity of Man* (1486). People now realized they were no longer members of a collective that imposed some predetermined identity upon them—an identity carried in the very names they bore: "You (and your children) will be a Smith, a Carpenter, a Baker." Now a person so named was no longer marked; he could take up a different occupation. For when knowledge and information became available through books, each person could take on a new identity; each could become what he willed. The collectivism of a feudal society was undermined by the knowledge that flowed freely from the printing presses of Europe. (Printers also furthered individualism when they—largely for their own economic self-interest—included portraits in their books as well as clear, careful, and correct identification of authors, their birthdates, birthplaces, and their personal histories.)

Printing also subverted another characteristic of the closed society: intellectual cooperation. In place of cooperation, the press encouraged competition, a characteristic of the open society. Printers published books and pamphlets that contained an ever-widening variety of different and often conflicting beliefs, theories, and attitudes, which ensured a continuous competition of ideas. Authors, printers, and booksellers all competed with one another, attempting to persuade readers that what they purveyed was correct, true, and valid—at least better than what their competitors offered. This intellectual competition for the minds of readers replaced cooperation. The printing press now produced more books than any one person could read, containing more different theories, ideas, and proposals than any one person could accept. As long as printers in competition with one another were free to publish whatever books they chose, there could be no universal guaranteed cooperation with orthodoxies of any kind. So it was to be from then on—except in those times and those places wherein some central authority re-established a closed society by securing total control over what came from the printing presses in its domain.

In addition to promoting individualism and competition, the printing press promoted the idea of equality—a third characteristic of the open society. This happened in at least two ways. First, the dissemination of ideas, knowledge, skills, and procedures, which allowed them to be publicly criticized and tested, led to the rejection of traditional knowledge. Paracelsus symbolized this when he threw a copy of Galen's work into a bonfire in 1527. Once printing had arrived, no knowledge could remain authoritative, no matter where it came from. All theories had to be equally tested and criticized. All claims to knowledge had an equal right to a hearing or a reading; and in the age of print, the intellectual hierarchies characteristic of closed societies became impossible—as long as no authority could claim that it was infallible.

A second way the printing press broke down hierarchy was by publishing books fom antiquity that informed people about the social ideas of the ancients—ideas that were different from those current in Europe at the time. Those social ideas of the ancients served as a counterenvironment from which people could critically appraise their own times. The ancient authors made people of the Renaissance period conscious of a nobility different from that which then existed. Thus, we find a number of writers of the Renaissance proclaiming a nobility of excellence, not of birth—a nobility of excellence is characteristic of an open society because it is a nobility open to anyone. Dante, for example, whose works were widely published during the Renaissance, argued that nobility had nothing to do with birth and everything to do with intellectual and moral eminence; and Poggio, who wrote a book called *On Nobility* (1440), reminded his readers that Aristotle called noble those who strove after that which is truly good. By disseminating and preserving such ideas, printing did much to subvert the social hierarchy of the middle ages and set afoot the modern idea of social equality of equality of opportunity, in which one's position in society depends on one's talents and virtue, one's merits, one's excellence.[7]

Finally—in addition to promoting individualism, competition, and equality— the printing press created the ideal of scientific objectivity. Scientific objectivity is not a psychological phenomenon. It does not inhere in a detached or disinterested point of view on the part of the scientist. (Scientists are no more detached or disinterested than the rest of us.) Rather, as Karl Popper has demonstrated, scientific objectivity is a sociological phenomenon: It depends on the existence of a critical community that will provide critical feedback to proposed theories, ideas, plans, and explanations. People, of course, had criticized knowledge before the printing press came along. But prior to the printing press, knowledge could only be encoded in speech or in writing. These media of speech and writing do detach knowledge from the knower and convert it into objective knowledge—something that can be examined, analyzed, and criticized by others. But the critics of speech and writing were necessarily limited in number: limited to those who heard the speech (the listeners), or limited to those readers who had access to the hand-written documents. Moreover, readers and listeners often erred in their understanding of what was said or written; and without readily available multiple copies, it was very difficult to corroborate what had actually been said or written. Printing made knowledge much more objective, for now knowledge was encoded in typographical fixity, in multiple copies that could be scattered everywhere, so great numbers of people could read the knowledge, corroborate their understanding of it, and criticize it.

With printing, it became clear that a world of knowledge did exist—a world whose denizens include theories, plans, problems, explanations, and proposals.

Fallible human beings create knowledge, so it can never be perfect—but it can be inproved through criticism. This is what scientific objectivity is: the continuous critical scrutiny of knowledge encoded in the medium of speech, writing, or—best of all—print.

The printing press not only facilitated scientific objectivity by enlarging the number of critics, it also created and maintained many different critical communities: in the arts, in the sciences, in politics, and in technology. The members of these various critical communities were artists, engineers, architects, instrument makers, mathematicians, philosophers, politicians, and statesmen. They read and then challenged and tried to refute, the theories of ancient and modern writers alike. I have already mentioned Paracelsus's treatment of Galen. The same critical scrutiny and rejection soon befell the works of Aristotle and Ptolemy and the writings of the Church Fathers, too. The critical reaction of Nathaniel Carpenter, an Englishman who published a book on geography early in the seventeenth century, is typical. Carpenter admitted that Lactantius (245-325), who had written about geography, was a pious, eloquent Church Father, but he claimed that "the childishness of his arguments will discover his ignorance in the very first rudiments of cosmographie."[8]

Criticism was not limited to the work of the ancients; the moderns experienced it too, which is clearly evident in the receptions given to the published books of Copernicus and Galileo. When the critics published their criticisms, they helped create a continuing critical dialogue in a field of study. Sometimes they even put forward new, better theories to replace those they had rejected. Witness Dürer, Alberti, Machiavelli, and Leonardo—to name only the most well known.

The case of Leonardo is instructive. He never published any of his writings, but instead concealed them in notebooks—in mirror writing, transcribed in a cryptic script. At his death, the five thousand pages of his manuscript notes were widely dispersed as collectors' items. Not until the nineteenth century did his notes reach a wide scholarly audience, who discovered his genius. But because he never published during his lifetime, Leonardo da Vinci never actually participated in the critical dialogues going on about mathematics, engineering, and anatomy. Although he had made great advances in these fields, he never contributed to the adancement of knowledge. Despite his genius, his knowledge remained subjective knowledge—knowledge never exposed to the critical scrutiny of others, but simply held as a belief.[9]

Subjective knowledge is characteristic of a closed society, in which theories and skills are closely guarded secrets transmitted only to chosen initiates. As long as knowledge remained subjective, it could not advance. Printing helped create an open society by making knowledge objective so that it could be more readily criticized. Printing made scientific objectivity possible on a scale that could never have existed before. Henceforth, knowledge advanced at a dizzying pace. The advent of the printing press demoted subjective knowledge to an inferior status. From then on, the only real knowledge was objective knowledge, and the only acceptable way to ascertain the worth of knowledge was scientific objectivity.

This state of affairs persisted as long as books were rapidly produced and readly accessible and as long as people could read.

THE PROTOTYPICAL MODERN MAN

I have argued that the printing press helped create the open society by facilitating the criticism of the existing social arrangements: the collectivism, the cooperation, the hierarchy, the subjectivism. All these characteristics of a closed society restricted the life chances of people. In place of these medieval characteristics, the printing press facilitated the rise of individualism, competition, equality, and scientific objectivity—the hallmarks of the open society of the modern world.

Probably no person of the Renaissance evinces these characteristics of the open society more clearly than Michel Eyguen, Seigneur de Montaigne (1533-1592), known simply as Montaigne. He disclosed himself as the prototypical modern man in his famous *Essays* (1580), in which, for the first time in the history of literature, an author wrote about himself—what he thought, felt, liked, disliked; his foibles and virtues; his faults and accomplishments. Here, for the first time in print—or writing—we find the celebration of an individual. Not part of any collective, not embedded in any hierarchical relationship, Montaigne had no predetermined identity imposed on him with which he was expected to cooperate. As he wrote in the Preface to his *Essays*:

> Had my intention been to forestall and purchase the world's opinion and favor, I would
> surely have adorned myself more quaintly, or kept a more grave and solemn march. I
> desire therein to be delineated in mine own genius, simple, and ordinary fashion, with-
> out contention, art, or study; for it is myself I portray. My imperfections shall therein
> be head to the life, and my natural form discerned, so far forth as public reverence has
> permitted.

Montaigne's rejection of the collectivism of the existing social order, his disavowal of hierarchy, and his repudiation of traditional roles mark him as a modern man. Yet many found the appearance of this new man upsetting. Coherence seemed to be slipping away. Here is how John Donne reacted to the emergent modern world:

> 'Tis all in pieces, all cohaerence gone;
> All just supply, and all Relation: Prince, Subject, Father,
> Sonne, are things forgot.
> For every man alone thinkes he hathe got
> To be a Phoenix, and that there can bee
> None of that kinde, of which he is, but hee:
> This is the world's condition now.

One can understand this reaction of John Donne. At that point, it certainly was hard to see that things were getting better, hard to recognize that collectivism, cooperation, and hierarchy—the values that modern people rejected—had all restricted and curtailed the life chances of most people.

Montaigne also personified the modern value of scientific objectivity. At the age of thirty-eight, he retired from public life to spend the remaining time in his library, where he studied the wisdom encoded in his books. He approached the contents of those books as objective knowledge, as knowledge that exists outside a knowing subject, as knowledge that could be criticized. That objective knowledge, he discovered, could not withstand his critical scrutiny. "What do I know?" became his motto. "Nothing with certainty," was his reply. Montaigne's skepticism was not a denial that the universe is rational, but only that its rationality is beyond the grasp of human reason. This critical approach of Montaigne disturbed people as much as his espousal of individualism. His thoroughgoing critical approach especially upset those who sought certainty in knowledge. Few at the beginning of the modern age recognized that criticism led to improved knowledge. Most instead saw it terminating in skepticism.[10] So philosophers anxiously searched for some new authoritative formulation for knowledge, some authority to replace the discredited authorities accepted before. At the beginning of the seventeenth century, Francis Bacon announced that he had found such an epistemological authority in sense experience; while later in the century, René Descartes declared that the foundation for certainty was human reason.

Here's how Bacon put it:

> I propose to establish progressive stages of certainty. The evidence of the senses, helped and guarded by a certain process of correction, I retain. But the mental operation which follows the act of sense, I, for the most part, reject; and instead of it, I open and lay out a new and certain path for the mind to proceed in, starting directly from the simple sensuous perception.

This "new and certain path" to truth, Bacon announced, was the method of induction:

> There are and can be only two ways of searching into and discovering truth. The one flies from the senses and particulars to the most general axioms, and from these principles, the truth of which it takes for settled and immoveable, proceeds to judgment and to the discovery of middle axioms. And this way now is now in fashion. The other derives axioms from the senses and particulars, rising by a gradual and unbroken ascent, so that it arrives at the most general axioms last of all. This is the true way, but as yet untried.

For Descartes, the authority for truth was not the senses but the mind. Therefore, he advised us to follow his method, which was "to accept nothing as true which I did not clearly recognize to be so; that is to say, carefully to avoid precipitation and prejudice in judgments, and to accept in them nothing more than what was presented to my mind so clearly and distinctly that I would have no occasion to doubt it."

Although both Bacon and Descartes are sometimes mentioned as the founders of modern philosophy, from the perspective I have presented here, both are better regarded as representatives of premodernity insofar as both construed knowledge as subjective beliefs that one could demonstrate to be true. I take this conception of subjective demonstrable knowledge to be characteristic of a closed society. Bacon went farthest in trying to construct a new intellectual closed society by attempting to get the English monarch, James I, to reform the universities and establish hierarchically organized collectives of scholars cooperatively engaged in gathering true knowledge. He made such proposals first in his *The Advancement of Learning* (1604) and then again in *De Augmentis Scientiarum* (1623), in which he proposed that all scholars should employ the true inductive method so that there will be a certain, authoritative knowledge base for the future advancement of knowledge.

One of the last treatises Bacon worked on was the posthumously published *New Atlantis*, a description of a utopian community that had as its centerpiece a model college, Solomon's House, whose function was "the finding out of the true nature of things."[11] Bacon staffed Solomon's House with a large collective of hierarchically organized scholars who worked cooperatively on assigned projects. There are "Pioneers," who undertake new experiments; and "Mystery Men," who collect the inventions made in the mechanical arts; and "Merchants of Light," who collect the inventions from foreign lands. Then there are the "Compilers," who draw all these findings on tables from which the "Benefactors" educe things for use for life and practice. The "Lamps" devise still more experiments to penetrate still more fully into the nature of things. The "Innoculators" execute these experiments, the findings from which the "Interpreters of Nature" raise into "greater observations, axioms, and aphorisms." In keeping with this intellectually closed society all these researchers take an oath to conceal "those inventions we think fit to keep secret." However, some of these secrets, Bacon admits, "we do reveal sometimes to the state, and sometimes not."[12]

While philosophers like Bacon and Descartes engaged in a fruitless and reactionary quest for certainty in knowledge, the scientists themselves proceeded apace with the critical approach characteristic of modern science. Here, too, the printing press helped things get better.

Chapter Five

Printing and Modern Science

"In the year 1500 Europe knew less than Archimedes," Alfred North Whitehead once pointed out; "yet in the year 1700, Newton's *Principia* had been written."[1] Traditionally, historians have explained the rise of science during this 200-year period by declaring that sometime during the Renaissance, people discarded dusty parchments and began to look at nature itself; and by dint of keen observations, they began to discover the laws that govern the physical universe. Actually, as Elizabeth Eisenstein has argued, modern science rose from those dusty parchments—from a critical reading of them made possible when the printing press began to encode them in typographical fixity, reproduce them in multiple copies and scatter them everywhere.[2]

THE RISE OF MODERN SCIENCE

In the field of astronomy, we find Copernicus publishing his *De Revolutionibus Orbium Coelestium* (1543) in an attempt to clear up the contradictions he had uncovered in Ptolemy's *Almagest*. In the field of anatomy, Vesalius published his *De Humani Corporis Fabrica* in 1543 to overcome the inadequacies he had un-covered in Galen's ancient text on anatomy. In the field of natural history, the recovered and published texts of Aristotle, Theophratus, Dioscorides, and Pliny gave rise to confusion and triggered the publication of new texts to solve some of the difficulties. The most famous was the *Commentary on Dioscorides* by Piet Mattioli, which appeared in 1554.[3]

By claiming that modern science came into being as a result of criticism of the science of the ancients, I do not mean to imply that there had been no criticism leveled at the theories of antiquity during the middle ages. As Pierre Duhem and A. C. Crombie have shown, some philosophers in medieval universities did teach theories about mechanics and optics that were based on criticisms of Aristotle's pronouncements.[4] So new scientific ideas had appeared during the middle ages. But the coming of the printing press changed the logic of the situation.

Prior to the printing press, most new scientific ideas were soon lost—encoded in some misplaced or forgotten manuscript, or corrupted by some scribe in the act of copying it. This happened to scientific criticism, too. As Dijksterhuis notes, "untenable and long refuted theories were revived time after time, to be refuted and rejected once again."[5] Once the printing press appeared, however, criticism could be encoded and preserved. This broke the cycle of making the same mistake over and over. The printing press enabled the entire community of scholars to learn from and forever thereafter avoid the mistakes of their predecessors. This gave birth to modern science.

Modern science did not arise because suddenly there appeared a generation of more intelligent people or because some scientists turned away from books and began to look at nature; nor did it arise as a slow, gradual growth out of the work of medieval scientists. No, modern science came into being because the printing press enabled people to encode criticisms of scientific ideas in typographical fixity, reproduce them in multiple copies, and scatter them everywhere. Now people had a better way of eliminating inadequate scientific theories. Western civilization had never lacked scientific theories—old theories and new theories—because people always have, and always will, make conjectures to explain or make sense of the goings-on they encounter. But what Western civilization had lacked was an effective medium for permanently eliminating those theories that were inadequate. The printing press thus came to serve as a means of selection: It helped wipe out those theories that were unfit. What remained was modern scientific knowledge: a body of objective knowledge (i.e., knowledge encoded in print) that had survived rigorous criticism.

The printing press created modern scientific knowledge by creating a community of scientists—a collection of widely scattered readers who, through reading, kept abreast of the state of knowledge in a given field. This community of scientists was a critical community. For in addition to informing people about the state of the field, the printing press provided them with a medium for participating in the critical dialogue through which scientific knowledge emerges.

Almost two thousand years before the invention of printing, scholars in Hellenistic Greece had accumulated vast manuscript collections in the libraries of Alexandria and Pergamum. These libraries had attracted a critical community of scientists who produced significant scientific treatises—Ptolemy, Archimedes, and Galen are some of the better-known scientists of that era. But the destruction of these Alexandrian libraries and the dispersal of their contents curtailed all scientific work. During the medieval period, many of those scientific works from the past all but disappeared, whereas many others remain hidden away in monasteries.

Without a traditional body of knowledge available to them, people could not surpass or even equal the scientific knowledge of the ancient Greeks. The coming of the printing press made scientific knowledge possible again. It reinstituted—on a much broader scale than ever before possible—the critical dialogue through which scientific knowledge emerges.

This critical dialogue was made possible by the new, elaborate, and widespread communication networks created by print shops, booksellers, and book fairs throughout Europe. These were convivial networks that any reader could plug into. Scholars could plug into these communication networks because the printing press had changed the logic of the situation for scholarship: Printing had increased the autonomy of the individual scholar. Now instead of wandering from monastery to monastery in search of manuscripts, scholars could stay at home and read the books in their library. Scholars had less need for teachers, too, because they could have portable books sent to them through which they could learn about the state of knowledge in a scientific field. And the ever-increasing output of book lists, reference guides, and other bibliographic aids allowed them to undertake a search of the literature on a scale not possible before. In addition, through grammar books, dictionaries, manuals, and handbooks, they could learn languages, mathematics, and any critical skill they needed to participate in the critical dialogue. Moreover, scholars could now study and analyze the books they read instead of spending countless hours slavishly copying manuscripts or memorizing the contents. The printed book became the warehouse of memory: Instead of storing them in their minds, scholars could turn to the readily available books that contained the rules of grammar, the formulas of mathematics, the laws of physics, and the anatomy of the body. Title pages, pagination, and indexes all facilitated retrieval.

PRINTING AND CRITICAL DIALOGUE

As we saw earlier, the printing press initially encoded, in multiple copies which were scattered everywhere, those same manuscripts from the past that scribes had labored over the centuries to preserve by hand-copying. So the messages first carried by the new communication networks were the messages from the past, the texts from antiquity. These earliest printed books included a vast amount of occult lore—works of alchemy, astrology, magic, cabala, and other arts—as part of the traditional wisdom.[6] So the intellectual ferment brought about by printing included much mystification and confusion as well as enlightenment. But the ancient texts in the so-called established fields of medicine, astronomy, and natural history also sowed confusion. For now that printing had multiplied the number of texts readily available to each scholar it was not long before scholars discovered diversity, conflict, and contradictions among the ancient authorities. Once Aristotle was compared to Ptolemy, or Averroes to Galen, the traditional transmission of received opinion suffered a breakdown. Confidence in old theories weakened; the creation of new theories quickened.

But what good were new theories without some way to decide among them? New theories only added to the confusion. What was needed, many insisted, was some new authority for scientific knowledge. If the authority of the ancients could no longer be sustained, then where could such an authority be found? Some scholars claimed to find it in the great book of nature itself. Here is how Tommaso Campanella (1568-1638) put it: "I learned more from the anatomy of an ant or a blade of grass . . . than from all the books which have been written since the beginning of time."[7]

The belief in nature as the authority for scientific knowledge was shared by many. Vives wrote, "I only call that knowledge which we receive when the senses are properly brought to observe things and in a 'methodical' way. . . . [This] knowledge . . . is called science firm and indubitable."[8] Here is what Peter Severinus, one of the followers of Paracelsus, wrote: "Burn up your books . . . buy yourself stout shoes, travel to the mountains, search the valley, the deserts, the shores of the sea, and the deepest depressions of the earth; note with care the distinction between animals, the differences of plants, the various kinds of minerals."[9] In one of its 1665 publications, the Royal Society, which traced its origins back to Bacon, claimed that its aim was "to study nature rather than books."[10]

In spite of such claims, however, it was the books of men that gave birth to modern science. For those new scientists of the sixteenth and seventeenth centuries who turned to nature did so to reconcile or decide among the competing and contradictory theories they found in the books the newly invented printing press made available to them.

The printing press not only initiated the observation of nature, it also directly influenced that observation. For when these scientists looked at nature, they looked at it with eyes different from those who had lived in the pre-print period. This is because no one can observe anything without a theory, a question, a problem.[11] So these observers now had their minds filled with theories, questions, and problems gathered from the books they had read or were reading. Moreover, the printing press influenced all observations insofar as it supplied scientists with new tools for observing, analyzing, and testing data. Printing, for example, hastened the discarding of Roman numerals in favor of Arabic ones, and it established uniform mathematical symbols and units of measurement. Before printing, surveyors and navigators had used their hands and feet to measure distance. Printing also supplied newly forged mathematical tools, like printed trigonometry tables, charts, logarithms, recorded tabulations, equations, and formulas that permitted more exact measurement and calculation. These new paper tools made observations more dependable and more rapid. Laplace once suggested that logarithm tables doubled the life of an astronomer.

Yet the observations these scientists made did not constitute "science." First, these observations had to be published in books or in periodicals—otherwise they had no meaning or significance. The printing press greatly improved all descriptions and explanations of observations by reproducing exact copies of pictures, diagrams, maps, and figures. Prior to printing, the astronomical texts of Ptolemy, the architectural texts of Vitruvius, and the natural history of Pliny had been often copied and translated without accompanying pictures. But when Vesalius published his *Structure of the Human Body* (*De Humani Corporis Fabrica*) in 1543, the book that inaugurated the modern science of anatomy, he sought the best artists to draw the illustrations—artists of the school of Titian—and engaged the most skilled Venetian wood block cutters to make the reproductions.[12] Agricola, commenting on his masterpiece on early technological writing, *De Re Metallica* (1556), explained that he not only described the "veins, tools, vessels, sluices, machines, furnaces" but also hired illustrators to delineate their forms "lest descriptions which are conveyed by words should either not be understood by the men of our time, or should cause difficulty to posterity."[13]

Just as printing initiated the observation of nature by confronting scholars with competing theories, explanations, and reports, so printing also directly affected the observations scientists made and, furthermore, encoded those new observations, theories, and explanations in typographical fixity, reproduced them in multiple copies, and scattered them everywhere. But this knowledge did not become scientific knowledge until readers subjected it to criticism and critical scrutiny. Once printed, it became part of the critical dialogue out of which scientific knowledge emerged: Scientific knowledge was that knowledge which, so far, survived criticism.

THE GROWTH OF SCIENTIFIC KNOWLEDGE

Printing made scientific progress possible. Scientific knowledge grows through criticism, and printing facilitated the procedure of criticism. Critical dialogue had gone on before, but the printing press changed the logic of the situation by enlarging the community of scholars to include more people and a wider variety of points of view. Printing created a worldwide critical dialogue, a dialogue from which none could be excluded—except by returning to the authoritarianism of a closed society.

Albrecht Dürer, for example, in his book on the proportions of the human body (*Vier Bucher von Manschlicher Proportion*, 1528) explained why a nonscholar such as he would undertake to publish a book. He did it "for the public benefit of all artists." He hoped his book "would induce other experts to do likewise so that our successors may have something to perfect and lead to further progress."[14] Dürer knew that his book would be criticized and that the criticisms would be published. But he also knew that this is how knowledge advances. Scholars in other fields recognized this, too. Simon Stevin (1558-1620), a military engineer, published his *Memoirs, Mathematiques* so that "his errors might be corrected and other inventions added, inasmuch as the joint efforts and the works of many scholars is required in this field."[15] The joint effort Stevin referred to was criticism.

When the printer Abraham Ortelius published his atlas, *Theatrum Orbis Terrarum* (*Theatre of the World*) in 1570, he asked readers to send in suggestions for corrections and revisions—criticisms. He received so many that he had to issue supplements and successive new editions. When Ortelius died in 1598, at least twenty-eight editions of the atlas had been published in Latin, Dutch, French, German, and Spanish.[16] The same course of progress is evident in the work of individual scholars and scientists. For example, each successive edition of the *Commentaries on Dioscorides*, which the botanist Pier Andrea Mattoli first published in 1558, contained revised and corrected descriptions of plants based on the criticisms readers had sent to the author.

This community of critics took no account of national boundaries—works presented in Latin were soon translated into vernaculars, and vice versa. The community transcended religion and class differences, too. Latin-reading astronomers, as well as vernacular-reading artisan-engineers, read and criticized scientific texts as they appeared in print; whereas surveyors, surgeons, and merchant adventurers consulted and criticized printed charts, diagrams, and maps that had been published to help them in their different lines of work. Astronomers and philosophers could now read and study both Aristotle and Ptolemy and uncover the contradictions never evident before when the (often incomplete) manuscript copies of each author had circulated only among small circles of experts in each field. Now professors of anatomy, physicians, barber-surgeons, and apothecaries could all study and criticize the works of Galen.

As a consequence of printing, there existed for the first time since the Hellenistic period a body of knowledge that comprised the state of the field in each discipline. But the knowledge was more widely diffused and more widely shared by greater numbers of people than had ever been possible before. Scientific progress, for the first time., was secured—precisely because the problem statements, the theories, and the critical discussions were all encoded permanently in print and open to continual critical scrutiny and dialogue.

By bringing more people into the critical commuhity to engage in the dialogue, the printing press heated up the critical dialogue and raised it to a new level—a meta-level—wherein people began criticizing the critical dialogue itself. This happened precisely because the critical community included not only pure scientists and mechanics, but pious and devout scientists and mechanics and even clergymen—all of whom criticized the emerging scientific knowledge because it conflicted with the Scriptures. This criticism led to new problems and questions: What is truth? What are the standards for truth? What is the relationship between science and Scripture? Controversies over questions like these led to initial efforts to demarcate scientific knowledge from nonscientific knowledge. These developments are best seen in the famous trial and condemnation of Galileo.

PRINTING AND ASTRONOMY

The story begins with the *Almagest* of Claudius Ptolemy (fl. 150 B.C.) which had put forth the geocentric theory of the universe that had become the traditionally accepted astronomical system in Western civilization. According to this theory, the earth was motionless and at the center of the universe. Actually, Aristotle (378-

322 B.C.) had first proposed the geocentric theory, and later Ptolemy had provided the mathematical structure to elaborate the theory.

Although all subsequent Arabic and Christian astronomers accepted and endorsed the Ptolemaic theory of a geocentric universe, the manuscript of the *Almagest* could not be found in the West until the twelfth century, when it was translated into Latin from Arabic. Few copies existed, and not many Christian astronomers had ever read the work in its entirety. Those who did spent much of their time making "copies, revisions, and epitomes of an initially faulty and increasingly corrupted translation."[17] In 1451, a new translation was made from the Greek and a carefully edited epitome based on the twelfth-century translation from the Arabic was printed in 1496.

The recovery and standardization of Ptolemy's work in print revealed that it was inadequate to predict celestial motions correctly. This was the state of the field around 1500 when Nicholas Copernicus (1473-1543) was a student. By this time, not only the *Almagest* but other Ptolemaic books as well had appeared. These had been written by Arabic and European astronomers, who had tried to overcome some of the inadequacies discovered in the *Almagest*. They had added or subtracted circles and epicycles or had altered the rates of rotation to account for planetary irregularities. This confusing array of books made the Ptolemaic system so diffuse that it was no longer clear what techniques an astronomer should use in computing planetary positions; nor did the system give results that corresponded with naked-eye observations. Moreover, astronomical tables—the Alphonsine tables, based on the Ptolemaic system—contained gross and obvious inaccuracies.

When he read the *Almagest*, Copernicus was sorely disappointed, not only because Ptolemy's system could not correctly predict celestial motion but also because the ancient Greek astronomer had claimed that there were ten thousand circles in the clockwork of the heavens. Copernicus could not reconcile this with his religious beliefs: "It would be altogether unworthy of the sublime Creator to have needed so many circles in order to make the sun, the moon, and the five planets move around the earth," Copernicus declared.[18] In other books made available to him by the printing press, Copernicus discovered that Cicero and Plutarch both mentioned that according to some philosophers—Nicetas of Syracuse, Aristarchus of Samos and the Pythagorean, Philolaus—the earth itself moved. If this were so, then the sun must be standing still, and it must be the center of the universe.

Drawn to this simpler conjecture of a heliocentric universe, Copernicus spent the rest of his life exploring the mathematical consequences of the earth's motion and fitting those consequences to an existing knowledge of the heavens.[19] He had no desire to overthrow Ptolemy. He merely sought to amend him, to reconcile astronomy with Christian beliefs about the Divine Creator. A heliocentric universe, he thought, answered the Christian criticisms of Ptolemy's system.

> How could this light [of the sun] be given a better place to illuminate the whole temple of God? The Greeks called the Sun the guide and soul of the world; Sophocles spoke of it as the All-Seeing One; Trismegistus held it to be the visible embodiment of God.

Now, let us place it upon a royal throne, let it in truth guide the encircling family of
planets, including the Earth. What a picture—so simple, so clear, so beautiful.[20]

Copernicus's theory, which he finally published as *De Revolutionibus Coelestium*
just before he died in 1543, claimed that the earth was a planet which moved
around the sun in a perfect circle—which was the only motion appropriate for
heavenly motion. Copernicus based his system on no new observations. He had
not read the book of nature; he had read Ptolemy's *Almagest* and other works of
astronomy recently printed. Printing had made the inadequacies of the Ptolemaic
system more visible. Copernicus's efforts to refine that system had led him ultimately to propose a new theory—a theory he had also found in the texts of antiquity made available to him by the printing press.

The immediate practical result of Copernicus's new system came about in the
form of a long-awaited calendar reform. Ever since the thirteenth century, proposals had been made to remove the cumulative errors of the calendar used since the
time of Julius Caesar. Over the centuries, the Julian calendar, like a clock that runs
too slow, had produced serious dilocations. By the time of Copernicus, the vernal
equinox had moved back from March 21 to March 11. The distortions were criticized by farmers, who could no longer rely on the calendar for planting and gathering crops; by merchants, who could not depend on the calendar in signing contracts for the delivery of seasonal products; and by clergy, who could not use the
calendar for accurately setting movable feasts, like Easter.

Early in the sixteenth century, when the Pope had asked for advice on calendar
reform, Copernicus had urged postponement of reform because existing astronomical observations and theories did not permit the design of a truly adequate calendar. In the preface to his *De Revolutionibus* (which he dedicated to the Pope),
Copernicus suggested that his system might be used for calendar reform. One of
his disciples, Erasmus Reinhold, used Copernicus's treatise to prepare a new set of
astronomical tables in 1551, which he called the Prutenic tables, named after his
patron, the Duke of Prussia. These tables became the basis for the construction of
the Gregorian calendar. In addition to solving the problems of the farmers, the
merchants, and the church, this new, printed, calendar helped scholars and others
to solve innumerable practical problems that were difficult, if not impossible, to
deal with before: problems like finding a day that corresponded to a given date, or
trying to keep straight the number of days in a month.

Although the Copernician system solved the practical problem of calendar reform, that same system created new theoretical problems. Presented with a fully
worked out theoretical system completely different from the Ptolemaic system,
astronomers had to decide who was correct: Ptolemy or Copernicus.

Copernicus was a mathematician who had made few astronomical observations
on his own. But when Tycho Brahe (1546-1601), at the age of sixteen, made some
measurements of a conjunction of Saturn and Jupiter in August 1543, he consulted
printed copies of both astronomical tables and observed that the Alphonsine tables
of Ptolemy were a whole month off in their predictions, and the Prutenic tables of

Copernicus were several days off. Thus, the printed tables of both systems had facilitated Tycho's criticisms of both Ptolemy and Copernicus. In consequence, Tycho developed a third cosmographical system in which planets revolved around the sun, while the sun orbited around the earth.

Only a century earlier, students of astronomy had been fortunate to have access to one astronomical theory. Now, through the medium of the printing press, all had access to three different theories—each with its own set of printed tables that allowed them to continually test each theory against the real world. Through such devices as printed open letters, this critical community of scientists could continually provide critical feedback to one another and keep abreast of the critical dialogue that determined the state of the field.[21]

The observations Tycho made while still a teenager were the first of many thousands he was to make and record. The son of a wealthy Danish nobleman, Tycho set up an elaborate observatory on the island of Hven, and his observations recorded there added more to the accumulation of astronomical facts than anyone before him. On his island, Tycho had an elaborate library, a workshop where artisans built the instruments, a chemical laboratory, a paper mill, and a printing press. With the the help of numerous assistants, he carefully cataloged the position of 1,000 stars, which he published along with descriptions of his observational methods and the instruments he used. This *Progymnasmata* (1603) displaced Ptolemy's catalog and brought astronomy to a new level.

At his death, Tycho bequeathed his voluminous observation records to one of his assistants, Johannes Kepler (1571-1630), with the request that they be used to construct improved astronomical tables that would demonstrate that his astronomical system was the correct one. Kepler did compose the Rudolphine tables by ingeniously combining Tycho's data with Napier's logarithms. (Logarithmic tables were a print-made mathematical innovation first published in 1614.) Unfortunately for Tycho, Kepler used the data and the tables to demonstrate that the system of Copernicus was the correct astronomical system. Kepler, however, had come to support the system of Copernicus only after he had made some modification of the original system. These modifications were generated in part by Kepler's own criticisms of all three astronomical theories.

The Ptolemaic system, Kepler believed, sullied the honor of God by having planets orbit around assumed points in the universe, which, in turn, revolved around another assumed point: "The Architect of the universe could not have had the heavenly bodies revolve around a nullity."[22] He accepted Copernicus's heliocentric universe and went Copernicus one better by claiming that the sun caused the motion of the planets. For Kepler, the system propounded by Copernicus was not spiritual enough. He preferred to see the unmovable sun—the source of Light and Power and Enlightenment—as God the Father, whereas the immovable fixed stars beyond were the Son, and the Son's moving force, which pervaded the spaces in between, was the Holy Ghost. This spiritual system produced a perfectly understandable mechanical universe. As Kepler saw it, "the Sun impells a body more violently as it is nearer but becomes ineffective in the case of the more distant bodies on account of the distance and the attendant weakening of its power."[23] This meant that the orbits of the planets could not be circular.

Kepler had originally accepted the dogma that movements in the heavens could be nothing but uniform and circular, but a difference of eight minutes between observations and calculations of the orbit of the planet mass had forced him, after a struggle of several years, to abandon the dogma of circularity and to postulate a nonuniform motion in eliptical orbits.[24] His precise calculations demonstrating that the orbits were elliptical destroyed the Ptolemaic edifice and established that no scientific claim was beyond criticism, not even a claim so longstanding and so deeply held as the belief that a perfect circle underlay all cosmic movement. Kepler published his findings as the *Laws of Planetary Motion* in 1609, a book, he said he wrote "to be read either now or by posterity, it matters not. It can wait a century for a reader, as God himself has waited six thousand years for a witness."[25]

Although his turgid prose was difficult to read, Kepler, unlike God, did not have to wait 6,000 years. He was plugged into the communication network that the printing press had established among scientists. (Kepler himself spent much time in print shops supervising scientific press work, and at one point he actually peddled his own books at the Frankfurt Book Fair.[26]) One of the scientists who read his book on planetary motion was Galileo Galilei (1564-1642). But Galileo, like others, was put off by "the long-winded theological speculatiions, mythical allusions and autobiographical meanderings in which Kepler concealed his genuine achievement."[27] But in time, the demonstrable superiority of Kepler's Rudolphine tables gradually converted most astronomers to his revised Copernican system, which he fully described in his *Epitome Astronomiae Copernicus*. (The superiority of the Rudolphine tables, especially for navigation, led to the disappearance of the Alphonsine tables, which were last printed in 1641.[28])

Armed with printed copies of the Rudolphine tables of Kepler, the Prutenic tables of Copernicus, and the Alphonsine tables of Ptolemy, astronomers could now compare the predictions of each with the actual observed positions of the sun, moon, and planets and thereby test the worth of the three different astronomical theories. The demonstrated superior acuracy of Kepler's tables led them "to undertake the laborious work of mastering Kepler's method."[29] But then, to corroborate this modified Copernican theory, astronomers needed more data—data that could conclusively refute the theories of Ptolemy and Tycho. Suddenly at the beginning of the seventeenth century these data became available, obtained by means of Galileo's telescope.

THE DEMARCATION BETWEEN SCIENCE AND NONSCIENCE

Galileo, a professor of mathematics at the University of Padua and a part-time instrument maker, was initially sympathetic to, but unconvinced by, the Copernican theory. In 1609, after having heard about such an instrument, he constructed a telescope and began viewing the heavens. In March of 1610, he published *The*

Starry Messenger (*Sidereus Nuncius*), a pamphlet of twenty-five pages that described what he saw: "stars in myriads which have never been seen before . . . the galaxy nothing else but a mass of innumerable stars planted together in clusters. . . . But that which will excite the greatest astonishment by far . . . I have discovered four planets, neither known nor observed by any one of the astronomers before my time, which have their orbits around a certain bright star." (These were actually the four moons of Jupiter.)

Although his observations convinced Galileo, the telescope did *not* prove the validity of the Copernican system, because both the Ptolemaic and Tychonian systems could have been modified to cohere with the observations Galileo had made. But as Kuhn points out, the telescope did provide an enormously effective weapon for the battle. "It was not proof, but it was propaganda."[30]

Wanting to reach astronomers and scientists all over Europe as quickly as possible, Galileo had addressed *The Starry Messenger* to them and had written it in Latin. The book brought him worldwide acclaim and popularized Copernican astronomy. The telescope became a popular tool, and amateur astronomers sprang up everywhere. In 1611, Galileo was invited to Rome, where he had an audience with the Pope, received an encomium from the Jesuits of the Collegio Romano, and was elected into the premier scientific community, the Academia dei Lincei. But soon a reaction set in against the Copernican system, not so much against the astronomical system itself—although many felt it went against common sense—but against the heretical implications people could draw from it.

Not long before, Giordano Bruno (1548-1600) had carried the Copernican system to its logical conclusion. Journeying throughout all of Europe, Bruno had preached the new astronomy in Switzerland, France, Germany, and in his native Italy. His message was that the Copernican system initiated a new revolution in science which brought about a new way of thinking, a breakthrough in the consciousness of the human race. Whereas Copernicus had banished the earth from the center of the universe, Bruno now did the same for the sun. Intuitively, he realized that the sun was only a star, one star among millions of other stars. From this, it was clear that the universe was boundless and infinite. Thus, Bruno explained, the universe is God.

Denounced by Catholics, Lutherans, and Calvinists as the incarnation of heresy, Bruno was finally apprehended by the Inquisition and brought to Rome, where he was imprisoned for seven years and then burned at the stake. But within a decade of Bruno's death Galileo announced that his telescope demonstrated that Copernicus, and Bruno was correct, too: The universe is infinite. People were shocked and upset. Assent to Copernicanism meant the destruction of a cosmology that for centuries had been the basis for everyday practical and spiritual life. The reaction of John Donne was typical:

> And new Philosophy calls all in doubt,
> The Element of fire is quite put out;
> The Sun is lost, and th'earth, and no man's wit
> Can well direct him where to look for it.

And freely men confess that this world's spent,
When in the Planets and the Firmament
They seek so many new; then see that this
Is crumbled out againe to his Atomies.
'Tis all in pieces, all cohaerence gone.

Because the universe Galileo described did not conform to the sense perceptions of common sense, some people simply denied he had seen what he had claimed.
One explanation was that the telescope simply deceived people. Or it may have
been sheer deception on Galileo's part: One professor of mathematics at the Collegio
Romano said that he, too, could show what Galileo had seen if he were given time
first to build it into some glasses.

In 1613, Galileo published his *Letters on Sunspots*, in which for the first time he
actually endorsed the Copernican system in print. Bypassing Latin, the language
of scholars, he wrote this book in Italian, disclosing the new astronomy to a wider
critical community. The growing controversy now became a popular subject of
discussion, with the arguments focused not on the complex questions of astronomy
and physics but on the scriptural difficulties involved in the new system.

The Scriptures contradicted Copernicus. In Joshua 10:12-13, Joshua commanded
the sun to stand still, and it did. In Psalms 92:1, the Lord was said to have "made
the world firm, not to be moved." Again in Psalms 103:5, "God fixed the earth
upon its foundation, not to be moved forever." And Ecclesiastes 1:5, states that the
sun rises and the sun goes down; then it presses on to the place where it rises.
There were other passages, too, that contradicted the Copernican system.

The critical discussion had obviously moved to a new level. It had become a
discussion about the nature of science. Could a scientific theory be heretical? Could
a scientific theory be true? Or was a scientific theory only a hypothesis? How can
we tell if one theory is better than another? The entire debate was made more
confused by the fact that the *De Revolutionibus* had been initally published with a
preface, which was mistakenly attributed to Copernicus, but was actually written
by his disciple, Nicole Gresme, and which claimed that the system was merely a
hypothesis. This became the quasi-official position of the Catholic Church: The
Copernican system is a hypothesis; it has not been proved to be true. Only if it
were, in Cardinal Bellarmine's words, "a true demonstration that the sun was in
the center of the universe . . . and that the sun did not travel around the earth but the
earth circled around the sun "would the Church consider reinterpreting the passages of Scripture which seemed contrary." "But," the Cardinal added, "I do not
believe that there is any such demonstration. None has been shown to me."[31]

Although these remarks showed up in a letter addressed to Father Paolo Foscarini,
who had written a book advocating the Copernican system, Cardinal Bellarmine
was clearly appealing to Galileo At that time, April 1615, Cardinal Robert
Bellarmine was seventy-three years old, a General of the Jesuit Order, consult of
the Holy Office, and the most respected theologian in Christendom. His opinion,
Koestler says, "carried more spiritual authority than Pope Paul V's."[32] Bellarmine
clearly believed that the phenomena observed through the telescope were really in

the sky, but he denied that they proved that the Copernican theory was true.

In Galileo's notes there is a point-by-point reply to Bellarmine's letter to Foscarini. Here we find the outlines of Galileo's earliest efforts to explain how scientists choose between competing theories:

> Not to believe that a proof of the earth's motion exists until one has been shown is very prudent, nor do we demand that anyone believe such a thing without proof. Indeed, we seek, for the good of the Holy Church, that everything that followers of this doctrine can set forth be examined with the greatest rigor, and that nothing be admitted unless it far outweighs the rival arguments. If these men are only ninety percent right, then they are defeated, but when nearly everything the philosophers and astronomers say on the other side is proved to be quite false, and all of it inconsequential, then this side should not be deprecated or called paradoxical simply because it can not be completely proved.[33]

In this passage Galileo clearly says that we cannot prove (i.e., confirm) a scientific theory but can, through criticism, demonstrate it or its competitors to be false. In his "Letter to the Grand Duchess Christina"—an open letter he wrote in 1615 that circulated widely but was not printed until it appeared in Strasbourg in 1636— Galileo elaborates this conception of scientific argument. He explains that he has demonstrated the Copernican system "not only by rejecting the arguments of Ptolemy and Aristotle, but by producing many counterarguments."[34]

Repeating an argument first made by St. Augustine, Galileo went on to explain that the Scriptures do not teach us scientific information, simply because such information is not relevant to our salvation. In an epigram he appropriated from Cardinal Bronius, Galileo quipped, "the intention of the Holy Ghost is to teach us how one goes to heaven, not how heaven goes."[35] Fom this, it follows that there can be no criteria in the Scriptures for declaring any scientific theory to be heretical. Thus no scientific theory can be contrary to the faith unless it has first been proven to be false. (A false scientific theory could not be in harmony with truth divinely revealed in the Scriptures.) Once again, Galileo quotes St. Augustine: "A theory is not proven contrary to the faith until disproved by most certain truth."[36] "Disproved by certain truth" means that a proposition or a theory must be falsified if it is to be shown to be contrary to the Catholic faith.

If a scientific theory that has not been falsified does seem to contradict Holy Scipture, then Augustine (and Galileo) admit that the meaning of the Holy Scripture may have to be modified. This, however, does not mean that Holy Scripture had falsely claimed something to be the case. Rather, as Augustine explained, when that happens "it was not Holy Scripture that ever affirmed it, but human ignorance that imagined it."[37] Then, in a passage that has been sharply criticized by some recent commentators, Galileo states that

> Now if truly demonstrated physical conclusions need not be subordinated to biblical passages, but the latter must rather be shown not to interfere with the former, then before a physical proposition is condemned, it must be shown to be not rigorously demonstrated—and this is to be done not by those who hold the proposition to be true, but by those who hold it to be false.[38]

Both Arthur Koestler and Jerome Langford have argued that this passage reveals how weak Galileo's case was. He could not offer a single argument in support of the Copernican system, so he shifted the burden of proof to the theologians, demanding that they must disprove it.[39] But Galileo did not ever try to prove the Copernican system by confirming it. He recognized that scientific theories cannot be confirmed or verified. The way to prove them—the way to "rigorously demonstrate their truth"—is to try to falsify them or the theories that compete with them. In the foregoing passage, Galileo is saying that those who hold the Ptolemaic theory to be false have shown via criticism that that theory has not been "rigorously demonstrated"—hence it should be condemned. And if the Copernican theory is to be condemned, it must be likewise criticized and shown not to be "rigorously demonstrated." When a theory resists attempts to refute it while other competing theories are refuted, we can conclude that the unrefuted theory has been "rigorously demonstrated." That this was Galileo's understanding of the nature of scientific theories is clear from the fact that someone whom Drake identifies as an unbiased contemporary observer, who heard many of the debates Galileo continuously engaged in, reported that although Galileo had not managed to prove (confirm) the Copernican system, he had "conclusively destroyed every argument on the other side."[40]

THE CONDEMNATION OF GALILEO

Galileo the scientist had become Galileo the philosopher, joining the critical dialogue about the demarcation between science and religion. Galileo's argument is that we cannot prove (confirm) a scientific theory any more than we can prove (confirm) the Scriptures. So proof or confirmation cannot be used to demarcate science from religion. The situation seems to be this: A believing Christian, as Galileo professed to be, does accept the Scriptures as true, as revealed truth which we can neither confirm nor refute, but can only accept on faith. Scientific theories, however, are not revealed and must be "rigorously demonstrated." For although we cannot confirm them, we can try to falsify them. So for Galileo, a scientific theory is "rigorously demonstrated" when it resists all efforts to disprove it and when, at the same time, other competing theories can be refuted or disproven. Therefore, Galileo concludes, the Copernican theory has, indeed, been "rigorously demonstrated."

This was not, however, how the Church saw this matter. All of Galileo's open letters and vigorous debates were of no avail. In 1616, the Theological Consultors of the Holy Office censored the Copernican system as heretical and the *De Revolutionibus* was placed on the index of prohibited books. At the same time, Cardinal Bellarmine, at the request of Pope Paul V, ordered Galileo to abandon the opinion "that the sun is the center of the world and unmoveable by local motion; and that the earth moves, even with a diurnal motion."[41]

Chastened but undaunted, Galileo continued to write and publish polemical tracts on the philosophy of science: *A Discourse on Comets* in 1619 and *The Assayer* (*Il Saggiatore*) in 1623. He did not, of course, discuss the Copernican theory in print. When, in 1623, his early defender Cardinal Barbarini became Pope Urban VIII, Galileo sought and obtained permission to write a book on the Copernican system as long as he treated it as a hypothesis.

Galileo promptly set to work on his monumental *Dialogue on the Great World Systems*. He followed the philosophy of science he had outlined in previous books and pamphlets, presenting devasting arguments against Aristotle's physics and Ptolemaic astronomy—not to convince others that the Copernican system was correct, but only to show that those who accepted it had carefully considered and examined the arguments of the other side. It is through such critical dialogue that knowledge advances, Galileo explains: "Philosophy itself cannot but benefit from our disputes, for if our conceptions prove true, new achievements will be made; if false, then rebuttal will further confirm the original doctrines. . . . As to science itself, it can only improve." Yet no matter how much scientific knowledge improves Galileo insists that human knowledge can not be perfect. "[There] is not a single effect in nature, even the least that exists, such that the most ingenious theorists can arrive at a complete understanding of it." He repeats this as his final conclusion of the dialogue, pointing out that God grants us the right to argue about the constitution of the universe, but we can never discover the work of his hands: "Let us, then exercise these activities permitted to us and ordained of God, that we may recognize and thereby so much the more admire His greatness, however much less fit we may find ourselves to penetrate the profound depths of His infinite wisdom."[42]

The *Dialogue Concerning the Great World Systems* was published in February 1632. By August, publication was suspended and all unsold copies confiscated. In October, Galileo was summoned to Rome. In June 1633, he was sentenced by the Inquisition as "vehemently suspected of heresy, namely of having believed and held the doctrine which is false and contrary to Sacred and Divine Scriptures, that the sun is the center of the world and does not move from east to west and that the earth moves and is not the center of the world." The Inquisition ordered him to "abjure, curse, and detest before us the aforesaid errors and heresies." His *Dialogue* was placed on the index of prohibited books.

Rome had not accepted Galileo's philosophy of science. The Catholic Church had asked for confirmation of a scientific theory before it would accept it as true; but Galileo had supplied only refutations of the Ptolemaic theory. Galileo's argument that we do not affirm scientific theories, we try to refute them, was lost until the philosopher of science, Karl Popper, revived it in the twentieth century and made falsifiability the criterion for demarcating science from nonscience: Scientific theories are falsifiable, nonscientific theories (like those of religion) are not falsifiable.[43]

As long as critics like Cardinal Bellarmine and the Roman Inquisition demanded confirmation of scientific theories, there could be no rational explanation of why any theory wins acceptance over competing theories; nor could there be any rational explanations of how scientific progress takes place.[44]

Rome had not only rejected Galileo's philosophy of science; it condemned a scientific theory for being heretical. This shattered the critical community in all Catholic countries. That critical community, I have argued, depended on the free, open, competitive publication of books and pamphlets. Religious censorship created an atmosphere of suspicion, secretiveness, and suppression. Libraries were ransacked and printers imprisoned, while the fear of persecution brought on self-censorship by both authors and printers. Descartes's *Monde*, for example, never appeared in print, even posthumously. Marco Aurelio Severino, the Italian physiologist, left seventy-seven volumes of unpublished manuscript materials when he died in 1656. His pupil, Tommaso Cornelia, postponed publication of his own work to the point that he "lost credit" for significant work in physiology and anatomy. Severino's mentor, Tommaso Campanella, had to smuggle his *Apologia Pro Galileo* to Frankfurt to get it published.[45]

Risks, uncertainties, confusions, and interminable delays led to the ruin of booksellers and printers. Deprived of both printers and patrons, science declined rapidly in all Catholic countries, which retreated to become closed societies, reasserting the values of cooperation, collectivism, and hierarchy.

Among Protestants, Luther, Melancthon, and perhaps Calvin had all condemned the Copernican theory; but in Protestant lands, no strong central authority existed that could impose censorship on books. So in the Protestant countries, the printing presses continued to roll and modern science continued to advance. Many of the northern Protestant printers continued to publish the books of Catholic scientists that were already on the index of prohibited books or were likely to appear there. A mixture of anti-Catholicism and financial interest probably motivated such actions—books on the index were eagerly sought by readers. But there is also evidence of a devotion to the advancement of science—as when the Royal Society of England published the works of the Italian embryologist Marcello Malpighi in the late seventeenth century. Nevertheless, Protestant printers and publishers profited greatly by purveying titles listed on the Catholic index of prohibited books. In 1617, the Amsterdam printer Blaeu brought out a third edition of Copernicus's *De Revolutionibus*. In Strasbourg, Bernegar published the first Latin translation of Galileo's *Dialogues*, and there, too appeared the first printed edition of Galileo's *Letter to the Grand Duchess Christiana*.

In 1637, Galileo's *Discourse on Two New Sciences*, which he had smuggled out of Italy, first appeared in print in Strassbourg. Two years later, Galileo complained that he had not been able to obtain a single copy of the book, although it circulated through all the northern countries.[46] Italy and the other Catholic countries had withdrawn from the critical community of scholars. The advancement of knowledge had shifted to the Protestant north to be carried on by scientists like Isaac Newton, who, explained his nephew, "had the happiness of being born in a land of liberty where he could speak his mind—not afraid of the Inquisition as Galileo." This land of liberty was, quite simply, the open society created by a free press—a modern society that prized the values of individualism, competition, objectivity, and equality that had triumphed over the closed society values of collectivism, cooperation, subjectivism, and hierarchy.

Chapter Six

Printing and the Modern State

The modern European states emerged in diverse manners and from various local conditions. For the most part, they were the outcome of the disintegration of medieval realms and empires and the consolidation of local independencies. They were constituted in "conquest, rebellion, secession, the murder of heirs, multiple treaties, purchases, surrenders of rights to commercial exploration, acts of parliaments, the intermarriages of ruling families, hereditary succession to estates thitherto unconnected, the extinction of palatine independencies, the consolidation of expired fiefs, and the falling in of feudal inheritances."[1]

But these kinds of goings-on were not new. They had been common for centuries when, at different times, various kings and princes and several emperors had secured power over large numbers of people by acquiring control of extensive territories. But none had been able to preserve their domains. Suddenly, in the sixteenth century, rulers succeeded in gaining a purchase on political authority more secure and more lasting than any others before them. The advent of the printing press explains this. First, the printing press helped destroy with great rapidity the medieval political order by undermining its legitimacy. Second, the printing press quickly enabled the new rulers to establish, for the first time a permanent sovereign state.

THE RESPUBLICA CHRISTIANA

Medieval Europe identified itself as a Christian commonwealth, a *respublica Christiana*. This Christian commonwealth was not a state; it was a territory held together by adherence to the Christian faith. The bonds of religion created a transregional unity and brought about real cooperation that superseded any national identity.

In this *respublica Christiana*, each person had a station to which he had been called: There was an ecclesiastical hierarchy made up of priests, bishops, cardinals, and the Pope; along with this, there was a secular hierarchical order stretching from the serfs up through the barons, princes, kings, and emperor. Each position or station in the hierarchy had its attendant rights, privileges, and duties. This created a distinctive form of human association—a feudal order—in which men are personally related to one another through oaths of loyalty embedded in a hierarchical arrangement of lords and clients.

This feudal order had its own military, financial, and administrative arrangements. In theory, the king was the sole landowner. He granted most of the lands to his barons or princes in return for specific services. The barons, in turn, would have tenants or clients under them, and so on down the order until the serfs, upon whom the whole system rested. The typical service rendered to the lord was military. Each baron supplied and commanded his own troops. Finances for the kingdom came from dues or reliefs that the king's tenants had to pay on fixed occasions. Each baron administered justice within his own feudal domain, usually with an immunity from interference by the king's officers.

This feudal order was not only hierarchical and subjective (bound by ties of personal loyalty) but also cooperative: The obligations between lords and clients were mutual. In return for military service and various payments clients made to their lords, the lord was obliged to give aid and protection to his clients and to abide by the customs or the charter which defined the clients' rights and immunities.

Finally, in addition to being hierarchical, subjective, and cooperative, the medieval order was collective. By this I mean that the *respublica Christiana* had one common purpose: to ensure the heavenly salvation of all members. As head of the Church, the Pope ruled the *respublica Christiana*, steering it, like a ship, toward its destination or goal.[2] As the Pope saw it, each and every human action should have a Christian import and be motivated by Christian norms: Everything one did had consequences for one's eternal life.[3]

In the *respublica Christiana*, spiritual interest stood above all other interests, and the temporal powers—the kings and princes and the emperor—contributed to the goal of salvation by preserving the purity of the Christian faith. In the famous papal bull, *Unam Sanctam* (1302), Pope Boniface (1294-1303) wrote, "We learn from the words of the Gospel (Luke 22:38) that in this Church and in her power are two swords, the spiritual and the temporal. . . . Both are in the power of the Church . . . but the latter is to be used for the Church, the former by her; the former by the priest, the latter by kings and captains, but at the will and by the persuasion of the priest. The one sword, then, should be under the other, and temporal authority subject to spiritual."[4] His predecessor, Innocent III (1198-1216), had put it more succinctly: The Pope, he explained, was the mediator between God and man.

Ever since the time of Pope Leo I (440-461), the papacy had claimed plentitude of power (*plenitudo potestatis*) to rule the *respublica Christiana*. And since the time of Leo, the power and authority of the papacy exceeded that of any king or emperor. The Pope had the power to depose kings from their offices, to excommunicate them, to place realms under interdict, to discharge subjects from their allegiances—all with terrible effect.

The Pope alone could license universities to award degrees, and he presided by proxy at every coronation and was party to all agreements made under oath between rulers.[5] He could annul laws, confiscate property, and impose taxes on all domains. No secular prince was, or could be sovereign during the middle ages: No temporal ruler was independent, and all public acts of temporal rulers were open to censure and punishment by the Pope.

Yet in the sixteenth century, the kings of several territories successfully repudiated the authority of the papacy and gained sovereign rule over their own states. The emergence of the modern state destroyed the *respublica Christiana* and created a new form of human association: a civil society. As the feudal society gave way to the civil society, the hierarchy of rights and privileges was replaced by equality before the law. In a civil society, clients became subjects, while lords became rulers; and, as a result, the subjective relationship of personal loyalty turned into the objective relationship of simple obedience to the law. In a civil society, the collectivism and cooperation characteristic of feudal society also disappear and people find themselves in a world where they can make choices and perform self-chosen actions in pursuit of the satisfaction of their own substantive wants: Civil society is characterized by individualism and competition. In civil society, human beings become agents engaged in individual self-enactment instead of partners in some cosmic process of divine salvation.

So with the destruction of the feudal order of the *respublica Christiana* and the emergence of the civil order, things got better: People lived in a social-political order in which they enjoyed and prized equality, individualism, competition, and objectivity. In such a world, a civil society, everyone had more life chances—more than had ever been possible in the medieval world.

The printing press played a distinct role in the destruction of the *respublica Christiana* by facilitating criticism of the four pillars that held up the social-political order: scholasticism, papal authority, Roman law, and the Bible.

SCHOLASTICISM AND THE PRINTING PRESS

Scholasticism is a way of thinking that is appropriate to a scribal culture. The scholastics accepted certain written texts—the Bible, the writings of the Church Fathers, and Roman law—as true and correct, and sacred as well. In a scribal culture where texts are few in number, most scholarly activity consists of copying manuscripts and perhaps making comments to explain them. There is little time or incentive to criticize them, to subject them to critical analysis. Hence, in a scribal culture, the texts become authoritative.

The scholars of these texts did, however, uncover difficulties with them, difficulties in the form of contradictions or antinomies. Nevertheless, they had to accept both sides of any contradiction as true, because both sides came from authoritative sources. Consequently, the task for the medieval scholar was to reconcile the contradictions, to show that, when properly understood, no contradictions existed. This called for highly subtle, abstract, and abstruse analyses and syntheses of the textual materials.

The scholastic method was not a method to prove the truth of a given proposition; rather, it was a method to demonstrate that seemingly contradictory truths were not, in fact, contradictory. The method used dialectic reasoning to devise abstract, universal principles from the authoritative texts, universal principles that could accommodate, and thus reconcile, the seeming contradictions.

Scholasticism began in the twelfth century, and the first scholastic treatise was Peter Abelard's *Sic et Non*, which was nothing more than a list of 150 inconsistencies and discrepancies in the Bible and in the writings of the Church Fathers and other authorities. Abelard assumed all of these to be true and left it up to the reader to harmonize them.

Medieval lawyers, as well as theologians, used the scholastic method both to reconcile contradictions among the various doctrines, rules, and proposals found in the authoritative manuscripts of law and religion and to systematize the theological doctrines and laws into an integrated system. Thus, every decision, every rule, every proposition, every doctrine rested on some universal principle which was part of a coherent system of thought. These systems of thought provided intellectual order to the medieval world and legitimacy to the *respublica Christiana*.

Printing destroyed this magnificent intellectual order that the scholastics had created by introducing a new approach to the contradictions uncovered in the sacred texts: the historical approach. Medieval scholars had never used a historical approach. Indeed, the historian Peter Burke has gone so far as to claim that during the medieval period, people had no sense of history. They lacked the sense that the past is different from the present—they had no historical perspective or sense of the past. Of course, they did know that the past was over and gone, but they confused and paid no heed to the differences between past eras and cultures. They assimilated Hector, Caesar, Alexander, Joshua, David, Arthur, and Charlemagne. They called Aristotle a schoolman, a clerk.[6]

Printing created the new sense of history that appeared in the late fifteenth century simply because this sense depends on the availability of written history. The Greeks and Romans had written histories, and they had shared a sense of history. Yet, although writing existed when Christianity had first begun—indeed, Christianity is a religion based on written texts—Christianity had made written history unnecessary.

According to Christianity, God had become man, the infinite had become finite, and the eternal had become temporal, disrupting the course of human events. Such goings-on had occurred in other religions, it is true, but these other instances had taken place in oral cultures, whereas Christianity was embedded in a scribal culture: Its doctrines were encoded in writing, and it had a sacred written tradition that not only described the whole story of how God had become man but recorded in writing the words of God himself. These manuscripts, therefore, contained a message that was not historical but eternal, and not temporal but sacred. These writings—the Bible, as well as the works of the Church Fathers and the letters of the popes—were accepted as given, as authoritative pronouncements from God himself or through his vicars on earth.

Printing changed all this. By reproducing these manuscripts in multiple copies and scattering them everywhere, printing enabled some Christians to approach them critically—as historical documents to be weighed and tested, not as sacred pronouncements to be accepted as true. This historical scholarship destroyed scholasticism. Henceforth, when scholars uncovered contradictions in texts, they no longer attempted to reconcile them as the scholastics had. Instead, they assumed that a contradiction indicated that a proposition was false, or that the proposition that contradicted it was false, or that both propositions were false. That is, these early modern scholars assumed, like the scholastics, that the ancient manuscripts did encode the actual word of God, the true thoughts of the Church Fathers, and the real laws of the Romans; but they also recognized that these ancient manuscripts had been copied and recopied by fallible human beings, who had made mistranscriptions, errors, transpositions, and other mistakes. They blamed the scribes for corrupting the original texts, thereby introducing the seeming contradictions found among the authoritative writings.[7] So instead of using dialectical reasoning intended to reconcile these contradictions as the scholastics had done, these modern scholars called for a careful examination of the documents to get to the true, original meanings. Erasmus put it succinctly: "If anyone wants to learn piety rather than disputation, let him straight away go to the sources and those writers who drank immediately from the sources."[8]

Erasmus's advice, of course, was only feasible in an age of printing. Before printing, there was no incentive for anyone to prepare a definitive edition of any ancient text, because any so-called definitive edition would, in turn, have to be hand copied by scribes and thus subject to the inevitable corruption and drift that accompanied the copying of all manuscripts. Printing, as noted before, created what Elizabeth Eisenstein has called "typographical fixity"—the exact duplication in multiple copies of a text as originally prepared and edited. Encouraged and even driven by the possibilities of preservation provided by printing, these early modern scholars believed that they were doing for their age what St. Jerome had done for his: restoring and purifying the Christian tradition.[9]

But, of course, they were doing much more. They were laying the axe to scholasticism, which for centuries had impeded all intellectual progress simply because it had accepted and tried to reconcile contradictions. Knowledge advances through the elimination of errors and mistakes in our present knowledge, and we become aware of errors and mistakes when we uncover contradictions in that present knowledge. Contradictions can always be argued away, as the subtleties of the scholastics demonstrate, but only at the expense of the advancement of knowledge, as the legacy of scholasticism also demonstrates. Instead of spinning subtle webs of dialectical reasoning to reconcile contradictions found in the sacred texts, these early modern scholars took these contradictions as a sign that more research was needed. Indeed, they deliberately and consciously looked for contradictions in the texts they studied—this is what scholarly criticism is. And this is how knowledge advances: through criticism and the elimination of errors and mistakes uncovered by the criticism.

Printing facilitated criticism, which is to say that it destroyed scholasticism and made modern scholarship possible. With printing, things got better: Knowledge could, and did, advance.

THE PAPACY AND THE PRINTING PRESS

The decline in the political power of the papacy was the most salient development in the emergence of the modern state. How did this come about? It is true that the Babylonian Captivity (1309-1377), the Great Schism (1378-1417), and the Conciliar Movement (1309-1449) had all weakened the power of the papacy.[10] It is also true that the Turkish seizure of Christian domains and the extension of European domains overseas tested and stretched papal responsibilities beyond their capabilities.[11] Yet the question remains: Why did the authority of the papacy disappear? For over a thousand years, Christians had accepted the authority of the office of the Pope. At the end of the fifteenth century, that authority began to disappear.

What happened, I suggest, is that the printing press destroyed the legitimacy of papal authority. The Pope's claim to plentitude of power was a product of a scribal culture, which meant that it could not survive in an age of printing. The Pope's *plenitudo potestatis* rested on written records that had been preserved since the earliest days of Christianity. With the coming of the printing press, many of these documents were reproduced in multiple copies and made available to the critical scrutiny of scholars, who revealed that the claim of papal supremacy was based on forgeries, misconceptions, specious reasoning, and fraud. Once the printing press scattered these charges throughout all of Europe, the *plenitudo potestatis* of the papacy was destroyed forever.

Criticisms of the plentitude of power of the papacy had begun as early as the eleventh and twelfth centuries, during the fierce jurisdictional struggle between the Pope and the Emperor over the matter of investiture, each side claiming the right to appoint (invest) bishops. This dispute was not between temporal and secular powers, because both the Pope and the Emperor viewed themselves not as different agencies, but as different officers of the same *respublica Christiana*. Nevertheless, this battle produced numerous written claims and counterclaims, arguments and counterarguments in the form of letters, proclamations, depositions, signed oaths, pamphlets, and tracts about the proper or legitimate authority of each office.

The controversy began in 1075, when Pope Gregory VII prohibited lay investiture and then the following year excommunicated Emperor Henry IV and absolved his feudal vassals from their feudal oaths. Gregory based his actions on the traditional Petrine theory of the papacy, according to which Christ had given Peter the "keys of the kingdom," and Peter, in turn, bequeathed this legitimate authority to all succeeding popes. Justification for this lay in the Gospel of Matthew (16:19): "You are Peter and on this rock I will build my church, and the powers of death shall not prevail against it. I will give you the keys of the kingdom and whatever you bind on earth shall be bound in heaven, and whatever you loose on earth shall be loosed in heaven."

From this authority to bind and loose in heaven and earth, Gregory VII concluded that he had the power "to take away or to grant empires, kingdoms, principalities, dukedoms, marches, counties, and the possessions of all men according to their merits."[12] Later, Honorius of Augsburg claimed in his *Summa Gloria*, written about 1123, that all temporal authority derived from spiritual authority. To support this claim, he cited the Donation of Constantine—the supposed gift by Constantine the Great (324-337) of the City of Rome and the western part of the empire to Pope Sylvester I (314-335). Some thirty years later, John of Salisbury wrote, in his *Policratus*, that the inherent superiority of spiritual authority means that the sacred *and* temporal sword belonged of right to the papacy and that the pope simply conferred the power of coercion on the prince. The most forthright declaration of papal authority came from Innocent III (1198-1216), who likened the relationship of popes and kings to that of the sun and moon and who announced that he, the Pope, was "lower than God but higher than man, who judges and is judged by no one."[13]

The Emperor, of course, rejected all papal claims to power over him. In a letter of 1076 to Gregory, Henry insisted that his power was derived from God directly and not through the Church. Therefore, he concluded, he was responsible for its exercise directly to God. Counterarguments to claims of papal authority came not only from the Emperor but also from scholars, theologians, and lawyers. In 1084, Peter Crassus, a teacher of law at Ravenna, wrote *Defensio Henrici IV Regis*, in which he argued that hereditary succession was an indefeasible natural right that the Pope could not interfere with. A more important antipapal argument appeared in the *York Tracts*, produced about 1100 in another investiture controversy—this time between Pope Anselm and Henry I of England. The anonymous author argues that all bishops are equal and that the Pope is, therefore, a usurper. Moreover, the spiritual authority of the Church, the author insists, is simply a right to teach and preach and not a right to exercise power of any kind.

In the fourteenth century, new written criticisms of papal authority appeared. This began when Pope Boniface VIII prohibited Phillip the Fair of France from taxing the clergy. This contest between the Pope and French king led, finally, to the Babylonian Captivity of the Pope at Avignon and, eventually to the Great Schism from 1378 to 1417, when there were two and sometimes three rival popes. So many pamphlets and tracts attacking papal claims to authority appeared during this period that Sabine had said, "Barely to mention them would be unprofitable and to discuss them all would be impossible."[14] The most significant works came from Dante, John of Paris, Marsilius of Padua, and William of Occam.

Distraught by the endless dissension between the papal and imperial parties in Italy during his lifetime, Dante saw no hope for peace except through the unity of the empire under the all-embracing authority of the emperor. In his *De Monarchia* (1318), Dante justified this position by arguing that the Church should possess no temporal power whatsoever because its kingdom is not of this world.

In *De Potestate Regia et Papali* (1303), John of Paris cited forty-two reasons that had been given for the subordination of secular to spiritual authority and then went on to refute them one by one. Of all his arguments, the central one was that secular power could not be derived from spiritual power (hence could not be subordinated to it) because secular power was older than the Church. Moreover, he added, spiritual power resides in the Church as a corporation, not in the Pope; and, therefore, a council could depose a pope.

In *Defensor Pacis* (1324), Marsilius of Padua, Rector of the University of Paris, applied a thoroughgoing Aristotelian argument against papal authority. Religion, he says, is exclusively concerned with other worldly interests, so it is logically irrelevant to human society, which is self-sufficient in the fullest sense. "The function of the clergy," he wrote, "is to know and teach those things which, according to scripture, it is necessary to believe, to do, or to avoid, in order to obtain eternal salvation and escape woe." Yet, although the clergy has a mission concerned solely with the other world, they do comprise a social class, like the class of farmers or artisans; so their actions do affect temporal matters. Therefore, Marsilius concludes, all clergy, like the artisans and the farmers, should be subject to control by the temporal powers.

William of Occam (1285-1349), in a number of tracts and pamphlets attacked papal sovereignity as a heresy. The Pope, William wrote, had set himself up as a tyrant. Like John of Paris and Marsilius, William proposed a Church council to check the power of the Pope; but unlike them, he did not think such a council could issue infallible decrees—for the members of such a council would be fallible human beings.

Early in the fifteenth century, a group of scholars connected with the University of Paris—all of whom were conversant with the scholarly writings of their predecessors on the matter of papal authority—convened the Council of Constance (1414-1418) to resolve the Great Schism. The council proclaimed that it, as the representative of the clerical hierarchy, had authority over the rival popes and proceeded to restore unity to the *respublica Christiana* by deposing the reigning popes and seting up a legitimate one in their stead.

From the foregoing, we can see that for over 350 years, papal authority over the *respublica Christiana* had come under severe attack. Yet few Christians had read these written criticisms, and the legitimacy of papal authority remained unshaken. Printing changed all this.

First practiced in the German city of Mainz, printing spread to all of Europe. By 1500, sixty German towns had printing presses, and migrating German printers had established presses in another 150 European centers. During this first half century following the invention of printing, an estimated 6 million books were printed. Half of the thirty thousand different titles were on religious subjects.[15] Moreover, a growing educated public existed and was reading this flood of books and pamphlets. Between 1300 and 1500 monarchs, princes, and wealthy merchants created forty new universities in Europe, raising the total to seventy. Literacy increased slowly throughout all of Europe during this time, rising most dramatically in the sixteenth century as the vernacular language triumphed over Latin.[16]

During the first century of printing, more old than new texts were duplicated, in both Latin and vernacular translations. These included some of those discussed above. So for the first time, the numerous attacks made on the legitimacy of papal authority during the preceding four centuries became widely available to the public.[17] One of the most influential texts was Marsilius's *Defensor Pacis*, which first appeared in print in 1522. An abridged translation came out in England in 1535 during the reign of Henry VIII.[18]

The impact of these newly printed older works of criticism was heightened and strengthened by the new criticisms made by scholars like Erasmus and his friends. These modern scholars wanted to restore the sacred documents to the pristine purity they had when they first appeared, before they had been corrupted by the scribes. Valla (1407-1457), for example attributed the grammatical misunderstandings and mistranslations he found in the vulgate Bible not to Jerome but to the copyists. In their efforts to restore the documents to their original state, these scholars discovered that much of what earlier scholars had accepted was, in fact, false. In a letter commenting on his own new translation of the New Testament, Erasmus pointed out that both Augustine and Aquinas had made mistakes because they had used faulty translations of the Bible.[19] Inevitably, it was those mistakes and errors that became the focus of public attention. If the Church Fathers had erred, how could they be accepted as authorities?

These Renaissance Christian scholars found not only mistakes, but they also found forgeries. The most famous forgery uncovered was that of the Donation of Constantine, which had been used numerous times by the defenders of papal authority. Lorenzo Valla conclusively demonstrated that this document was a forgery, probably concocted in the eighth century. Using his vast philological knowledge of Latin, Valla showed that the document could not be genuine: In every line he found flagrant anachronisms, words that could not possibly have been used in Constantine's time.[20]

Valla's scholarship uncovered other forgeries that had been part of the Christian tradition: He demonstrated that the Apostles' Creed was the work not of the Apostles but of the Council of Nicea; he proved that a letter from King Abgar of Edusa to Jesus was apocryphal; and he revealed the grammatical misunderstandings and unhappy translations present in Jerome's Latin translation of the Bible. Valla conducted his researches on medieval manuscripts, but his critical writings were published in print: *The Donation of Constantine* first appeared in 1517; his *Notes on the New Testament* appeared in 1505.[21]

Other Christian scholars soon discovered other forgeries that undermined the historical evidence for legitimate papal authority. Erasmus and others uncovered the fact that many of the letters of the popes were forgeries—the so-called false decretals, composed by the pseudo-Isidore sometime in the ninth century and ascribed to Isidore of Seville (c. 560-636). These false decretals had been used over and over to substantiate the right of the Pope to invest bishops.[22]

Coupled with the publication of these old and new attacks on the legitimacy of papal authority were the printed criticisms of the personal morality of the popes. Prior to the fifteenth century, the papacy had successfully defended the doctrine that the person of the Pope was separate from the office. Thus, during the papacy of Boniface VIII (1294-1303), the French had charged him with twenty-nine specific moral offenses, ranging from fornication to sodomy. But these moral offenses could not impair his ecclesiastical authority.[23] No one could judge the Pope (i.e., the office of Pope). But beginning with the papacy of Sixtus IV, who became Pope in 1471, the infamous Renaissance popes were subject to continuous judgment, criticisms, and condemnation. Their corruption, immorality, and venality were taken as a condemnation of the office of the Pope.

Why had this changed? After all, the corruption, the immorality, and the abuses were not new.[24] What was new was the fact that these accusations now appeared in print for the first time. Moreover, the publication of these old charges and criticisms stimulated new attacks, such as the book *Concerning the Vices of the Pope* by Bartolomeo Sacchi (1421-1481), Poggio Bracciolini's (1380-1459) *Dialogues against Hypocrisy*, and Erasmus's *Julius Excluded from Heaven* (1517), a satire against Pope Julius. In a class by itself as a European bestseller was *In Praise of Folly* (1509), in which Erasmus satirized all medieval institutions, but especially the Church.

This swelling of criticism of the personal morality of the popes, together with the attacks on the legitimacy of papal authority, created for the first time a community of critics ready and willing to subscribe to Luther's call for reformation. By the time Luther tacked his ninety-five theses to the door of the church in Wittenberg in 1517, the legitimacy of papal authority had all but disappeared—so much so that in the same year Luther could write, "Since the Roman bishop has ceased to be a bishop and become a tyrant, I fear none of his decrees."[25]

The wholesale selling of indulgences—which is what initally promoted Luther's attack on the papacy—had been made possible by the printing press, which not only mass produced letters of indulgence but also turned out pamphlets and leaflets to promote their sale. In addition, the printing press rapidly duplicated Luther's ninety-five theses in multiple copies and scattered them everywhere. They were known throughout Germany in two weeks and throughout Europe in a month. As Elizabeth Eisenstein has noted, the printing press was both a precondition of the Protestant Reformation and a precipitant.[26]

The printing press not only ended the rule of the Pope over the *respublica Christiana*, but it destroyed the *respublica Christiana* itself, which, as a product of a scribal culture, gave way to the modern state—a product of a print culture.

LAW AND THE PRINTING PRESS

From the early centuries on, the Church had accumulated a great many laws. These had come from canons (rules) and decrees of the church councils and synods; decrees and decisions of bishops, including the Bishop of Rome (the Pope); and decrees from Christian Emperors and kings concerning the Church. All these laws were subordinate to the precepts contained in the Bible and in the writings of the Church Fathers, especially those of Augustine.

Although some attempts had been made to codify these laws, none had succeeded. The basic problem was the absence of a clear and comprehensive scheme of organization. A model finally appeared in the late eleventh century, when someone recovered a manuscript that reproduced the enormous collection of legal materials that the Roman Emperor Justinian had compiled about 534 A.D.

This rediscovered Roman law was highly developed and sophisticated, in marked contrast with the Germanic folklaw and existing Church law of the eleventh century. Understandably, then, this digest of the legal system of an earlier civilization became the object of Europe's first legal studies. Those who now studied it believed that the Roman law had a permanent and universal quality applicable to all times and places. These Christian scholars regarded the Roman law as authoritative, just as they regarded the Bible.

The newly discovered legal texts were copied and disseminated to various Italian cities, where scholars began to study, cross-index, gloss, and write commentaries on the Roman law. The most famous of these centers for the study of law was Bologna, where, in 1140, the Bolognese monk Gratian—following the example of the Christian jurists of Roman law—composed the first comprehensive and systematic legal treatise in the history of the West, *A Concordance of Discordant Canons*, known as the *Decretum Gratian*. This was an attempt to collect all the laws of the Church into a single book.

To do this, Gratian had to set forth an organized hierarchy of all the different kinds of law. Following the Christian tradition, Gratian presented divine law as superior to natural law, which, in turn, superseded human law, whether the enactments of the Church or of temporal powers. At the bottom of the hierarchy was customary law. This hierarchy of law did three things. First, it provided a means for weeding out customary law, which was the most prominent law of the time. ("Natural law absolutely prevails in dignity over customs and constitutions. Whatever has been recognized by usage or laid down in writing, if it contradicts with natural law, must be considered null and void."[27]) Second, it subordinated the law of the temporal powers (secular law) to the canon law of the Church. Third, it allowed the Pope, the vicar of Christ, to be the final judge to determine which enacted laws were, and which were not, in accord with divine and natural law. As the canon lawyers now viewed it, the Corpus Juris Canonica granted the Pope supreme governance (*imperium*) in the Church, full authority (*plenitudo authoritati*), and full power (*plenitudo potestatis*): The Pope was the supreme legislator, the supreme administrator, the supreme judge. [28]

In the following century, Thomas Aquinas (1224-1274), in his great *Summa Theologica*, made Gratian's hierarchy of law a central support for papal authority. According to Thomas, all law comes from God—either directly as divine law, which is embodied in the revelations of scripture and in the dogmas of the Church; or indirectly as natural law, which we ascertain through observing the natural order of things. All positive law, he explains, is but an elaboration or implementation of God's law. Positive law can vary and change, but divine and natural law are eternal and immutable. All positive law, therefore, should be in accord with divine and natural law.

> The validity of a law depends upon its justice. But in human affairs a thing is said to be just when it accords aright with the rule of reason: and as we have already seen, the first rule of reason is the Natural law. Thus all humanly enacted laws are in accord with reason to the extent that they derive from the Natural law. And if a human law is at variance in any particular with the Natural law, it is no longer legal, but rather a corruption of the law.[29]

Then, agreeing with the tradition, Thomas acceded to the plentitude of power of the Pope:

> To the Supreme Pontiff, who has this authority, major difficulties are submitted. . . . One faith should be held by the whole church: *that ye all speak the same thing, and that there be no divisions among you,* cannot be ensured unless doubts about the faith be decided by him who presides over the whole church, and whose decisions will be accepted by all. The publication of articles of belief is like the convocation of a General Council or any other commitment affecting the Universal Church: no other power is competent but that of the Pope.[30]

After the invention of the printing press this medieval legal order came under attack from a number of quarters. Before printing, when manuscripts of the *Justinian Digest* were scarce, medieval lawyers could do no more than excerpt, summarize, define, and try to explain what the *Justinian Digest* contained. This was called the period of the glossators. Later in the thirteenth century, as they uncovered contradictions and antinomies in the *Digest*, a new school of postglossators or commentators emerged, who attempted to reconcile the contradictions through abstract analyses and syntheses: scholasticism.

In the fourteenth century, Petrarch complained that the lawyers paid no attention to the history of Roman law.[31] Again in the fifteenth century, Valla accused the lawyers of not knowing ancient history and implored them to return to the sources to find out what the laws really meant. But it was not until printing made documents available in abundance that lawyers were able to be scholars of the law. Guillaume Bude (1468-1540) and Andrea Alciate (1492-1550), the founders of the new historical school, were the first to write books on the Roman law texts that explained the laws by describing the historical situation each law was designed to meet.

The inevitable consequence of the work of this historical school of law was the recognition that Roman law had no relevance to present-day society—the historical past, the context in which Roman law had emerged, was so different from the present that Roman law was of no practical use whatsoever.[32]

Ever since they had recovered it at the end of the eleventh century, Christians had regarded Roman law as *jus*, the system of justice or right. But now the work of the critics made clear that Roman law was not *jus*, but *lex*—enacted law, the creation of fallible human beings. The criticism of the historical school had destroyed the medieval notion that Roman law was an ideal law, a universal unified system for testing the validity of all other laws.[33] Roman law, like all law, was a historical creation, the creation of human beings who, at different times and in different places, tried to solve various different problems. Moreover, if Roman law was not sacred, not *jus*, then it followed that canon law, too, was simply the creation of fallible human beings, not a law that was superior to, or higher than, any other positive law. This was the conclusion dramatically drawn by Martin Luther when he publicly burned a copy of the *Decretum Gratian.*

A second source of criticism of the medieval conception of legal order emerged from the voluntarist or nominalist philosophy of William of Occam. This philosophy swept through the universities in the fourteenth and fifteenth centuries, and then, with the advent of printing, achieved even wider influence in the second half of the fifteenth century.

Nominalism was primarily an epistemology, a theory of knowledge which claimed that only individual entities exist (this person, that house, these beds). The nominalists insisted that universals or essences (man, woman, house, cat, bed) have no existence in reality, but are only names (*nomen*) for collections or classes of individual objects. The nominalists taught that all knowledge comes from sense experience, and from this they concluded that it was impossible rationally to prove the existence of the soul or of God. But as Christians, they accepted that both the soul and God do exist. Moreover, as Christians they believed that God is omnipotent and supremely free. And if God is all powerful and totally free, then his laws cannot be restricted by the bonds of rationality or reason, as Thomas Aquinas had taught. The divine law is to be obeyed, the nominalists insisted, not because it is rational or reasonable but because it is God's law. This is voluntarism: Laws have no other foundation than the will of whoever imposes them. There is no rational, no natural, no historical foundation for any law: Only divine law (the will of God) and positive law (the will of humans) exist. The so-called natural law, the bridge between God's law and human law, did not exist. There was no evidence, the nominalists insisted that an eternal and immutable natural legal order exists.[34]

By denying the existence of natural law, the voluntarists further weakened one of the foundations of papal authority—a foundation used by Thomas Aquinas, as we saw above. Moreover, the notion that all law is nothing more than the expression of the will of the lawmaker helped pave the way for the third area of criticism of papal authority: the populist theory of the origin of all law.

Although the theory that all law came from the people had been around at least since the recovery of the *Politics* of Aristotle in the second decade of the thirteenth century, it was only with the *Defensor Pacis* of Marsilius of Padua that the populist theory came to be fully developed and, with the help of the printing press, widely known and subscribed to.[35]

Marsilius distinguished divine law from human law in terms of the kinds of penalties entailed. Divine law is sanctioned by the rewards or punishments meted out by God in the afterlife. Therefore, he concluded, the spiritual teachings of the Church have no power or authority in this world. Only human law involves an earthly penalty, so only human law has power and authority in this life. And human law, he pointed out, comes from the people; the people are the legislators, and legitimate authority lies with the people.

So, according to Marsilius, the plentitude of power—the power limited by no law whatsoever—belongs to the people. Here we can see that nothing remains of the traditional idea promulgated by lawyers and theologians, that human law is subject to an eternal and absolute order of value expressed in divine and natural law. Law, Marsilius insisted, derived from the people of the realm, not from God. Moreover, the people of the realm are not a collective joined in the pursuit of some common goal. Rather, they are a multitude formally associated in terms of laws which they make for themselves, laws to which they subscribe in the pursuit of the satisfaction of their individual wants.[36] In Marsilius's work, the hierarchical, collective, cooperative, subjective feudal order has given way to a vision of a new form of human association: a civil order, with its postulates of equality, individualism, competition, and objectivity.

All three of these movements of the fifteenth century—popularism, voluntarism, and the historical school of law—combined to unveil the irrelevance of Roman law to any science of government. This not only ended the monopoly of lawyers over all governmental questions, it also destroyed acceptance of that hierarchical legal order constructed by the medieval lawyers and theologians. And it all happened at precisely the point that tribal culture ended. For with the advent of printing, this whole legal order erected in the twelfth century following the recovery of Roman law, had come under continual critical scrutiny in a way never possible before. This criticism revealed that the medieval legal order had been constructed on certain misunderstood texts, was completely unrelated to the original meaning of those texts, and could never be derived from those texts.

THE BIBLE AND THE PRINTING PRESS

Gutenberg produced the first printed Bible in Mainz in 1456. Mentelin published the first German Bible in 1460. Zainer, a printer of Augsburg, produced the first illustrated Bible in 1475. An Italian Bible appeared in 1471. By 1500 ninety-four Latin editions of the Vulgate Bible had been printed, whereas thirty Bible translations, mostly in German, had appeared.[37]

Yet Christian scholars, like Erasmus, worried about the publication and dissemination of so many Bibles. It is obvious "even to a blind man," Erasmus noted, "that the Greek text has often been badly rendered because of the ignorance or careless-ness of the translator, and that often the genuine, true reading has been corrupted by unskilled copyists—this we know is a daily occurrence."[38]

Erasmus, therefore, set out to make a new Latin translation of the New Testa-ment, which finally appeared in 1516. His work, and that of his fellow Christian scholars, he believed, would usher in a new "age of gold." "What a world I see dawning!" he exclaimed in a letter to Leo X in 1517. There will be, he predicted, a true Christian piety and a united Christendom. True piety and true unity, he thought, were the inevitable product of the new "learning" hitherto "partly neglected and partly corrupted."[39]

Erasmus translated the New Testament into Latin "not for the crowds, but for the erudite." Yet he also hoped that the "true" scriptures would be made available to all in the vernacular. In his introduction to his New Testament, he wrote,

> I utterly disagree with those who do not want the Holy Scriptures to be read by the uneducated in their own languages, as though Christ's teachings were so obscure that they could hardly be understood even by a handful of theologians, or as though the strength of the Christian religion consisted in man's ignorance of it. I wish that every little woman would read the Gospels and the Epistles of St. Paul. And I wish these were translated into each and every language so that they might be read and under-stood not only by Scots and Irishmen, but by Turks and Saracens.[40]

In 1523, Lefevre d'Etaples complied with Erasmus's wishes, producing the first French translation of the New Testament. The year before, Luther using Erasmus's Latin edition, had completed his famous German translation. After 1522, Steinberg reports, every European nation received the scriptures into its mother tongue: The New Testament was printed in Dutch in 1523, the Old Testament in 1525; Tyndale's New Testament appeared in English in 1524, and Cloverdale's Bible in 1535; the New Testament was published in Danish in 1524, in Swedish in 1526, and in Ice-landic in 1540; the first printed Bible in Hungarian came out in 1541, in Spanish and in Croatian in 1543, in Finnish in 1548, in Polish in 1552, in Rumanian in 1561, in Lithuanian in 1579, and in Czech in 1579.[41]

But the golden age Erasmus had envisioned never came about. As early as 1526, he admitted that his optimistic prophecy had been shattered. In a letter to Martin Luther, he lamented the "irremediable confusion of everything," for which, he declared, "we have to thank only your uncontrollable nature."[42]

Erasmus blamed Luther for the "irremediable confusion of everything" only because he failed to understand the logic of the printing press. The printing press had made the new learning possible. But then, instead of ushering in a golden age, the printing of the Bible subverted Christian piety and destroyed Christian unity, leaving in its wake skepticism and fragmentation.

In the scribal age, scholars had spent their time slavishly copying the Scriptures from generation to generation. But in the age of print, scholars could engage in the open-ended quest for the true meaning of the Scriptures. Each successive published edition of the Bible claimed to be more accurate than its predecessors. Erasmus, for example, in defending his new translation of the New Testament to Leo X, maintained that he was not trying "to do away with the ancient vulgate edition," but rather had "only emended some corrupt passages and clarified several others where the text is obscure."[43]

The quest for the true meaning of the Scriptures led to the construction of an index to the vulgate and a lexicon, both compiled by the printer-scholar Robert Estienne. Grammars and dictionaries for Greek and Hebrew appeared so that scholars could trace the Scriptures to their original sources. The first polyglot edition of the Bible—Hebrew, Greek, and Latin versions of the Old Testament, and Greek and Latin versions of the New Testament, printed in parallel columns—appeared in Spain in 1517.[44]

Yet the more Greek and Hebrew studies progressed, the more wrangling there was over the meaning of words and phrases. The recovery of thousands of manuscripts of the Bible, each with variant readings, created uncertainty, confusion, and disarray in the ranks of Christian scholars. Instead of lighting up the true meaning of the scriptures, biblical scholarship increased perplexity about the Divine Word. As Elizabeth Eisenstein has pointed out, the production of one generation became the object of criticism of the next, with each succeeding generation pressing against continually receding frontiers in a never-ending, impossible quest for the true meaning of the Scriptures.[45]

Scholarly disputes were not limited to the meaning of the text; they extended to a lack of agreement on many factual details. Prior to printing, there had been severe restrictions on data collection—scribes garbled, transformed, and even lost data. With printing, however, scholars could for the first time carefully and continually accumulate accurate data in all fields of scholarship. But Bible scholars now recognized that it was impossible to compile accurate data about the events and persons discussed in the Scriptures: The date of creation, the name of the fruit that led to Adam's fall, the year of Christ's birth were all factual questions that remained unanswered. So even strictly factual matters became areas for scholarly dispute and, of course, beyond the scholar's grasp.[46]

Moreover, printed Bibles which were available to all, made possible the critical scrutiny of the content of the Scriptures by a European-wide community of scholars who began to raise probing and disturbing questions: How did the creatures from the Ark get disseminated all over the world—especially over the oceans and seas? How could Moses have calcined the golden calf if gold does not turn to powder under high temperatures? Some scholars suggested rational explanations for some of the miracles reported in the Scriptures: Manna is an actual plant, so this is how the people of Moses were fed in the desert; Elijah may have kindled the fire on God's altar by means of naphtha.

The printing of the Bible, therefore, increased skepticism, not piety. Encoding the sacred text in print allowed scholars to view it with detachment. This brought forth questions, problems, objections, arguments, and criticisms that had never been asked before. Moreover these criticisms often appeared in print, which then spread the seeds of skepticism.

The critical detachment of scholars toward the sacred texts complemented the detachment of the salesmen of the Bible. For now—at least for the printers, as well as the editors, translators, and commentators—the Bible became a commodity: something to be packaged, merchandised, marketed, and sold for a profit. Both Erasmus's and Luther's printers made fortunes, for example.[47] This, too, reduced Christian piety.

The printing of the Bible not only spread skepticism among Christians, it also developed dogmatism among them. Lay scholars with their knowledge of grammar, philology, and history now challenged theologians, while ordinary men and women "began to know their scriptures as well as most parish priests." And because they read little else, the Scriptures had an inordinately strong influence on half-educated people, creating an independence of mind often partnered with a literal fundamentalism that was hard to contain within the church. New sects appeared that raised the "infallible sciptures to a more lofty position than Catholics had ever ever elevated their popes.[48]

Both Luther and Calvin claimed that the Scriptures were the fundamental authority for all Christians. Here is Luther's famous declaration in his trial at the Diet of Worms in 1521:

> Your Imperial Majesty and your Lordship demand a simple answer. Here it is plain and unvarnished. Unless I am convicted of error by the testimony of scriptures or (since I put no trust in the unsupported authority of pope or or councils, since it is plain that they have often erred and often contradicted themselves) by manifest reasoning, I stand convicted by the scriptures to which I have appealed, and my conscience is taken captive by God's word, I cannot and will not recant anything, for to act against our conscience is neither safe for us, nor open to us. On this I take my stand. I can do not other. God help me. Amen.[49]

The printing of the Bible in the vernacular exacerbated this scriptural dogmatism. Instead of unity, Christendom became fragmented into warring factions, splintering the *respublica Christiana* into a multitude of sects, each with its own authoritative vernacular Bible. The European-wide unity that had been ensured by a common Latin language came undone.

As head of the *respublica Christiana*, the only response the Pope could make was to censor and prohibit the publication of the Scriptures. This simply broadened and deepened the fragmentation and darkened and strengthened both the skepticism and the dogmatism. As early as 1515—before the publication of Erasmus's New Testament and before the Lutheran revolt—Leo X had issued a sweeping censorship decree on all translation of the Scriptures into Latin or into the vernacular. All such translations were to be censored by the bishops, their delegates, or the Inquisitiion. In 1520, the papal edict against the Protestant heresy included the prohibition of unauthorized biblical editions and vernacular translations. Finally, the Council of Trent, convened to preserve the "purity of the gospel," declared that the Latin vulgate of St. Jerome was to be the authorized Catholic Bible.

When the first papal index of prohibited books appeared in 1559, it included the French Bible of Lefevre d'Etaples, Luther's German Bible, and the New Testament of Erasmus. The 1564 index included a prohibition against Bible reading as well as Bible printing. These papal actions effectively eliminated all biblical scholarship and vernacular translations of the Bible in all Catholic countries.

The Protestant lands copied the authoritarian actions of the Catholic Church in response to the printing of the Scriptures. Over the course of the sixteenth century, each ruler who broke with Rome sooner or later officially authorized a particular vernacular translation of the Bible. This further balkanized Christendom, fragmenting the *respublica Christiana* not only into Catholic and Protestant religions but into national religions as well.

Yet although the printing of the Scriptures did not usher in the golden age of Christian unity Erasmus had anticipated, it did help make things better. For example, the printed vernacular editions of the Bible conferred a new dignity on the various vernacular languages of Europe. This promoted the conversion of the texts of law and medicine, as well as the texts of the liberal arts and science, into the vernacular so that they were no longer hidden in Greek or Latin and were made available to the "vulgar people." This destruction of the academic monopolies and professional elites increased the life chances of those unacquainted with the classical languages. Henceforth, too, a national literature emerged in every European nation, written by and open to those who, like Shakespeare, had "small Latin and no Greek."

The printing press helped to create a more pluralistic world, in which there was more freedom and equality for more people. And this was true of the realm of religion itself. In place of a monolithic, hierarchical Church imposing a common or collective goal on all, with which all must cooperate and to which all must subscribe with complete fidelity, there now existed many different individual Christian religions, all equal, all in competition with one another, among which Christians could freely choose. This religious pluralism did not, of course, immediately lead to the toleration of free choice among religions, but it was inevitable once the printing press had fragmented the *respublica Christiana*.

THE EMERGENCE OF THE MODERN STATE

During the sixteenth century, the papal *plenitudo potestatis* was extinguished: Declared enemies and even otherwise faithful members plundered ecclesiastical property; civil courts took over what had belonged to the jurisdiction of ecclesiastical courts; wills and treaties ceased to be semiecclesiastical documents; the Pope's authority as an arbitrator between the rulers of realms lapsed; civil rulers proscribed papal taxation; ecclesiastical offices became royal appointments; and henceforth "excommunication had no terror and interdict no peril."[50]

It was the rulers of the newly emerging European states who had dispossessed the papacy of its plentitude of power. After the anarchy of the fifteenth century—

the Hundred Years' War in France, the War of the Roses in England, the troubles in Spain—the monarchs in each of these countries had led the way in centralizing power into their own hands and establishing relative order.[51] The monarchs were no longer merely lords of a domain; they had each become rulers of a realm. The primary role of the ruler of each state was to get his new title (and himself as holder) acknowledged by his subjects. This was no easy task. The reluctance of the English, for example, to acknowledge Tudor rule is evident in the De Facto Acts of the second year of the reign of Henry VII, which recognized him only as "the King and Sovereign lord of the land for the time being." One of Henry's first actions on becoming king in 1485 was to appoint Peter Actors of Savoy as the first royal printer. The king gave him the right to "imprint, as often as he likes, from ports beyond the sea, books . . . and to dispose of the same by sale without paying customs." (Actually, Actors was not a printer. The first official printer was William Facquer, who held the office from 1504 to 1508.[52]) Henry used the printing press to establish his legitimacy: issuing multiple copies of edicts and proclamations—like the DeFacto Act— and scattering them everywhere. But it remained for his son, Henry VIII, to recognize the propaganda uses of the printing press. Henry VIII had a more difficult time than most monarchs in securing the acceptance of his subjects. This was not so much a matter of the legitimacy of his authority as it was the radicalism of his actions: his long and vicious dispute with the Pope over his divorce from his brother's widow, Catherine, which ended with Henry declaring himself head of the Church of England.

Under Henry VIII, the government of England undertook a full-scale propaganda campaign using the printing press in an intensive fashion to secure acceptance of the new order. The statutes that wrought these dramatic changes were printed in multiple copies—including their long, highly propagandistic preambles—and put on public display throughout the land. But more than this, the king's printer published pamphlets, sermons, and books that defended the revolution Henry had wrought. The published books included the ponderously entitled *The Determination of the Most Famous and Excellent Universities of Italy and France That it is Lawful for a Man to Marry his Brother's Wife and that the Pope hath no Power to Dispense Therewith* (1531), as well as the lively *A Little Treatise Against the Muttering of Some Papists in Corners* (1534). These works, along with *De Vera Obedience (Oration of True Obedience, 1535)*, were all commissioned and paid for by Thomas Cromwell, Henry's chief officer of state. During this period, Cromwell also had the antipapal tracts of Marsilius and Valla translated and published in English. One book explaining the monarch's side in the divisive dispute with the Pope was called *The Glass of Truth* (1532), which was probably written by Henry himself. According to Elton, this propaganda campaign in print did help to reconcile most people to Henry's divorce and persuaded them to accept the Act of Supremacy, the act wherein Henry declared himself head of the Church of England.[53]

In France, Claude de Seyssell, one-time minister of Louis XII, published *Le Grand Monarchie de France* (1518), a book explaining why monarchy was the best form of government for France and why Louis was the ideal monarch. Other justificatory works followed, many of them written by French lawyers. Jean Ferrault wrote *Jura regni Franciae*, the first book published in sixteenth century France to claim for the king rights almost unlimited. In *Regalium Franciae* (1538), Charles de Grassaille described the king of France as *imperator in sero regni*, as well as the viceregent of God. In the *Livres des dignities* (1551 in Latin, 1561 in French), the lawyer Vincent de la Laupe declared that the king can make war or peace, impose taxes, and make laws as seem good to him—and all he says is esteemed "as the laws and the sayings of the oracle of Apollo himself." In all these books proclaiming the authority of the ruler of the state, the claims of the papacy are ignored.[54]

In Italy, Roderico Samcius, Bishop of Calahorra, wrote a book, titled, *Speculum Humanae Vitae*, which extolled the monarchy and described the king as an image of God. It was printed in Paris in 1472 and in Lyons in 1477. But the most famous Italian work on the virtues of the new European state was Machiavelli's *The Prince* (1532). The state, he explained, is necessary because only it can give the security and stability all people desire. Rulers should strive to be popular, Machiavelli says, but those rulers that give the most security will be most popular. "Let a prince, therefore, aim at conquering and maintaining the state, and the means will always be judged honorable and praised by everyone."[55]

As they set out to become rulers of their realms, the heads of the new European states paid heed to Machiavelli's advice. In state after state, the king became supreme in both theory and fact. He ruled through his councils and great offices of state. But this was not new. Powerful kings had existed before. What was new was the creation, at this point, of agents who carried out the administrative and judicial tasks of the government at the local level—aiding the monarch, in the words of Thomas Elyot, "in the distribution of justice in sundry parts of a huge multitude."[56] In Spain, this officer of local government was called *corregidor*, and in England the *justice of the peace*, in France, the *baillis* and *senechaux* were the officials of local government, but the *lieutenant du roi es bailliage* performed the real work of administration.[57] The local agents in each country were university graduates in law, usually bourgeois, not members of the landed aristocracy. All were appointed and paid by the crown, responsible and accountable only to the king.

The media of communication always determine or limit the degree and the extent of control that a government can exercise from a central source. Thus, just as the feudal arrangements of the medieval period had been the product of a scribal culture, so the creation of these local agents in the sixteenth century was the direct result of the invention of the printing press. Only when commands, orders, proclamations, edicts, and ordinances were printed, rather than handwritten and handcopied, could government be centralized.

With the printing press, the number of comunications from the central government could and did increase, and the number of recipients of these communiques increased in number, too. Moreover, typographical fixity guaranteed that the messages received would be uniform, so all agents could be held accountable for carrying out the orders issued by the government. This increase in the availability, rapidity, and reliability of communication enhanced the certainty with which the government could forecast the outcome of the course of events. Now the government could more efficiently control the goings-on in the state.

It is true that much of the daily work of the central government continued to be done by clerks, who hand wrote, copied, and transcribed correspondence, petitions, warrants, and the like. But it is significant to note that in spite of the vastly increased number of governmental communications, there seems to have been no increase in the number of writing clerks in the employ of the government of England during the sixteenth century, and Elton reports that in some cases, the amount of work these clerks had to do acually diminished by mid-century.[58] What had happened, of course, was that much of their work had been taken over by the royal printer, who duplicated and disseminated statutes, proclamations, edicts, ordinances, and acts—all of which made the centralized government a reality and established the monarch as ruler of the realm.[59]

During the sixteenth century, the monarchs in each state established what was to become a monopoly over the law. The state could and did extricate itself from its legal past as each ruler asserted and exercised the power to release subjects from entrenched, but now unwarranted, obligations. From that time forward, no other authority could prescribe laws to the state or challenge its authority to create laws. The ruler of each state became a single inalienable authority, without superior, partner, or competitor. It was by means of the printing press that the monarchs of Europe succeeded in making themselves the source and custodian of the laws of the land.

These laws of the land created the modern state, a new form of human association called civil society. Jean Bodin (1530-1596) was one of the first to perceive this European-wide transformation from domains into states. A state, Bodin recognized, is a human invention: Its laws are man made. This new form of human association—in terms of (man-made) laws—necessitates that there be a sovereign authority for law. Otherwise, there can be no association. This authority, Bodin added, must be not only sovereign, it must be absolute and continuous. Without absolute, continuous sovereignty, the state cannot persist, and the civil association cannot exist.[60]

In the civil society of the modern state, people were no longer clients of a lord as they had been in feudal society. In civil society, people became subjects of a ruler, which meant that they were free and independent agents associated in terms of laws, not in terms of some collective purpose imposed on them, as had been the case during the period of the *respublica Christiana*. Indeed, the modern state is different from all previous political constructions insofar as it is not a form of association to pursue a superordinate satisfaction, a general prosperity or happiness; nor is it a form of association to stimulate people to virtuous conduct or salvation. Under the civil association of the modern state, each becomes a free individual. The laws of the modern state prescribed no purpose or goals, they prescribed only conditions to which each subject must subscribe in pursuing his or her own individual wants.

The law of the land had not only to be proclaimed and administered, it had to be interpreted to local conditions, and transgressors had to be punished. The modern state needed modern courts, and with the help of the printing press, each state was able to create a national judicial system to replace the inherited patchwork system of independent courts of the feudal period with their overlapping jurisdictions and conflicting codes of ancient laws and customs.

Each state secured a national court system by setting up a central court that would be supreme in the land—a court to which plaintiffs could appeal when they failed to receive satisfaction in some other court. In England, this was the Court of Common Pleas; in Germany, it was called the *Reichskammergericht*; in France, the *Parlement*. All lower courts then had to begin to decide cases more or less in accord with the decisions of these supreme courts. The cases decided by these courts became "binding authorities."[61] But this was possible only because of the printing press

During the middle ages, jurists had declared that like cases should be decided alike. But before the advent of the printing press, court cases were recorded in manuscript plea rolls, which were unavailable and inaccessible to any except legal scholars.[62] With the coming of the printing press, these court cases could be duplicated in multiple copies and scattered throughout every court in the land, where they could be studied and readily consulted as precedents for similar cases. The doctrine of precedent—the fundamental doctrine of every modern state's judicial system—came into being in the sixteenth century, following the invention of the printing press. This doctrine of precedent guaranteed that like cases would be decided alike. The significance of this, of course, is that all people would be equal before the law.[63]

So with the emergence of the modern state, things got better. For the first time, people were both free and equal—free to pursue their own choices and wants, and equal before the law.

In addition to using the printing press to secure acceptance, to establish the law of the land, and to provide equal justice for all, the early monarchs used the printing press to create the apparatus of governing. Through the printing press, governing was converted from an activity conducted by the king's household into a bureaucratic enterprise.

Rudimentary instruments of bureaucracy, like licenses and permits, had existed before printing, but the Reformation had caused the cancellation of many of these—licenses to preach, for example, that had been issued by the Church were no longer valid in Protestant countries. This made it necessary for the state to issue new pemits, licenses, and the like. The printing press allowed the state—both Catholic and Protestant—to do this rapidly and efficiently, while at the same time the typographical fixity of printed forms reduced the possibility of forgery.

In addition to issuing printed licenses, permits, and certificates, the state governments of the sixteenth century began keeping records as a way of maintaining surveillance over their subjects. The printing press supplied the forms for recording births, deaths, marriages, addresses, and occupations—which were often maintained by the local church or parish. In addition, local agents of government used printed forms to record deeds, leases, contracts, etc., which reduced the possibility of fraud and deception.

One of the most important forms now printed was the tax form, which allowed governments for the first time to obtain income by regular taxes at stipulated rates through extractions of definite amounts. Taxation required that each country be divided unto counties and districts for the purpose of rating and collection. This could be done only because the printing press made it possible to construct, duplicate, and disseminate correct maps of each territory in the state.

Another means of revenue raising made possible by the printing press was the sale of government bonds and the floating of public loans: In the sixteenth century, the Spanish government sold bonds called *juros.* and the French issued bonds they called *rentes sur l'hotel de ville.*

One reason that states needed new sources of income was the cost of maintaining military forces. (The administrative and judicial bureaucracies were not a drain on the treasury; indeed, they were a source of income, because many of these offices were sold to those who ran them.) The monarchs of Europe now relied on professional, trained mercenaries, so the task of clothing, supplying, and equipping soldiers added a tremendous burden to the royal treasuries. By the late sixteenth century, some 70 percent of Spanish state revenue was spent on the military, and two thirds of the revenue of other European countries went the same way.[64] Moreover, the task of maintaining a professional army also required a massive number of printed forms and records. The printing press did not create the large military forces of the modern state, but they could not have been created and maintained without the press.

In sum, the printing press made governmental bureaucracy and professionalism possible on a national scale by supplying the forms and records and other paper apparatus necessary for the functioning of the councils, commissions, committees, secretaries of state, advisors, clerks, constables, diplomats, and the bureaus in which they worked. The printing press allowed government officials to develop their routines and their expertise, and it enabled them to conduct inquiries, collect information, store it, and retrieve it with relative ease. Moreover, each state preserved the bureaucracies it had created by publishing printed manuals, guides, and handbooks to explain the workings of the various bureaus and departments and to prepare people to staff and use them.

Bureaucracy objectified the people in the modern state. In place of the personal, subjective loyalties that had bound people together in feudal society, men and women now experienced an objectification never possible before. Each person's life now became nothing more than a series of entries on forms and records. Each person's identity was encoded on the certificates, licences, and permits he or she possessed. Although many felt dehumanized by being reduced to the data inscribed on printed forms and records, for many more this objectification confirmed their identity as human beings. This objectification in the records and files of the government bureaucracy was the first recognition that large numbers of people existed: They were no longer unknown serfs working in the fields, each living out a life unacknowledged and unrecognized as a person. So with governmental bureau-cracy—made possible by the printing press—things got better; life chances im-proved.

PRINTING AND ROYAL ABSOLUTISM

As happened with both speech and writing, the medium of print helped make things better by encoding descriptions of, and arguments about, the existing ar-rangements and scattering them everywhere; this facilitated criticism of those ar-rangements. Criticism destroyed the *respublica Christiana* and created the inde-pendent modern states of Europe. But, as happened with both speech and writing, after bringing about radical political change, the medium of print became an agent for conserving the status quo.

Through the medium of the printing press, the rulers of the modern states had become the residuary legates of the *plenitudo potestatis* of the Pope. As the all-embracing authority of the *respublica Christiana* receded, the ruler of each state centralized his control over the administrative, judicial and military organizations within his realm, assuming responsibility for the temporal peace of his subjects. In time, rulers even assumed responsibility for the souls of their subjects. This came about when each ruler claimed the sacerdotal authority of the Pope. This was the direct result of the Peace of Augsburg (1555), in which the notion first appeared that all subjects should subscribe to the religion of the ruler of the realm (*cuius regio, eius religio*). Later, the doctrine of Divine Right, enunciated by both the monarchs of England and France, intensified this claim to sacerdotal authority.

This acquisition of the sacerdotal authority intimated a transformation of the character of the government—a return to the more closed society of the premodern era. By the seventeenth century, rulers not only had the right to appoint ecclesias-tical officers but also the right to direct their activities. Now, in every European state, clergy received from the government a continual stream of printed requests, orders, rules, and laws regarding such matters as religious services, the content of sermons, and pastoral responsibilities. By this time, the state not only owned large quantities of property taken from the church, but it also regulated schools and universities, charities, public holidays, marriage laws, baptismal names, usury, and many other goings-on hitherto regulated by the Church. The printing press made all this possible. The royal printer could disseminate throughout the realm those edicts, statutes, and regulations that the state wished to impose on all subjects. The jurisdictional authority of the state thus extended, in Michael Oakeshott's words, "not only over persons hitherto exempt, but over causes previously ignored: her-esy, blasphemy, moral delinquency, and intellectual deviance."

Along with the new laws and extended judicial authority came an increase in the bureaucratic apparatus of the state—records, dossiers, files, documents, pledges, affidavits, oaths, and tests—used to identify and suppress aliens (like the Jews and Morescos in Spain), witches, and all varieties of cults. The state controlled the publication of authorized Bibles, catechisms, and prayer books; it established censorship of art, literature, and entertainment; and it suppressed languages (like the *langue d'oc* of France).

Early in its history, then, the modern state used the medium of print to impose a collective goal or purpose to which all subjects had to subscribe, the administration and adjudication of which undermined freedom and deprived the people of their traditonal and customary rights. All this, of course, was a throwback to earlier forms of human association, forms that had first emerged in oral and scribal cultures and that harkened back to tribalism. Now that these authoritarian characteristics could be implemented by the printing press, the modern state was able to become more despotic, more tyrannical, more totalitarian than any previous form of human association.

In asserting their authority and assuming responsibility for both the temporal and spiritual well-being of their subjects, the monarchs of Europe assumed that these actions ensured the safety, stability, and welfare of the state. Most of their subjects agreed, for most actually subscribed to royal absolutism. In England, for example, William Tyndale, who had suffered much from the monarch and was to suffer more, wrote a tract in 1528 called *Obedience of a Christian Man*, in which he announced that "the kyng is in thys worlde without lawe . . . for god hath made the kyng in every Realme judge over all, and over him there is no judge." And Tyndale's words, Professor McIlwain assures us, "did not stand alone." In the seventeenth century, royal absolutism was endorsed and strengthened by the political writings of political theorists—Bodin and Bossuet in France, Bacon and Hobbes in England—who declared that all law was the expression of the unlimited will of the sovereign.[65]

PRINTING AND CONSTITUTIONALISM

But if the printing press had made royal absolutism possible, it was the printing press that also helped create the antidote: constitutionalism. For by the seventeenth century, the printing press had created a new critical movement, an environment in which the acts of the crown increasingly came under critical scrutiny. Now, for the first time, people began to view the actions of the monarch as arbitrary. It was not that those actions were much different from those of earlier kings and queens, but that by the seventeenth century, people could read printed criticisms of those actions.

The printers themselves were responsible for much of this criticism. Their opposition to the crown stemmed from the practice of issuing royal licenses to printers. This licensing of printers had worked in the sixteenth century, when printing was in its infancy. During that period, the absolute monarchs of Europe had used licensing to control the printing presses in their realms and had successfully prevented the publication of political tracts critical of the government. But as the logic of licensure unfolded, it led to increased political criticism. For as the printing trade flourished, more and more printers found themselves denied licenses.

These unlicensed printers then set about composing and printing "illegal" tracts and pamphlets denouncing the existing arrangements, which they declared to be "contrary to the laws of God and nature." But when the crown relented and issued new licenses, this made matters even worse by creating conflicts and overlapping jurisdictions among license holders. As a result, some printers began to claim that all attempts to control printing were arbitrary, "being contrary to the Magna Carta, the Petition of Rights, and other statutes."[66]

The absolute monarchs themselves heated up the critical dialogue by using the printing press to assert what they considered to be their traditional rights. Thus, James Stuart of Scotland, before he became King James I of England, published *The True Law of Free Monarchies, or the Mutual Duty Betwixt a Free King and his Subjects*—a political treatise that announced the divine right of kings: the doctrine that monarchy is divinely ordained, so kings are accountable to God alone. The book provoked an extended controversy between the Crown and Parliament. First came a reply from Parliament—a printed "Apology" that asserted the traditional rights and privileges of that body. James replied to this in a speech, later printed, that reiterated the doctrine of divine right. In response, Parliament, under the leadership of Edward Coke, then proceeded to reaffirm the "Ancient Constitution"—that body of common law that derived from the Magna Carta of 1215. Coke, one-time Chief Justice of the Court of Common Pleas, did much to reconstruct—some say to fabricate—and make public that "Ancient Constitution" through his *Institutes of the Laws of England*, which were published under the aegis of the House of Commons.[67]

During the reign of James I and his son, Charles I, actions commonly taken by previous monarchs came under severe critical scrutiny and were condemned as arbitrary violations of traditional rights encoded in common law: jailing people without a trial; issuing acts of attainder (statutes passed to condemn a person to death without any legal trial); imposing taxes; selling benefices; extorting "forced loans; selling monopolies; suspending laws, or dispensing some actions from law; and controlling the courts. Initially, the critics argued that the cure for despotism was rule by Parliament. But this did not work; for after beheading Charles I and abolishing the monarchy in 1649 the English created the Commonwealth, which lasted only until 1653, when it was succeeded by the Protectorate of Oliver Cromwell, a period of military dictatorship. In 1660, the monarchy was restored to Charles II.

From 1640 to 1660, the volume of printed political criticism increased tremendously. The incomplete collection of tracts assembled by the bookseller George Thomson for this twenty-year span contains more than twenty thousand titles. As Sabine says, the printing press became the organ of government discussion.[68] Through printed declarations, agreements, proposals, manifestoes, political critics gained followers, who both subscribed to their criticisms and advocated their solutions. The medium of the printing press thus created the first modern political action groups: the Levellers, the Diggers, the Presbyterians, and the Independents.

The members of these groups were all disciples of the ancient Roman Republic.

The printing press had made the work of the ancient poets, philosophers, orators, and historians available and, as Hobbes noted, the members of these various political action groups had all read "the books of policy and the histories of the ancient Greeks and Romans." Milton, too, declared that they were "men more than vulgar—bred up . . . in the knowledge of ancient and illustrious deeds." They printed pamphlets, tracts, and books to bring, in Milton's words, "civil virtues" to the modern world from " the examples of past ages."[69] Each group had its own identifiable slogans and quotations, culled from the printed speeches and manifestoes of its leaders: "The poorest that lives hath as true a right to give a vote as well as the richest and the greatest" (Levellers). "True freedom lies where a man receives his nourishment and preservation, and that is in the use of the earth" (Diggers). "Posterity will say that to deliver them from the yoke of the King we have subjugated them to that of the common people" (Presbyterians).

Each group believed that a good state could come into being only if those who shared its ideas were to become rulers, or if rulers were to adopt its ideas. But arbitrary acts and despotic rule did not cease—not during the time of the Commonwealth, not during the Protectorate, and not with the Restoration. This fact made clear to some that the fundamental question of government is not "Who should rule?" but rather, "How can we restrain the rulers, no matter who they might be?" The political theorist James Harrington was one of the first to see this clearly. In his *Oceana*, the highly influential political treatise he published in 1657, he wrote, "Give us good men and they will make good lawes is the maxim of a Demagogue."[70] Gradually, more and more Englishmen came to realize that changing rulers could not protect against despotism. In 1688, these "whigs" carried out the Glorious Revolution. After deposing James II, they established a new form of government, a constitutional monarchy—a monarchy that could be held accountable through constitutional checks.[71]

Constitutionalism had actually begun in England with the Petition of Rights of 1628, when Parliament forced Charles II to confirm the "ancient principles" of trial by jury, due process, and taxation only with the consent of Parliament. The Petition of Rights was only a restatement of the rights Englishmen believed they already possessed. The Petition was not a statute that made those rights absolute; it carried no guarantee that the king would not, in the future, as he had in the past, violate those rights. This became evident the following year, when Charles disbanded Parliament and ruled without it for eleven years. The second step toward constitutionalism came with the first written (printed) constitution, *The Instrument of Government of 1653*, which launched the Protectorate. In the official defense of this constitution, entitled *A True State of the Care of the Commonwealth* (1654), Marchamont Nedham wrote that the "grand" secret of liberty and true government "lies in the doctrine of the separation of powers contained in this instrument."[72] People now began to see that when the function of laying down the rules and the function of applying them to individual cases is combined in one power and one body, the government becomes arbitrary. By separating the powers of government, it becomes easier to identify arbitrary actions and hold them in check (arbitrary actions being those that were not in conformity with existing general principles of law).[73]

A constitutional government is a limited government, in which arbitrary power is proscribed and procedures are prescribed for the legal exercise of power.[74] Constitutional government could not exist before the advent of the printing press because the proscriptions and prescriptions directed at the exercise of power work only if they are encoded in typographical fixity, for only then can they become permanent, known to all, and accessible to all who seek protection from the actions of government. Through the printing press, rulers, for the first time in history, became accountable to their subjects. The printing press, in short, made possible, and guaranteed a rule of law, not men.

After the Glorious Revolution of 1688, the English composed and published the Bill of Rights, which enumerated the specific liberties that citizens possess— liberties that should be protected: the right to petition the king, the right of free speech in Parliament, the right to free elections, no quartering of soldiers, no cruel and unusual punishments, and no changes in religion by fiat of the crown.[75] A few years later, the Act of Settlement of 1701 established an independent judiciary.

Following the lead of England, both the United States and France constructed constitutional governments in the eighteenth century. Both nations used the medium of print to proclaim to the world and to make permanent the rights accorded to all citizens and to encode the doctrine of the separation of powers in written (printed) constitutions.

With the advent of the printing press, things got better: Government improved. Through the medium of print, people were able to create constitutional governments. The rule of law replaced the arbitrary power of men and made government limited. The outcome of this was the emergence of an abstract society. In an abstract society, people are independent, free to pursue their individual ends and goals. No shared or common purpose exists, and no subjective bonds of cooperation join people together as in a tribal society. In a nation with constitutional government, what one may do is not dependent on the approval of any person or authority and is limited by only the same abstract rules that apply equally to all.

Chapter Seven

Printing and Capitalism

Markets, as we saw, were the product of alphabetic writing. But the market system did not exist until the modern era, when land, labor, and capital came into being. Land, labor, and capital—in the sense of soil, human beings, and tools—certainly were around prior to modern times, but what is new is the idea of abstract land, abstract labor, and abstract capital as impersonal, dehumanized, economic entities: as agents of production.[1]

During the middle ages, all land belonged to the king, who held it (he did not own it) as a temporary trust from God. The king distributed most of the land to others, as a benefice, and they, in turn, redistributed some of it to still others, as a benefice. Land was not bought and sold: There was no land market. In return for his benefice, each recipient owed service to the benefactor. This service consisted of labor in one form or another, but it was not labor to be bought and sold. People cultivated the soil, prepared the food, made clothing for others—all as a service, a duty. Workers were not free agents contracting to sell their labor: No labor market existed.[2]

The tenants lived tied to their lord's estate, and each estate was more or less self-sufficient. People owned bullion, animals, clothing, horses, equipment, and so on, but these specific goods were not capital: No one used them to create wealth. They were not valued because of their capability of earning interests or profits. Without a market where such transactions could take place, private wealth could not become capital. Lacking a market for land, capital, or labor, all economic transactions during the middle ages followed custom and tradition. Some economic growth did occur, but it was not sought after or planned for: Capitalism did not exist. It was the commercialization of the land, the commutation of labor, and monetarization of the economy that brought capitalism—and the resultant growth in wealth—to the nations of Europe. Printing facilitated all these changes.

THE QUASI-MARKET OF THE LATE MIDDLE AGES

The decline of the military might of Rome in the fifth century in the face of successive raids and invasions from the north, east, and south tore apart the European countryside and made life unsafe and insecure. In southern Europe, once-thriving ports around the Mediterranean sank to the level of fishing villages. In the north, cities all but disappeared as people retreated to the manorial estates of the local lord for protection. Trade and commerce over any distance became hazardous, which meant that each manor had to become self-sufficient, with its own farms, mills, ovens, and workshops for feeding, clothing, and equipping all who lived on the estate. The tenants usually paid their obligations to the lord in kind. Everyone owed the lord a fixed number of days of labor—repairing bridges, roads, and moats, caring for stables and herds, supplying firewood, doing laundry, and so on—or they owed him a fixed quantity of natural products or manufactured goods: corn, eggs, geese, chickens, lambs, pigs, and hempen, linen, or woolen cloth.[3]

Feudal laws bound each member of the community to the manor. No peasant could migrate from it without paying a fine or marry a person from another manor without both paying a fine and obtaining the lord's consent. When holdings passed from father to oldest son, the new holder had to give his lord the best article of clothing. If he died childless, his house, tools, and other possessions reverted to the lord. These taxes, fines, and dues all underlined the unfree condition of the peasants.

By the eleventh century, various technological innovations—the heavy-wheeled plow, the three-field system (rotating crops among three fields instead of between two), the horse collar, the tandem, and the horseshoe—all contributed to a great increase in farm productivity. More available food led to an increase in population and the spreading out and migration of the people. Some moved to new villas, where they became day laborers or landholders; others joined mercenary armies; and some ended up in new towns, where they became craftsmen and traders. The shrunken descendents of Roman towns had continued to exist throughout Europe, as stopping places for itinerant traders who traveled in armed caravans selling spices, textiles, dyes, and silks from India and Arabia. These goods came into Europe by way of Venice, Genoa, Pisa, and Amalfi, towns that had established trade with the East. The stopping places the merchants used became the nuclei for the new towns and small cities, where merchants, craftsmen and artisans established networks of markets.

By 1150, Europe had moved beyond self-sufficiency to the stage in which the feudal estates were marketing their surplus production in the towns in exchange for the luxury items available there. According to one estimate some 300 or so trading cities came into existence between the eleventh and thirteenth centuries. In the early thirteenth century, trading fairs—held every two months at a different place—became the center of all wholesale trade activity for the sale and exchange of commodities as well as for the exchange of money. By the end of the thirteenth century, the itinerant merchant had become a rare figure. Merchandise now traveled alone, controlled from a distance by written documents—instruments of credit.[4]

So between the eleventh and fourteenth centuries, both agricultural production and commerce grew slowly but steadily throughout Europe. One of the consequences of this was the monetarization of the economy. Once the manoral estates began selling their surplus crops at the market for cash, other economic transactions underwent monetarization. Thus, in locality after locality, feudal obligations to the lord were converted from payments in kind to money dues and money rents. The lord of the manor was glad to receive cash because he, in turn, could then buy the luxuries available in the town markets.

The monetarization of the economy gave rise to a quasi-market system, in which land, labor, and an increasing number of commodities could be bought and sold. Yet a full-fledged capitalist system did not emerge until the sixteenth century, as Karl Marx noted.[5] In a capitalist economy, the market is free, whereas the markets that had come into being by the beginning of the fourteenth century were protected, not free. The guilds that merchants, craftsmen, and artisans had formed in the towns strictly controlled the labor market, determinng who could and could not enter every occupation. The guilds also established wages and prices, unlike the free market of a capitalist economy, where competition sets both prices and wages. Nor did a free market exist for land. All land continued to be the property of the lord, who could not sell it because of the law of entail. He merely leased or rented it to tenants, and he could, and sometimes did, reclaim the land and expropriate the tenants.

In a capitalist economy, all goods are viewed objectively, with concern solely for their market value. This requires that all goods, including labor, be sold for what they are worth—for what they will bring in the market. Thus, in a free market, all goods are treated equally, solely in terms of their market value. But in the fourteenth century, ties of place and roles of status prevented this: There could be no equal treatment in economic transactions between lord and peasant. Contracts between consenting adults had not yet replaced the kinds of status dictated by the hierarchical feudal order. Moreover, the religious beliefs of the middle ages persuaded people to regard all economic transactions subjectively, viewing them through the prism of noneconomic customs, traditions, laws, beliefs, rules, and doctrines. St. Augustine had taught that "business is itself an evil," and medieval Christians believed that profit beyond a minimum necessary to support the dealer was avarice, that to make money out of money by charging interest on a loan was the sin of usury. Canon law condemned buying goods wholesale and selling them unchanged at a higher retail price. All in all, St. Jerome's dictum summed up the official Christian attitude toward commerce and trade: "A man who is a merchant can seldom, if ever, please God" (*Homo mercator vix aut numquam potest Deo placere*).[6]

The quasi-market system that had slowly developed in Europe between the eleventh and fourteenth centuries never became more than a severely limited economy. The limits, as I will try to show, were the limits of a scribal culture. The printing press, invented in the fifteenth century, removed those obstacles to economic growth and allowed the free market system of capitalism to emerge. It all began with the economic crisis of the fourteenth century—the century of adversity.[7]

THE CENTURY OF ADVERSITY

Famine, endemic in the middle ages, reached epidemic proportions in the fourteenth century. It engulfed all of Europe in 1315 when excessive rain, followed by floods and bitter cold, destroyed all crops. Thereafter, almost every year for the next three decades, crops repeatedly failed, reducing many people to begging, some to thievery, and some to cannibalism. Not only agriculture, but trade, too, declined—dramatically curtailed by the rise of the Ottoman Turks, who spread throughout much of eastern and southern Europe, threatening and restricting European trade on the Mediterranean and Adriatic. Another malignant influence on economic growth was chronic war—among Italian cities, German princedoms, and western monarchies. According to Lerner, the wars of the fourteenth century were more frequent, longer, and more bloody than any since those of the tenth century.[8]

Yet all of these adversities were nothing compared to the Black Death, or bubonic plague, which befell Europe in 1347. Entering Europe from Constantinople, it spread rapidly along trade routes, reaching as far as Greenland, Iceland, and Russia. Nearly everyone infected died. Out of 80 million people who lived in Europe before the plague, roughly 25 million disappeared in little more than three years. Plague broke out again six times over the next ten decades, reducing the population of Europe by about 4 percent in 1380 and by 50 percent at the end of the century.[9]

The combination of famine, wars, and epidemics devastated all of Europe. Contemporary texts describe the chill horror of a countryside where "neither cock crowed nor hen clucked." Everywhere, villages were deserted, sometimes for generations. On countless village lands, there was nothing to be seen but "thorns, thickets, and other encumbrances."[10]

The Black Death had a more dramatic impact on the economy than all the other calamities. Famine and war reduce population and food, but plague destroys population without touching goods and property. As a result, barns and warehouses remained full, while the number of people decreased. This meant an oversupply of goods combined with an acute shortage of labor, resulting in a contraction of markets. In consequence, the initial impact of the Black Death was improved economic conditions for the lower classes: The shortage of labor and the oversupply of products brought them both higher wages and lower prices. At the same time, the plight of the landlords and the merchants worsened. The landlords had fewer serfs and therefore less rental income. Bound by customary law, they could not raise rents—and if they did their serfs migrated. The plight of the merchants came from having fewer markets and fewer customers and having to pay higher wages.

In light of our present-day economic theories, the rational solution to this economic crisis would have been to look for new markets. But because they did not share our theories, the ruling classes did not do this. From our angle of vision, they reacted irrationally—exploiting and expropriating workers and peasants, and establishing monopolistic controls. Rather than trying to enlarge the economic pie, they fought bitterly to retain or expand their share.

The royal ordinances of the time tell the story. England issued an ordinance in 1349, later repeated in 1351 as the Statute of Laborers, requiring everyone to work for the same pay as in 1347. Penalties were imposed for refusing to work, for leaving a place of employment to seek higher pay, and on employers who offered workers higher pay. France similarly tried to maintain the system with a statute of 1351 that imposed wage and price controls. During this period, England also passed sumptuary laws that regulated the sort of clothing various classes were allowed to wear.

Some landlords withdrew lands from cultivation, driving the serfs away. Sometimes the landlords then used the lands to raise sheep, which required less labor. Other landlords defied customary laws by raising rents while at the same time extracting new dues from their tenants. Some lords sold off some of their lands to merchants, peasants, or yeomen, some of whom acquired enough property to enter what came to be called the gentry. The decline of the manor estate meant that the lord was no longer a protector of those who lived on his estate but simply the landlord who collected rents and dues with no obligations to his tenants. The tenants, however, frequently had to perform service for him.

For their part, the merchants and traders reacted to the decline in trade by establishing monopolies and pursuing protectionist policies that curtailed economic growth. In some towns, the boatsmen's guild claimed the exclusive right to tow all boats and even to transfer cargoes to their own boats. In 1381, England proclaimed the first of its navigation acts by requiring goods in trade with England to be carried in English ships. Also in England, a company of merchants, known as the Staple, secured a royal grant to control the wool trade. The crown, persuaded by the Staple, forbade foreigners to export wool from England and prevented the importing of continental wool. The guilds, who had secured political power in many European towns, kept out all competing goods by raising import taxes to prohibitive levels. They also banned foreign workers from migrating to their towns and even prevented producers from opening shops outside the town boundaries or from selling any commodities that had not been produced within the town walls. At the same time, guild manufacturers put out work to women and children to do at home—at wages below the subsistence level—and withheld wages to cover all waste and damage to new materials. On top of all the exploitation and expropriation they suffered at the hands of the landlords and merchants, workers and peasants also had to pay additional tax levies to finance the frequent wars and to contribute to ransom money for their often kidnapped rulers.

Not unexpectedly, the lower class revolted. The peasants—like the landlords and merchants—did not try to create new wealth: They tried to preserve their share of what existed. "Matters cannot go well in England," declared John Bull, one of the leaders of the peasant revolt, "until all things are held in common."[11] In France, a wild outburst of peasant fury, known as the *Jacquerie*, took place in 1358. In Florence, poor workmen, known as *Ciompi*, staged a revolt against the guilds. All these revolts failed—and each revolt deepened the economic depression and darkened the economic outlook for all.

Europe did not come out of the economic depression until the second half of the fifteenth century, after the arrival of the printing press brought about a more rational reaction to the economic crisis by removing the obstacles to economic growth inherent in a scribal culture. It all began with the expansion of the geographical world of Europe.

PRINTING AND THE AGE OF DISCOVERY

In the thirty years between 1492 and 1522, Christopher Columbus discovered America, Vasco da Gama sailed around the tip of Africa to India, and one of Ferdinand Magellan's ships completed the first circumnavigation of the world. In this same period, John Cabot crossed the North Atlantic, Amerigo Vespucci visited South America, and Vasco Nunez de Balboa discovered the Pacific Ocean.

Earlier, other Europeans had completed distant explorations, but the memories of their exploits had faded, and their impact on economic development had been nil for they had taken place in a scribal culture. In contrast, the printing press broadcasted those explorations of Columbus, da Gama, Magellan, and Cabot everywhere and made them a permanent part of the public memory. Even more important, the charts and maps that recorded these explorations were reproduced in multiple copies and scattered everywhere. This allowed others to replicate their journeys to establish new trading routes and markets throughout the world.

Technological developments in the tools of navigation had made these late-fifteenth-century explorations possible. In addition to the faster and more navigable three-mast ship with its fixed rudder, navies of the fifteenth century had the compass to give them direction and the astrolobe to help them establish their position in latitude. They also had the hand-made portolan maps that sailors had used since at least 1300.[1,2]

Employing mathematicians, makers of nautical instruments, and cartographers from all over Europe, the Portuguese Prince Henry, known as Henry the Navigator, had modified and refined those portolan maps in the first half of the fifteenth century. Searching for a sea route around Africa to India, Henry had sent out one expedition after another. Each tested the portolan maps, uncovered errors, and eliminated them. Yet although this procedure of trial-and-error eliminatiion brought these maps to a remarkable level of accuracy, they were of limited use: They described only the coastline, so mariners could not use them to fix the position of a ship out of sight of land.

As for the rest of the world, European knowledge of its shape, size, and configuration was fuzzy, vague, and inaccurate. During the middle ages, cartographers had constructed "Christian" maps: maps that depicted the world as a flat circle divided by a cross, with Jerusalem as its center. The cross, or T, divided the circle into three parts representing Europe, Africa, and Asia. More accurate information about the east appeared in manuscript chronicles that recounted the experiences of merchants and clergymen who had traveled to those distant lands—like the brothers Polo, who traveled to China in 1256 and remained there for fourteen years. This travel literature led to the composition of a series of maps, the *Catalan Atlas*, made in 1375 by Abraham Cresques of Majorca. The *Catalan* maps of Europe and the Mediterranean are accurate, but the southern part of Africa is conjectural, and Asia is distorted. Moreover, the maps depict imaginary islands peopled with pygmies and griffins.[13] The small stream of medieval geographical literature based on travelers' tales and legends consisted largely of myths and fables about the orient—most of them tales of fantastic wealth and utopian marvels. The last of these fabulous tales, *Imago Mundi* by Pierre d'Ailly, appeared in 1410. Amid the myths and fables, there was a passage in which d'Ailly argued that the world was round— a passage that Christopher Columbus duly marked in the margin of his printed copy. Yet in the history of cartography, the year 1410 is less notable as the year *Imago Mundi* appeared than it is as the year Europe recovered a manuscript copy of the famed *Geography* of Ptolemy.

Written about 150 A.D., Ptolemy's work surpassed all medieval geographical knowledge. His map of the world presented a reasonably accurate picture of the Roman empire and adjacent countries, but beyond these limits he, too, had created myths. He invented a vast southern continent joined at one end to Africa and at the other to China, making the Indian Ocean a landlocked sea; he declared the whole southern hemisphere to be unnavigable because of the heat; and, most important, he contradicted his predecessor Erastosthenes' more accurate estimate of the circumference of the globe, substituting his own—which was an underestimate of about one sixth. Ptolemy's underestimation of the earth's circumference convinced Columbus that he could reach India by sailing west across the Atlantic.

The first printed edition of Ptolemy's *Geography* appeared in 1472, followed by many other editions—seven before the end of the century, and at least thirty-three in the sixteenth century, including one in rhyme.[14] Once printed in multiple copies and scattered everywhere, the *Geography* helped break down medieval conceptions of the world. The publication of the *Travels of Marco Polo* in 1485—making this work more widely available than it had been in manuscript copy—furthered this breakdown. This reconstruction of the picture of the world in the minds of Europeans brought about by the printing press launched the age of exploration— Columbus, da Gama, Cabot, Magellan, and others. These explorations, in turn, brought modifications and corrections of Ptolemy's picture of the world. Indeed, until 1570, all published world maps were presented as modifications of Ptolemy's map. In that year, Abraham Ortelius published his atlas, *Theatrum Orbis Terrarum*, which set off the ancient maps in a section separate from the contemporary representations of the known world.[15]

The cartographic work of Henry the Navigator belonged to the scribal age: The portolan maps were all hand drawn, and the chronicles and logs of journeys were kept in manuscript form, hidden from public view. The Portuguese, consistent with a scribal culture, practised what Boies Penrose has called a "conspiracy of silence," withholding all detailed information about their new discoveries.[16] Most scholars believe that they did this to establish an ocean empire and maintain their monopoly over trade with India.[17] When King Manuel developed plans for a pepper monopoly in 1504, he ordered that no one could send any sea charts abroad, under penalty of death.[18] Spain likewise discouraged the publication of maps and charts, including publication of the map of the Americas made by Juan de la Cosa, who accompanied Columbus on his second and third voyages. Nor did the Spanish permit publication of the diaries and journals Christopher Columbus kept during his voyages. They allowed publication of only a short letter describing the discoveries, which was, of course, a bestseller (printed in Barcelona, Rome, and Paris in 1493, in Basel in 1494, and in Strasbourg in 1497).[19]

But no nation could maintain a monopoly of geographical knowledge in the age of print. In 1504, an Italian, Amerigo Vespucci, who had joined a Spanish expedition in 1499, published a letter announcing that he had found "what may rightly be called a New World." (Columbus apparently went to his death in 1506 convinced he had reached the coast of Asia.) The letter was widely read and translated into several languages. Sixty editions appeared all over Europe—but none in Spain or Portugal.[20] In 1507, a German cartographer, Martin Waldseemuller, produced a world map depicting a rough rendition of the new world, which he labeled "America," explaining later, "I do not see why anyone should object to its being called after Americus, the discoverer, a man of natural wisdom."[21]

The printing press helped disclose Portugal's secrets, too. In 1502, for example, the Italian Duke of Ferrara had a Portuguese cartographer, Alberto Cantino produce a map accurately depicting the whole Africa coastline. This Cantino map was, in part, the model for the world map produced by Nicholas D'Caneiro, a Genoese. The Caneiro map, in turn, became the basis for the printed maps of Africa, Asia, and America that Waldseemuller published in Strassbourg in his 1513 atlas, *Ptolemy*—which was the first set of printed maps to bring the new geographical findings to the commercial market.[22]

Further disclosures of geographical explorations appeared in the *Paesi Novamente Retrovati*, compiled by the Italian Francan da Montalboddo and first printed in Venice in 1507. It contained accounts of the Portuguese discoveries as well as those of Columbus and Vespucci. The *Paesi* had six Italian editions, six French, and two German ones. Penrose called it the book par excellence by which the news of the great voyages and the great discoveries—east and west—was disseminated throughout Europe.[23]

Between 1520 and 1540, great growth took place in the printing industry, first in Italy and then, after 1540, throughout all of Europe. Publishers began producing catalogs which made it easier for scholars to determine what actually appeared in print at that time. Febvre and Martin found eighty-three geography books printed in France before 1550, whereas 282 more appeared by the end of the century and another 112 in the first ten years of the seventeenth century.[24] In the second half of the sixteenth century, as the centers of publishing shifted to the northern Protestant countries, Christopher Plantin set up the largest and most famous of publishing houses in Antwerp, the center for world commerce, a city of merchants, traders, and manufacturers. Antwerp boasted of having the best line engravers in Europe, so after 1550, most maps published there were put on copper plate instead of wood blocks.

Abraham Ortelius, a native of the Netherlands, worked as a map illustrator and salesman of maps, traveling all over Europe, buying the maps locally produced, and selling his own products. In these turbulent times of religious and dynastic wars, the merchants of Antwerp needed reliable, up-to-date maps so that they could plan the shortest, safest routes for their merchandise. But the large maps, which had to be rolled, proved unwieldy while the small ones were illegible. Ortelius, at the behest of a friend, published a collection of the most reliable maps in a uniform size—producing the first modern geographical atlas, the *Theatrum Orbis Terrarum* (*The Picture of the World*). Its immense popularity led Plantin to republish it. The *Theatrum* went through twenty-eight editions before Ortelius died in 1598, and other editions appeared after that, the last one in 1612. The first edition contained fifty-three maps, the last 166.[25]

After the Spanish sack of Antwerp in 1576, many of the publishers left; some moved to Amsterdam, which became the map publishing center of Europe. In Amsterdam printers put out atlases and single maps used by mariners all over Europe. Luke Wagenaer's *Spieghel der Zeervaerdt*, first printed in Amsterdam, contained detailed sea charts of the Atlantic and Baltic coasts from North Africa to Scandinavia. Translated into English as *The Mariner's Mirror* in 1588, the word *waggoner* came to mean any volume of sea charts or sailing directions. The Amsterdam printers secured copies of the Portuguese portolan maps and produced the first printed maps of Africa, Southern Asia, and the East Indies as well as Spanish maps of the new world.

These pioneer cartographers, map printers, and dealers brought the discoveries of Columbus, Vespucci, Balboa, and Magellan to the public, transforming the economic arrangements of Europe. The economic consequences of the age of discovery are well known and their importance for the economic history of Europe is frequently noted. Adam Smith declared that "the discovery of America, and that of a passage to the East Indies by the Cape of Good Hope are the greatest and most important events recorded in the history of mankind."[26]

The first and foremost consequence of the exploration was the importing of precious metals. The plunder of the Aztecs and Mayas of Mexico, as well as the setting up of mines in Peru and Africa, brought vast amounts of gold and silver into Europe, such that Europe's holdings more than tripled from 1500 to 1650. As these precious metals spread through all parts of Europe in exchange for goods, gold and silver began to lose their value; that is, prices began to go up.

THE EMERGENCE OF A MARKET ECONOMY

Advancing prices encouraged more people to go into business. In England, for example, the price of wool went up so high that many large landowners turned to sheep raising, calculating that there was more profit in that than in renting the land to peasant farmers. This shift in the agrarian economy usually encroached on the land over which the manoral population had common rights. So, where there had been teams of villagers who plowed their strips in the open fields, there came to be only a handful of shepherds to watch sheep in the enclosed pastures. During the course of the sixteenth century, between 5 and 10 percent of the English country-side underwent enclosure.

The enclosure movement threw the manoral system out of working order. The serfs became free—no one needed their services any longer. Some became cottage workers, receiving an income from the home manufacture of textiles, stockings, hats, and other woolen items. Some acquired land of their own and became yeoman farmers. But some sank to beggary, and others roamed the land, stealing, robbing, and terrorizing people. The increase in pauperism in England—where enclosures were the most extensive—forced Queen Elizabeth to put forth the first poor law in 1601.

And the lords? The lords became capitalists: For the first time, they looked at land as a commodity, as something to be bought and sold to make a profit. The enclosure movement created a land market. Furthermore, the purchase of land by bourgeois merchants increased the likelihood that land came to be viewed as an investment: They ran their estates like a business. This was especially the case in France, where the new owners enclosed land to raise cattle and crops for sale.

It is true that some enclosures had taken place as early as the thirteenth century in both England and France, but the enclosure movement began in the latter half of the fifteenth century, after the advent of the printing press. At that juncture, the lords of the manor began to employ a variety of legal and semilegal methods to deprive the peasants of their rights: the right of cultivation in the open fields, the right to use the commons for pasture of their cattle, the right to collect wood and fuel. From this time onward, the landlords resorted to methods of expropriation that would have been unthinkable in a scribal age. In the scribal age when few were literate, no one possessed a deed for land except for the lord of the manor himself. All rights of the serfs depended on traditional oral agreements with the lord. No written document existed to prove that a serf had a legal right to his land. Even the so-called copyholders—those who had the name of an ancestor inscribed on a manoral parchment roll as a legal leaseholder—could not prove that they had inherited legal title to the land.

In the latter half of the fifteenth century, when, with the coming of the printing press, literacy had become more common, written or printed documents alone could establish legal ownership.[27] And when they could not expropriate the peasants from the land because of the absence of legal titles, the landlords undertook extensive searches of their own original deeds and documents to uncover and revive ancient rights that exacted long-forgotten dues and obligations the peasants owed them. The landlords used these legal documents to harass the peasants and harry them from their lands. These "freed" peasants created the beginnings of a labor market.

In addition to a land market and an incipient labor market, the sixteenth century saw a vastly expanded commodity market. For Europe now imported not only precious metals from the new world, but also a host of raw materials that had to be processed: Timber, cotton, tobacco, minerals, furs, chocolate, sugar, coffee, and rice came into the European ports, creating new industries and expanding old ones.

Perhaps the most significant economic development of all took place in trade and commerce—so remarkable that economic historians have called it a revolution, the commercial revolution. Trade and commerce offered opportunities for the highest profits, and the most profitable ventures were the large ones. But to secure the capital for undertakings of any magnitude, budding entrepreneurs had to sell shares of stock to interested investors. This kind of large-scale enterprise required methods and procedures for the rational accounting of all economic transactions. These methods of rational accounting are the basis for what Max Weber has called the "spirit of capitalism." This spirit could not have come into being without the help of the printing press.

PRINTING AND ECONOMIC RATIONALITY

During the later middle ages, Italy had become the center of long-distance trade and, understandably, the Italians had developed the most advanced techniques of commerce: bills of exchange, maritime insurance, and bookkeeping. Through these commercial techniques, the Italian merchant of the middle ages had become orderly to the point of meticulousness, a shrewd observer and a clear thinker.

Italian merchants had formed partnerships (*commenda*) and companies (*compagnie*) during the middle ages—originally just among family members, or with outsiders for the duration of a single venture. These early economic organizations increased the opportunities for wealth, but such arrangements were unsuitable for the large enterprise ventures made possible by the opening of new overseas markets in the sixteenth century. As the center of trade shifted to northern Europe, a network of trading companies appeared in England, Holland, and France: the Muscovy Company was founded in 1553, followed by the Spanish Company in 1577, the Eastland Company in 1579, the Levant Company in 1581, and many others, including the greatest of all, the East India Company in 1600. As joint stock companies, they launched the beginning of a market for shares of stock—something inconceivable without the printing press. Printed private newsletters listing stock prices appeared first; later, in 1585, the Amsterdam Commodities Exchange, the central market, began publishing its own bulletin of prices, which circulated throughout Europe.[28]

These large enterprises not only required vast amounts of capital, but they also needed technical procedures for management, control, and accounting. The book-keeping practices of the early partnerships and companies founded by the Italians had been crude, though adequate for the purpose. But now, with large companies engaged in continuous ventures financed by numerous stockholders, sophisticated methods of bookkeeping became necessary.

The biggest obstacle to more complex methods of bookkeeping were the Roman numerals merchants used to keep accounts. It is not possible to compute with Roman numerals, so merchants or their associates made all their calculations on the abacus, or on the counting board, and then copied the results into their books in Roman numerals. Thus, the merchants' accounts were no more than documentary records of the results of these computations.

With Arabic numbers, however, one can combine the writing of numbers and the making of calculations in a single procedure. Indian or Arabic numerals had appeared in some monastic manuscripts as early as 1000.[29] But they had fallen from use, as frequently happened with new knowledge during the scribal age. It is, however, easy to understand why people did not abandon Roman numerals: they were clear, easily read, and could not be tampered with (an important consideration for commercial recordkeeping); also, the absence of paper made calculation on counting boards more practical. Paper had appeared in Europe early in the eleventh century but was used sparingly until the fourteenth century.[30] However, people could calculate as efficiently and correctly on counting boards as they could with written Arabic numbers—except for multiplication and division. One monastic author lamented that division was so extraordinarily difficult that "its hardness surpasses that of iron."[31] But with the place value notion of the Arabic numeral system, even a child can perform the operations of multiplication and division.

Arabic numerals reappeared in a manuscript, *Liber Abaci*, written by Leonardo of Pisa in 1202. Leonardo explained and demonstrated all the mathematical operations one could perform with Arabic numerals and showed their practical application. Leonardo's work made exact calculation possible. Werner Sombart declared that, if pressed, he would say that capitalism began with *Liber Abaci*. But as Elizabeth Eisenstein points out, a hand-copied manuscript like the *Liber Abaci* was "not much easier to obtain than Ptolemy's *Almagest* during the thirteenth and fourteenth centuries."[32] Nevertheless, toward the end of the thirteenth century, some Italian merchants began using Arabic numerals. This gave those merchants such a decided advantage over others that people suspected fraud and deception, as can be seen by the ordinance issued by the City of Florence in 1229 prohibiting the use of Arabic numerals in account books.[33]

Calculation with Arabic numerals paved the way for the invention of double-entry bookkeeping sometime between 1250 amd 1350.[34] Double-entry bookkeeping for the first time separated business finances from the personal or household finances of merchants, actualizing the firm as an autonomous unit. This was vital to the operation of large joint-stock companies, where profits and losses had to be divided among shareholders. Double-entry bookkeeping provided a check on the accuracy of the entries for each transaction: One member of each pair of entries recorded a change in assets (or income) and the other an equal change in liabilities (or expenses). Entries of the two types could be separately totaled, and if the totals did not match, an error must have occurred.

Even more important, double-entry bookkeeping created the concept of capitalism. Now all goods and services were viewed as capital—converted to quantities and entered in the accounts as debits and credits. When they became capital, goods and services came to be valued solely in terms of their profitability. This is the "spirit of capitalism" talked about by Weber and Sombart. Sombart wrote that "one cannot say whether capitalism created double-entry bookkeeping as a tool in its expansion, or whether, perhaps conversely, double-entry bookkeeping created capitalism."[35]

Sombart somewhat confuses the notion of the spirit of capitalism by equating it with acquisition. In criticism of this, Weber wrote, "this impulse [acquisition] exists and has existed among waiters, physicians, coachmen, artists, prostitutes, dishonest officials, soldiers, nobles, crusaders, gamblers, and beggars. One may say that it [acquisition] has become to all sorts and conditions of men at all times and in all countries of the earth, wherever the objective possibility of it is or has been given."[36] But Weber himself further confused this notion of the spirit of capitalism by adding to it the doctrine of the calling.[37] Capitalism, or the spirit of capitalism, as I understand it, is simply economic rationality; the construing of goods and services solely in terms of their profitability—a construction that is possible only when goods and services can be measured mathematically.

Both Sombart and Weber agree that profitability is the essence of capitalism, and both further agree that one can readily ascertain profitability only by means of mathematical tools like double-entry bookkeeping and the rapid mathematical operations possible with Arabic numerals. Double-entry bookkeeping is more comprehensive and orderly than earlier forms of bookkeeping. Even more important, double-entry bookkeeping permits a check in the technically most perfect manner on the profitability of each individual step or measure.[38] Profitability thus becomes a concept that is "applicable to every discrete act which can be individually evaluated in terms of business accounting techniques with respect to profit and loss, such as the employment of a particular worker, the purchase of a new machine, the determination of rest periods in the working day, etc."[39] Double-entry bookkeeping encodes every economic transaction in a form such that all can critically appraise the profitability of each transaction. It reveals a firm's financial history and its fnancial capacity.

This critical approach made businessmen more rational about their actions. This is not to say that rationality did not exist before, but *economic* rationality did not exist. Before these mathematical tools for ascertaining profitability came into use, those who raised sheep, for example, cared only about the "visible grandeur" and size of their herds, not about profitability. To ascertain profitability requires mathematical calculations with several variables, calulations not possible with Roman numerals.[40] Merchants and traders, too, prior to the appearance of such mathematical tools could simply not practise economic rationality: They measured their success by their personal possessions and their hordes of gold bullion; they did not measure it in terms of profitability.

These mathematical tools had existed since the early thirteenth century, and many Italian merchants had begun using them by the second half of the fourteenth century, becoming thereby the most widely admired and feared entrepreneurs throughout Europe. Italy became the "school for merchants," as businessmen from all over Europe sent their sons to Italian cities to learn about bookkeeping and computation. Sombart claims that six "arithmetic" schools were in operation in Florence in the fourteenth century teaching the elements of commercial arithmetic to some 1,200 boys.[41]

But before the advent of printing, scientific bookkeeping spread slowly—most future merchants learned it in Italy through apprenticeship or from schoolmasters. However, once this knowledge could be encoded in print and scattered everywhere, the Italian hegemony on the capitalist spirit ended.[42] The first printed arithmetic text appeared in Italian in 1478, the *Arte de la Mercadantia* (*The Mercantile Art*): "Here begins a very good and useful book of instruction for everyone who wishes to learn the mercantile art, which is popularly known as the abacus."[43] The first printed German arithmetic text—also directed at the keeping of accounts—appeared in 1483. In 1494, Luca Pacioli published his *Summa de Arithmetica, Geometria, et Proportionate*, explaining the use of arithmetic and algebra in trade reckoning, money exchange, and bookkeeping.[44] Pacioli's book was the first theoretic treatise on double-entry booking.[45]

In addition to books explaining the secrets of commercial arithmetic and the mysteries of double-entry bookkeeping, printers published almanacs containing valuable information for businessmen: calendars, uniform tables for computing the cost of goods and labor, conversion charts (for currency, weights, measures), and mileage lists of distances between towns.

Printers also put out handbooks and manuals for merchants. One of the earliest appeared in German, translated into English in 1576 as *The Past of the World. Wherein is contayned the Antiquities and Originall of the Most Famouus Cities in Europe. With their Trade and Trafficke. With their Ways and Distance of Myles, From Country to Country. With the True and Perfect Knowledge of their Coynes, the Places of their Mynts: With All their Martes and Fayres: And the Raignes of All the Kings of England. A Book Right Necessary and Profitable for All Sorts of Persons, The like Before this Tyme Not Imprinted.*

Other practical guides for merchants traveling in foreign countries were Thomas Palmer's *Essay of the means how to make our traviles into Forraine countries the more profitable and honourable* (1606); James Wadsworth's translation from the Italian, *The European Mercury. Describing the highways and stages from place to place, through the most remarkable parts of Christendome. With a catalogue of the Principall Fairs, Marts, and Markets for all Gentlemen who Delight in seeing Forraign Countries: And Instructing Merchants where to meet with their conveniences for trade* (1641); and James Howell's *Instruction for Foreeine Travell* (1642). Some of the handbooks stressed living the kind of life that leads to worldly prosperity—like William Scott's *An Essay on Drapery: On the Complete Citizen.*

Trading Justly, Pleasingly, Profitably (1635), or William Loe's *The Merchants Manuell, Being a Step to Steadfastness* 1628). The most imposing and widely read handbook came from Lewes Roberts, who published the *Merchants Mappe of Commerce* in 1638, which also has one of the longest book titles on record: *The Merchants Mappe of Commerce: Wherein, The Universal Manner and Matter of Trade is Compendiously Handled. The Standard and Current Coines of Sundry Princes, Observed. The Reall and Imaginary Coines of Accounts and Exchanges, Expressed. The Naturall and Artificial Commodities of All Countries for Transportation Declared. The Weights and Measures of All Eminent Cities and Townes of Traffique, Collected and Reduced One into Another: And all to the Meridian of Commerce Practices in the Famous Citie of London. By Lewes Roberts, Merchants. Necessary for All Such as shall be Employed in Publique Affairs of Princes in Foreigne Parts: For All Gentlement and Others that Travelled Abroad for Delight or Pleasure, And for all Merchants or their Factors that Exercise the Art of Merchandizing in any Part of the Habitable World.*[46]

Printed directories and maps like the *Guide de Chemins de France* (1533), appeared to quicken the wheels of commerce. By helping those involved in business to practice economic rationality, this avalanche of printed tools spread the spirit of capitalism throughout all of Europe.

But the rational calculation of profitability—the spirit of capitalism—could not proceed far without the existence of a free labor market.[47] None had existed during the middle ages. It is true that the enclosure movement had gone some way toward creating a labor market when the first freed serfs took up cottage or domestic work in return for wages. But the greatest obstacle to a free labor market, and thus to the development of capitalism, was the guild system established in every town of Europe. Printing helped destroy the guilds.

PRINTING AND THE BREAKUP OF THE GUILDS

Artisan guilds existed as early as the eleventh century, when craftsmen formed fraternities along lines determined by the goods produced for sale: Bakers, tailors, cobblers, cabinetmakers, blacksmiths, and boatmen, each had their own guild. Some guilds were highly specialized—the saddlers, bridlers, and trunk-makers, for example, functioned as separate guilds in some large towns; in others, they were all members of the leather workers guild. In some towns, the cloth workers guild included the shearmen, the fullers, the weavers, the drapers, the hatters, and the upholsterers. However they were organized, each guild had a town monopoly for the production and retail sale of its special products.

In return for granting a monopoly to a guild, the town made specific demands to see to it that the guild provided adequate supplies at reasonable prices: There were to be no middlemen, no forestalling (buying goods before they reached the towns), and no engossing (hoarding); all traders in food were subject to inspection; night work was outlawed because it produced inferior products; artisans had to work in shops facing the street; and craftsmen could not practice more than one trade.[48]

Once a guild obtained a monopoly, there could be no free labor market in that occupation in that town. This effectively prevented economic growth. However, each guild pursued its own self-interest by imposing additional restrictions on its members—restrictions that prevented improvement in the existing practices, procedures, policies, and products. Each guild limited its membership and created elaborate training programs—apprenticeships that lasted, on the average, seven years. After serving his apprenticeship, the worker became a day laborer or journeyman (no longer living with the master) and, eventually, he might become a master and member of the guild. To ensure equality among members, the guild required all to have the same amount of equipment and to use the same techniques—members were forbidden to introduce any new techniques. All guild members had to work the same number of hours. The guilds prohibited all advertising and imposed price restrictions on all products.

By the sixteenth century, the guild restrictions had become more oppressive: Entrance to many guilds had become limited to relatives, entrance fees had escalated to prohibitive levels, and the period of apprenticeship extended to unbearably long periods. Paradoxically, the guilds themselves had come largely under the control of the merchant traders. Throughout the middle ages, the guilds had fought off control by the merchants, who wanted both to supply the artisans and craftsmen with the raw materials they needed and to sell the finished manufactured products themselves. By the sixteenth century, the merchants had available a large labor force—made up of freed serfs, disgruntled journeymen, and ex-monks—that they employed to work in their own houses and cottages, usually outside of town. In the towns, too, merchants now found guild members ready to work for them. In some cases, guild members themselves had become merchants, no longer practicing their trade but employing numbers of workers on a wage basis. And yet this new hegemony of the merchant class did not, itself alone, create a free labor market—it required the help of the printing press.

The guilds were a product of the scribal age founded on subjective knowledge, or know-how, passed on from master to apprentice. In formal ceremonies and rituals, each guild member pledged to protect the secrets of his trade. The restrictions the guilds imposed on their members—the long training period, the high standards for becoming a master, the quality control of practices and products—were all designed to maintain these secrets. This was possible in a scribal age, but not in an age of print. The arrival of the printing press made it possible to obtain large profits by revealing the secrets of the trade. Perhaps more important, writing and publishing a book on one's trade could spread one's name everywhere: Fame as well as fortune became possible. Moreover, such self-seeking activities appeared socially useful insofar as they contributed to the public good by scattering everywhere those secrets that would help the nation increase the production of goods for sale.

For all these reasons, as Elizabeth Eisenstein reports, the coming of the printing press brought forth "an avalanche of technical treatises and teach-yourself books," which revealed the secrets of all the arts, all the trades, and all the crafts.[49]

Technical works written in the vernacular appeared: Ambrose Pare (1510-1590) published eight different works on surgery, beginning with *La Methode de Traichter les Playes* in 1545; Bernard Palissy's *Discourse Admirables* (1580) covered pottery making as well as procedures for extracting metals and minerals from the earth; Lazarus Ercher wrote a book on assaying, mining, and smelting, *Beschreibung aller furnsten Mineralischen Ertzt und Beichwercksarten* (1574), with lavish illustrations; Albrecht Dürer wrote and printed a book on surveying, *Un weysungde Messung mit dem Zirckel und Richtscheyt* (1525) and a book on fortifications, *Etliche Underricht zu Befestigung* (1527); the Italian Vannocio Biringuccio published a comprehensive text on military engineering, *De la Pirotechnia*, in 1540 which went through four more editions in Italian, one in French, and one in English; Agostino Ramelli wrote a book on the construction of buildings and machines, *La Diverse et Artificiose Machine* (1588); in 1607, another engineer, Vittorio Zonca, explained the process of silk making in *Nuovo Teatro di Machine et Edifici*.[50]

In addition to the vernacular publications composed by practicing craftsmen, printers turned to Latin scholars to translate and make available ancient treatises in arts and crafts. The prolific Thomas Hill, for example published books on gardening, bee culture, Hippocratic medicine, and animal husbandry—all culled from the works of Aristotle, Galen, Pliny, and others for those "that lacke the Lattine Tungue."[51]

These new handbooks, manuals, and teach-yourself texts not only revealed the trade secrets long protected by guilds but, even more important, they laid bare the entire process of production in the various trades, crafts, and occupations. Once encoded in print, people could critically analyze these processes and procedures and then reconstruct and reorganize them in more rational ways. Instead of one master performing by himself all the steps of manufacturing, the labor could be divided into different stages, with each worker specializing in one aspect of production. Or again, instead of the various stages of production being carried on at different places and locales, the production processes could be centralized in one location—assembling workers in one workshop meant, too, that they could be better controlled and disciplined. These rational calculations about the methods of production gave rise to the creation of the factory.

The first factories appeared as early as the end of the fifteenth century, as institutions to help the poor by providing work for them. The capitalist owner controlled the process of production and therefore both the quality and quantity of the output. The owner owned the means of production, supplied the raw materials, and owned the final product. Initially, because the guilds still exercised their monopolies, these factories manufactured only new products that did not compete with them: cotton, porcelain, brocade, and substitute goods.[52]

The rational calculations that brought capitalist manufacturers to the notions of specialization and labor discipline led, in time, to the mechanization of the means of production. Such rational calculation could take place only because, as a result of printing, manufacturers had a new critical understanding of the entire production processes. And, of course, the rational reconstruction of production they brought about could take place only because of the existence of a free labor market, itself in large part created by the printing press.

So, with printing, things got better; productivity, and therefore, the wealth of nations increased tremendously. As Adam Smith pointed out in 1776, whereas before one worker could make no more than twenty pins a day, in the capitalist era, when the division of labor and the use of specially designed machinery prevailed, ten factory workers could make "upwards of forty thousand, eight hundred pins a day."[53]

The elimination of the guilds diffused authority to the initiators and the innovators. This heightened experimentation and risk taking and overcame the resistance to change fostered by the guilds. New ideas introduced new products. New methods of production led to lower costs of goods. The lifestyles of the poor for the first time in history, began to improve.

PRINTING AND USURY

Printing established the spirit of capitalism throughout Europe. Increasingly, merchants improved the profitability of their enterprises by adopting the mathematical tools that made rational accounting possible; and increasingly, manufacturers employed workers from the free labor market whom they could direct and control in rational ways that improved profits for the capitalist owner. Yet one long-standing and persistent obstacle to the development of capitalism remained: the attitude of the Church. Earlier, I mentioned the Church's general disapproval of trade and commerce. The most crucial matter, however, was the specific proscription against usury. Usury meant that any accrual, great or small, above the principal of the loan. This total ban on usury prevented the emergence of a financial market.

During the late middle ages, loans were made to businessmen and interest was charged, but bookkeepers concealed the interest charges by various strategems. The word *interest* never appeared in financial records—it was replaced by several euphemisms: *prode* (yield), *costo* (cost), *guadagno* (gain), *dono* (gift), and *merito* (reward). The secrecy and skullduggery increased after 1310, when Pope Clement V decreed that lenders could be convicted of usury on the strength of their account books.[54] Even as late as 1594, when the author of a textbook on arithmetic submitted it to a deacon of the Cathedral at Antwerp for his imprimatur, he was told that "the rules and procedures for computation and for finding the answer to problems are admittedly useful for merchants and for their sake permission is granted to them to be printed; but they [the merchants] must see to it that they avoid usury and all other illicit transactions and exchanges."[55] Ultimately, of course, capitalism struggled free from the restraints of the Church. And, once again, the printing press played a significant role.

During the middle ages, people did not think of themselves so much as individuals but as members of a caste or class: One was a serf or a noble or a cleric. Each class had a specific function in the collective order: The serfs worked, the clergy prayed, the nobility fought. No group competed with another for economic rewards. Each received—rightly so—the means suited to its station. Within each class there existed an accepted equality, whereas the hierarchical feudal order preserved great inequalities between the classes. Yet there was a subjective loyalty of one class to the other that held the whole feudal order together. "The health of the whole commonwealth will be assured and vigorous," John of Salisbury (1115-1180) wrote, "if the higher minds consider the lower and the lower answer in like manner the higher, so that each in turn is a member of every other."[56]

When commercial trading emerged as an occupation, those who traded had difficulty accommodating to the existing social order made up of those who worked, those who prayed, and those who fought. Those who traded, the businessmen, posed a threat. For the new men were individuals, not members of any existing class. They seemed to have no loyalty to the collective order; nor were they anxious to cooperate with others for the common good. Instead, they sought only their own self-interest in a competitive struggle with one another.

Yet their activities did increase the wealth of the community. Their presence made things better for everyone. The schoolmen, therefore, struggled to accommodate intellectually the new group to the existing order. Starting with the assumption that economic interests are subordinate to the real business of life, which is salvation, the schoolmen concluded that the Christian rules of morality must bind all economic actions. As Thomas Aquinas put it, "It is lawful to desire temporal blessings, not putting them in the first place, as though setting up our rest in them, but regarding them as aids to blessedness inasmuch as they support our corporal life and serve as instruments for acts of virtue."[57] In those tortured treatises they laboriously produced, the schoolmen issued warnings, cautions, restrictions, and prohibitions: "Labor is necessary and honorable, but trade, though necessary, is perilous to the soul. A man should carry on trade for the public benefit; his profits should be no more than the wages of his labor. To seek more is avarice and avarice is a sin. Even more dangerous to the soul is finance, which, if not immoral, is at least sordid and at worst disreputable."[58] The schoolmen viewed finance as the most dangerous because finance was based on usury and usury was a dangerous sin—rejected by Christian theologians from Ambrose to Luther and prohibited by numerous Church Councils. The Councils of Lyons (1274) and Vienne (1212) issued the most severe injunctions: No one could rent a house to a usurer under pain of excommunication; usurers could not go to confession, receive absolution, or have a Christian burial; and any person who declared usury not a sin was to be punished as a heretic, with Inquisitors to proceed against him accordingly.[59]

Secular legislation on usury mirrored the ecclesiastical doctrines down at least to the middle of the sixteenth century. In Florence, the financial capital of medieval Europe, the secular authorities fined bankers for usury in the middle of the fourteenth century and went so far as to prohibit credit transactions in 1400, importing Jews to conduct a business forbidden to Christians.[60] But although public policy and Church doctrine agreed in condemning usury, various practices did surface that circumvented the prohibitions—practices that theologians then justified by complicated casuistic arguments: The increments given on public loans were not instances of usury, the schoolmen argued; nor were redeemable rent contracts or costs, gifts, gratuities, etc., usury. In the fifteenth century, the Franciscans actually set up their own Christian banks in Italy—the mounts of piety (*monti di pietà*)—after expelling the Jewish bankers out of the land. These banks soon spread to France, Germany, and the Low Countries. In 1515, Pope Leo X decreed that the interest these banks charged on loans was not usury.

These exceptions, however, remained just that: exceptions. Usury was never excused or accepted. What happened was that some transactions—like the interest charged by the mounts of piety—were simply redefined and thereby excluded from the ban on usury. Yet these casuistical concessions did tax the credulity of many Christians. The advent of printing brought this to a head. Christians based their opposition to usury on the Deuteronomic Commandments: "Thou shalt not lend upon usury to thy brother; usury of money, usury of victuals, usury of anything that is lent upon usury." (23:19). "Unto a stranger thou mayest lend upon usury; but unto thy brother thou shalt not lend upon usury, that the Lord thy God may bless thee in all that thou settest thine hand to in the land whither thou goest to possess it" (23:20).

As Benjamin Nelson meticulously demonstrates, this Deuteronomic Commandment has had a checkered fortune.[61] St. Jerome (349-420), who provided the first Christian exegesis, contended that the prohibition of usury among brothers had been universalized by the New Testament, so that usury now was prohibited to all people. His contemporary, St. Ambrose (340-397), however, claimed that one could exact usury from one's enemies, ("From him exact usury whom it would not be a crime to kill.") A later commentator, Rabanus Maurus (784-856), spiritualized the commandment, explaining that it meant that it was permissable to demand repentance, faith, and good works from the criminals and infidels upon whom we spend money in preaching the word.

At the time of the Crusades, Christians discovered that Ambrose's interpretation authorized them to demand interest from Moslems—but it also, at the same time, permitted Jews to exact usury from their Christian debtors. This double standard, some argued, made God's commandment paradoxical, contradictory, and vicious. Understandably we find theologians like Peter Lombard (1100-1160), Peter Comestor (d. 1176), and Peter Cantor (d. 1197) declaring that usury was a sin no matter who engaged in it. God, they explained, permitted the Jews to practice it only at that time and for special reasons. In the following century, other theologians—Alexander of Arles (d. 1249), Albertus Magnus (1193-1280), and Thomas Aquinas (1225-1274)—all came to the same conclusion, but each with a different explanation. However, the canon lawyers, beginning with Gratian (d.1179) and followed by the Decretists, declared that Christians could exact usury from aliens. Some popes, like Alexander III, agreed. The Fourth Lateran Council (1215) confused matters even more by introducing the term *heavy usury*—threatening Christians with ecclesiastical censure if they persisted in associating with Jews who failed to make satisfaction for "heavy usury."

In the second half of the fifteenth century, the 'usurious practices' of the *monti di pietà* came under heavy attack from many theologians. These attacks by Alexander de Nevo (d. 1456), Celsus of Verona, and Annius of Viterbo (d. 1502) appeared in print, as did the counterarguments of Bernardino da Basto (d. 1503) in defense of the *monti di pietà*. For the first time, the public at large could read the inconsistent and contradictory interpretations of the Deuteronomic Commandments as the antagonists in the dispute revived and cited the authorities from the past.

At this point, the debate became more intense and more confused as the Protestant reformers began to speak out on the matter of usury. Luther, Melancthon, Zwingli, Bucer, and Calvin all published tracts giving their different and contradictory views. The most inconsistent arguments came from Luther. Originally, he condemned all usury, which, he explained, stemmed from the usurious extortions of the Roman Church. The peasant revolt of 1525 modified his views, causing him to turn his back on the radical followers who had used his *Longer Sermon on Usury* (1520) to call—in print—for utopian civil reforms and to encourage people to stop paying charges owed to their creditors. Following this Luther joined his friend, Melancthon, in declaring that the Bible was not intended to take the place of civil law or to supplant existing authorities: Usury was a civil matter to be decided by secular authorities. Later, in 1539, Luther again modified his position, denouncing those who practiced usury—except for the aged, widows, orphans, and other unfortunates who derived their income from investments. He stated that those who took a "little usury" (5 or 6 percent) should not be treated so harshly as "gross usurers." What did remain constant in his writing was the warning that clergy should not usurp the functions of jurists, princes, and the individual conscience.

Calvin went even further than the German reformers. In 1545, he pointed out that "if we wholly condemn usury, we impose tighter fetters on the conscience than God himself," who condemned it only between brothers. The scriptures, he explained, forbid only "biting usury"—usury taken from the defenseless poor.[62]

Once the printing press had set all these interpretations in typographical fixity, reproduced them in multiple copies, and scattered them everywhere, people could not take them seriously: There were too many contradictions, paradoxes, inconsistencies, qualifications, and exceptions in both the contemporary and traditional explanations of what the Deuteronomic Commandments meant. If one consulted the explanations available in print, one could find authorization for any practice, or any exception, for any prohibition, or any permission. The common-sense reaction to religious pronouncements on economic activity became one of indifference—especially if one were engaged in business, commerce, industry, or finance. Francis Bacon, for example, in his essay published in 1626 entitled *Of Usury*, discussed the matter without introducing any ethical or religious considerations—illustrating, Heckscher notes, "his keen eye for realities." Bacon did list seven disadvantages of usury, but all of these were economic disadvantages. In the seventeenth century, all discussions of usury focused on how high the rate of interest ought to be and whether its height should be limited by a legal maximum.[63] The printing press had clearly helped free economic activity from restrictions imposed by the Church.

In destroying the authority of the Bible over economic activity, the printing press secularized the economic realm and released the spirit of capitalism—the rational calculation of profitability. Henceforth, people could transact their affairs in a solely rational fashion, calculating every course of action solely on the basis of its profitability with no consideration for noneconomic conditions or restrictions. In place of the authority of the Bible, a new authority appeared: the market. But many— including businessmen—feared the free competitive market and fought to prevent it from becoming the economic authority. So now with the help of the printing press those who had the power to do so sought protection. Historians call this the age of mercantilism, a period when capitalists struggled to protect their investments, their jobs, and their products. Only later did the age of modern capitalism fully emerge.

MERCANTILISM AND PRINTING

Earlier, we saw that the age of discovery opened up the possibility of large commercial ventures, which became possible only when entrepreneurs gathered huge amounts of capital by selling shares in joint stock companies. These large companies had to present reports to their stockholders detailing their exploits and accounting for all gains and losses. The compilation and analysis of these printed reports made it clear that the way to wealth was simple and commonsensical: One had to sell more than one bought. Merchants and businessmen extended this economic insight to the nation itself. As early as 1576, the Third Estate of France issued a mercantilist diagnosis and a mercantilist prescription for the current economic ills:

> As the strength of this kingdom . . . consists in the multitude of inhabitants and in the money which they can secure from neighboring countries . . . and as there is no better means of funding and maintaining a plentiful population of good and excellent workmen, and by this means to draw money from abroad than by employing them to work up stuffs and merchandise in the kingdom. . . . May it please your majesty to order that henceforth no goods may be exported from this Kingdom that have not been manufactured into a finished product there; and contrariwise, that it shall not be permitted . . . to bring in . . . any manufactured goods under penalty of confiscation.[64]

By the end of the sixteenth century, the arguments for mercantilism took on a new dimension. By this time, poverty was endemic throughout Europe, especially in England, where in 1601, Elizabeth put forward a plan for the public relief of the poor. The merchants saw an alternative way to solve the problem of poverty and, at the same time, to enhance the wealth, power, and glory of the nation: By exporting more manufactured goods than it imported and taking the difference in gold, the nation could provide jobs for the poor and bring wealth to everyone.

In books, pamphlets, tracts, and letters, the merchants of England proclaimed the economic wisdom of mercantilism, suggesting various policies the government might take up to encourage more exports: Monopolies and subsidies, for example, would do this, as well as commercial treaties with foreign states and the setting up of plantations and colonies in distant countries. They also urged the government, at the same time, to discourage imports by imposing high tariffs or by prohibiting the import of foreign manufactures that could be produced at home.

One of the leading mercantilists, Thomas Munn, a director of the East India Company, initially wrote a pamphlet in 1621, called *A Discourse on Trade From England Into the East Indies.* He followed this with his famous and influential *England's Treasure by Forraign Trade, Or the Balance of Our Trade Is the Rule of Our Treasures* (1664): "we must ever observe this rule: to sell more to strangers yearly than we consume of theirs in value."[65]

The governor of the East India Company, Josiah Child, also wrote a book promoting mercantilism, *A New Discourse on Trade* (1688), which went into five editions before the end of the century. He argued that the best way to measure the balance of trade was by the "number of hands' employed. It was, he wrote, "man's duty to God and Nature to provide for and employ the poor, whose condition is sad and wretched, diseased, impotent, useless."[66]

Other merchants—John Cary, William Goffe, and Peter Chamberlin—also wrote books urging the government to promote exports and reduce imports. This mercantilist theory spread to various European countries through the medium of print. When Genovesi began his school of economics at Naples in the 1750s, he translated John Cary's *Essay on The State of England in Relation to Its Trade* as a text for his pupils. In his own work, Genovesi, like Cary, distinguished useful commerce—the exportation of manufactures—from harmful commerce—the importation of manufactures. J. J. Becker and F. W. Von Schroder, two of the founders of German mercantilism, (where it was called *Kammeralism*), had resided in England during the second half of the seventeenth century. A modern economic historian, Charles Wilson, sees a carryover in their work of the ideas of Cary and Child. In Eastern Europe, the economic policies of Peter the Great and Catherine the Great owed their theoretical foundations to the writings of British mercantilists.[67] In France, V. D. Gournay published, in 1754, a French edition of the work of Child. Here, of course, British theories merely gave support to the mercantile practices that had been common in France since the ministry of Colbert, who had served as economic advisor to Louis XIV between 1661 and 1683.

Not only did the printing press scatter the policies and doctrines of mercantilism everywhere, but no government could have carried them out without the printing press. To provide loans, tax exemptions, subsidies, and monopoly privileges and to build roads, bridges, and canals the governments of Europe had to use the printing press to encode the many rules, regulations, ordinances, agreements, and announcements that promoted the protectionist policies of mercantilism. At this point, the printing press became an agent of the government to restrain and control. Colbert, for example, issued printed orders forbidding the emigration of skilled French workers; he encouraged boys to marry before they were twenty; and he exempted families of ten or more from paying taxes—as long as none became a priest or a monk because they were, he thought, unproductive occupations. During his tenure in office, he abolished seventeen holidays because, he said, they cut down the productivity of the nation.[68]

In addition to policies to stimulate productivity, the governments of Europe adopted policies to improve the quality of production—which also made demands on the printing press. Throughout Europe, each nation tried to unify the systems of weights and measures that towns had created during the middle ages. To do this, the governments issued edicts and printed charts and tables. Governments also fixed standards of quality. In England, for example, the government printed standards for regulating the manufacture of wool: standards of length, breadth, and weight. The same regulations forbade processes thought to injure quality and required every piece of goods to bear the mark of the maker and to be inspected and sealed by a public official before it was sold. In France, Colbert once issued an edict concerning the dyeing of cloth that contained 371 articles.[69]

Beyond actions intended to stimulate production and ensure quality control, the governments of Europe also acted to protect their own industries and trades by imposing high tariffs on imports that competed with home-made goods. In some cases, the government simply prohibited importation, as when England, in 1701, printed an order forbidding the wearing of imported calico cloth. Governments also formulated trade agreements or treaties that guaranteed the exchange of specific items between the nations—the Methuen Treaty of 1702 provided for the exclusive exchange of English woolens for Portuguese wines.

The colonial policies that all European nations shared provided yet another area of economic protectionism. Each nation reserved its colonial markets for its own industrial goods, discouraging all colonial industry but insisting that the colonies ship raw materials to the mother nation, in her ships. The English Woolens Act forbade transportation of wool, yarn, or woolen textiles from one colony to another. The Hat Act of 1731 forbade the export of hats (beaver hats) and prohibited a hat maker fom having more than two apprentices. These and many other rules, regulations, edicts, and proclamations had to be communicated across the sea and scattered everywhere among the colonies—a task not possible without the help of the printing presses in England and the new world.

Mercantilism did not make things better. It suffocated the entrepreneurial impulse. The regulations and controls that governments imposed and the monopolistic privileges they granted, restricted the progress of manufacturing processes and limited the improvement of manufactured goods. One can gather some idea of how mercantilist regulations discouraged innovation from a clause in the famous French statute of 1666 for cloth weaving in Amiens. It stipulated (Article 101) that "if a cloth weaver intends to process a piece of cloth according to his own invention, he must not set it on the looms but should obtain permission from the judges of the town to employ the number and length of the threads that he desires, after the question has been considered by four of the oldest merchants and four of the oldest weavers of the guild."[70] The tariffs, prohibitions, and privileged treaties the governments enacted curtailed the development of trade and slowed the growth of wealth among the European nations.

By the eighteenth century, a growing number of critics of mercantilism had arisen. In England, Bernard de Mandeville and David Hume both wrote books and tracts attacking the interference of government in the economy. In France, a group of writers, called "physiocrats," denounced government regulations and controls that interfered with the "natural" economic order. All these critics favored the policy of laissez faire—a free market economy.

The most far-reaching indictment of mercantilism came from Adam Smith in his *An Inquiry Into The Nature And Causes Of The Wealth Of Nations* (1776). Mercantilism, he argued, was a successful economic doctrine—for the producers. The restraints on imports, the subsidies, the bounties, the treaties to exchange imports, the monopolies, and the colonial policies designed to make the colonists "a nation of consumers"—all these mercantilist policies, he complained, profit the producers at the expense of the consumer. "Consumption," Smith wrote, "is the sole end and purpose to all production; and the interest of the producer ought to be attended to only so far as it may be necessary for promoting that of the consumer."[71]

The basic problem with mercantilism was that it construed economics as a zero-sum game. Mercantilists believed that the world contained only a fixed quantity of economic resources. So a nation could win only by exporting more than it imported from any other nation. The implication that a nation could increase its wealth only at the expense of another generated fierce competition, trade wars, reprisals, and, ultimately, economic stagnation.

The way out, as Smith saw, lay in the cultivation of continuous economic growth. But no one nation, no one group, no one person is wise enough to know what substantive economic actions will sustain continuous growth. It is true that a powerful nation can, by pursuing its own self-interest, maintain its own growth—for a time. And a group of producers, following their own self-interest, could maintain their own growth—for a time. The same with an individual. But no one has the omniscience to decide what will maintain continuous growth for all. Only the market can do this.

The market does this by determining wages, prices, rents, and interest rates according to supply and demand. When the supply of workers is greater than the demand for them, their wages go down in the labor market. The price of goods declines when the supply exceeds the demand. In the land market, rents diminish when there is more land available than there is demand for it. And the rate of interest decreases as the money supply increases. When people can be rational about their actions, they act in ways to increase their profits: as workers or as employers in the labor market, as buyers or as sellers in the commodity market, as renters or as landlords in the land market, as borrowers or as lenders in the financial market.

As each person rationally pursues his or her own self-interest in the market, production, sales, and investments increase. For the market not only works as a noncoercive, nonauthoritarian mechanism for determining wages, prices, rents, and interest, it also encourages the creation of new, different, better economic practices, policies, procedures, and products. In the market economy of capitalism people are free—neither serfs nor slaves, nor members of a collective of any kind. They can enter into contracts to buy or sell, to work or hire, to rent from or rent to, to borrow or lend. In a free market, people compete: Workers compete with one another for the wages of an employer, or—depending on the conditions of supply and demand—employers may compete with one another for the service of workers. The same competition takes place in the commodity market among buyers and among sellers, in the land market among renters and among landlords, and in the financial market among borrowers and among lenders. This competition for gain permits and encourages the competitors to try to outdo their rivals in some way— by coming up with a better product, a better practice, a better process, or a better policy. In a capitalist economy, as even Karl Marx admitted, competition helps make things better.

If the market is to be free and open to competition, then all people must have an equal opportunity to engage in economic transactions. No such opportunity existed in the hierarchical feudal period or in the mercantilist era. Social castes and primogeniture, entail, monopolies, guilds, government regulations, subsidies, and tariffs—all curtailed the equal opportunity for all people to enter the market.

In addition to being free, competitive, and offering equal opportunity for all to enter, a market economy is also objective or rational. By this I mean that all market decisions—to buy or sell, to work or hire, to lend or borrow, to rent from or rent to—are based solely on the rational calculation of profitability. Religion, politics, ideology, morality, or any noneconomic considerations have no place in any such calculations. As Karl Marx observed in a famous passage of *The Communist Manifesto*, "the bourgeoisie, whenever it got the upper hand, put an end to all feudal, patriarchical, idyllic relations, pitilessly tore asunder the motley feudal ties that bound man to his 'natural superiors' and left remaining no other bond between man and man than naked self interest and callous cash payment." Subjective loyalties, commitments, beliefs, and values have no place in capitalist transactions— except insofar as they enhance profitability. As Benjamin Franklin, Max Weber's prototypical capitalist, so succinctly put it, "Honesty is the best *policy*" (italics added).

So, with the coming of the printing press, the economic arrangements got better. Printing provoked the worldwide expansion of trade and the adoption of rational methods of accounting, and it destroyed both the monopoly of the guilds and the restraints imposed by the Church on economic growth. The printing press created the markets—the labor market, the land market, the financial market—and it greatly expanded the commodity market. The printing press created capitalism—a free market economy that brought undreamed-of wealth to the nations of the West.

Conclusion

Media encode information. Some of this information is information about the culture—information about the existing social, political, and economic arrangements; about the existing institutions; and about the existing knowledge. So when people encode the existing culture in a new medium—whether the new medium be speech, writing, or print (or television or the computer)—they distance themselves from the culture; it becomes objectified, and people begin to see it in a way not possible before. This objectification of culture allows people to uncover inadequacies, faults, and limitations heretofore unrecognized. And once they uncover them, people do try to eliminate those faults. Insofar as the inadequacies or faults are eliminated, the culture improves.

If I am correct about the dynamics of cultural change—that people modify or refine the existing culture when they uncover inadequacies in it—then media of communication not only facilitate cultural change, they also determine the dimensions—the size, the number, the speed, the scope, the permanency—of those cultural changes.

Each medium of communication has a structure that enables us to store, retrieve, transmit, and process information. The structure of each medium creates an information environment characterized by the amount of information that can be stored, the speed with which it can be retrieved, the speed and distance information can be transmitted, and the accuracy with which information can be processed. Because each medium of communication creates its own information enironment, when a new medium first appears it transforms the existing information environment. This enables people to uncover many new inadequaacies in their culture, leading them to make numerous, large-scale, extensive, and permanent changes.

The more information about their culture people have available to them, the more that culture is open to critical scrutiny and then to change. Some media provide more information than others simply because they have more storage capacity than others. With the invention of writing, for example, people could encode and store more information than had been possible in an oral culture. When the Sumerians invented cuneiform writing this opened the existing culture to increased critical scrutiny and brought about vast social, political, and economic changes; and later, after the Greeks developed the alphabet, enabling literacy to become more widespread, this, too, brought large-scale, sweeping, changes.

Some media allow us to retrieve information more rapidly and transmit it more widely. With the medium of writing, for example, people could retrieve information more rapidly and transmit it more rapidly than had been possible when speech was the sole means of communicaton. So the cultural changes that first took place in Mesopotamia and in Greece were able to be spread rapidly throughout the literate world, through writing.

Finally, some media can process information more accurately than others. Because writing allowed people to process information more accurately than they could through speech, this gave written criticisms more cogency and made them more compelling and more enduring than oral criticisms. As a result, the changes that written criticisms brought about were more lasting.

The invention of the printing press, much later, again changed the information environment in Europe and, thereby the dimensions of cultural change. The printing press made more information about the culture available for criticism, increased the speed of information retrieval, broadened the distances over which information could be transmitted, and improved the accuracy of information processing. These changes in the information environment wrought by the printing press led to such historical events as the Renaissance, which led to a more open society; it brought about the emergence of the nation-state; it gave rise to capitalism; and it gave birth to modern science.

In addition to having its own structure, which creates a distinctive information environment, each medium of communication has its own bias, which leads to distinctive kinds of cultural changes. By this I mean that each medium of communication focuses people's attention on different kinds of inadequacies in the culture, thereby disposing them to uncover certain kinds of faults therein. So with the emergence of each new medium of communication in history, different kinds of cultural change take place. Thus, when speech first emerged in history, it led to the improvement of human practices; later, the invention of writing and printing helped people make culture more rational.

With the emergence of speech, human beings could move beyond the basic language functions of expressing and signaling that they shared with other animals. With speech, human beings could describe things ("This is an axe"), relationships ("This is my sister"), goings-on ("It is raining"). Once they could speak, human beings could ask questions, issue commands, tell stories, and make promises. Above all, with speech, human beings could become better problem solvers. Prior to the emergence of speech, human beings had constructed weapons, tools, and utensils to solve the problems of securing food, clothing, and shelter; they had created social arrangements and political arangements to protect themselves and their offspring. But once they could speak, human beings began to improve their artifacts and their arrangements. They made them more practicable and more practical. This happened because human speech made the argumentative function of language possible. Once they could speak, human beings became critical; they deliberately sought out and uncovered inadequacies in the existing culture. ("This axe is dull." "This leader is too old.")

The media of writing and print, when they came along, focused people's attention on the rational inadequacies of their culture. When information about the existing culture is encoded in writing or in print, it becomes easier to uncover the contradictions or illogicalities it contains. Thus, first in ancient Greece, after alphabetic writing made possible widespread literacy, and then later in Europe, following the invention of printing, many people became critical of the irrationalities in their culture and tried to eliminate them by making changes in the existing arrangements, institutions, and state of knowledge.

With print, critical rationality reached a new level. Print enabled us to create new forms of critical rationality, new ways to criticize our intellectual, political, and economic arrangements. In the intellectual world, we criticize theories in terms of their testability—a theory proves its mettle by how well it withstands tests and experiments designed to refute it. In the political world, we criticize the policies, laws, and actions of the government with regard to their constitutionality—unconstitutional acts are illegitimate and prohibited. In the economic world, we criticize decisions with respect to profitability—decisions that make no profit are to be avoided. Testability, constitutionality, and profitability are all forms of critical rationality made possible only since the coming of the printing press.

Moreover, printing not only makes these modern forms of critical rationality possible, it has also helped us construct social inventions that have institutionalized these critical approaches. The printing press created the community of scholars that critically examines all proposed theories and ascertains their testability, and tests them. The printing press also created the independent juducial system found in all modern western nations. The judiciary examines the policies and laws of the government to determine their constitutionality. The printing press also created the market economy by means of which all who engage in economic transactions can ascertain the profitability of their decisions.

These forms of critical rationality that the printing press has made possible have made things better: By eliminating those theories that failed our tests, we have reduced our ignorance; by eliminating laws and policies declared unconstitutional, we have diminished injustice; by eliminating actions that prove unprofitable, we have reduced poverty.

Finally, I must note that, after bringing about the dramatic cultural improvements they did, all of these dominant media of communication became, in time, instruments to conserve culture against change. That is, in time, speech, writing, and print all became media to socialize people to the existing arrangements, to get them to subscribe to, accept, and even revere the traditional institutions as well as the customary policies and procedures and the reigning values, beliefs, and understandings.

Yet although media of communication do seem to wind up as preservers of the status quo, as means for preventing improvement, it is clear that they have helped improve culture. Our culture is not perfect, but these dominant media of communication have helped us make our culture more practical, more rational, more moral[1] and more safe.[2] Moreover, further improvement is always possible—as long as we continue to speak, write, and read.

Notes

CHAPTER ONE

1. Reproduced in Stamm (1976), 253.
2. Hewes (1975), Hewes (1974).
3. Annals of the New York Academy of Sciences, Volume 280.
4. Farb (1975), 267.
5. Premack and Premack (1983); G. Mournin (1976); Annals of the New York Academy of Sciences, Volume 280, Part X.
6. New York Times, May 31, 1983.
7. Hewes (1974); also Annals Part IX.
8. Bickerton (1987).
9. Brunner (1979).
10. Buhler (1965), and Bartley (1982).
11. Popper (1972), 120-121.
12. Rosenstock-Huessy (1981).
13. Jaynes (1976a).
14. Ibid., but see Leakey and Lewin (1979), 171.
15. Lieberman (1975), 159.
16. Revesz (1970); Rosenstock-Huessy (1981), 136.
17. Bronowski thought that the delay occurred much earlier in the evolutionary past. He believed that the pebble tools of Australopithecus indicated that this early humanoid had foresight, a characteristic that he says is only possible when there is a delay between input and output. But as Brunner (1979) has argued, animals have foresight. So, since foresight is possible without this delay between input and output, then it seems likely that this delay is a characteristic of human speech.
18. Bronowski (1967).
19. Jaynes (1976b), 62 ff.
20. Levi-Strauss (1973), 8; see also Moscovici (1976), 19.
21. Levi-Strauss (1973), 481.
22. Gombrich (1969), 2-3.

23. Marshack (1972), 131.
24. Crombie (1971), 151.
25. Vygotsky (1962), 26.
26. Bronowski (1967), 355.
27. Pfeiffer (1982).
28. Braidwood (1975), Chapter V.
29. See Pfeiffer (1972).
30. Marshack (1972), 131-132.

CHAPTER TWO

1.   Pfeiffer (1982), 240.
2.   Rosenstock-Huessy (1981).
3.   Marshack (1972), Chapter XIII.
4.   *Encyclopedia of Art*, XIII, 802, 830.
5.   Clark (1969).
6.   Harris, M. (1978), 30.
7.   Thomas (1977), 25.
8.   Ibid., 21.
9.   Boorstin (1983), 4-19; Frankfort (1946), 81.
10. Adams (1966).
11. Hawkes (1965), 3.
12. Harris, M. (1978), 101.
13. Oppenheim (1975), 37-38.
14. Polanyi (1957), 254.
15. Davisson and Harper (1972), 95.
16. Frankfort (1946), 221.
17. Harris, M. (1978), 101.
18. Jacobsen (1970).
19. Conteneau (1964), 19.

CHAPTER THREE

1.   Finley (1979).
2.   Gelb (1963),194.
3.   Havelock (1976), 29.
4.   Ibid., 43.
5.   Oppenheim (1975), 41.
6.   Durant (1939), 209.
7.   Solmsen (1949), Part I; See especially 809.
8.   Herodotus, 2:53.
9.   Butterfield (1981), 129.
10. *Theogony*.
11. Quoted in Guthrie (1967), 371.
12. Aristotle, *Physics III*.
13. Guthrie (1967), 142.

14. Hesiod, *Works and Days*, lines 37-39.
15. Ibid., lines 180-201.
16. Murray (1980), 60.
17. Hesiod, *Works and Days*, lines 280-285.
18. Ibid., lines 220-221.
19. Quoted in Linforth (1919), 165.
20. Solon, *Fragments*, 36: 18-20.
21. Solon, *Fragments*, 36: 24D.
22. Solon, *Fragments*, 4.
23. Quoted in Linforth, 143.
24. Jaeger (1947), 110.
25. Quoted in Guthrie (1967), 70.
26. Jaeger (1965), Book II.
27. Guthrie (1971), Chapters III and VIII.
28. DeRomilly (1975).
29. Guthrie (1971), Chapter VII.
30. Durant (1939), 118.
31. Murray (1980), 65.
32. Ibid., 120.
33. Tyrtaeus, *Fragments*, 12, 13-20D.
34. See French (1964), Chapter I, also Finley (1974), 131.
35. Solon, *Fragments*, 4: 1-10.
36. Davisson and Harper (1972), 123.
37. Murray (1980), 244.
38. Davisson and Harper (1972), Chapters 6, 7, 8.
39. Finley (1974), 23.
40. Davisson and Harper (1972), 131.
41. Quoted in Thomson (1955), 195-196.
42. Aristotle, *Politics*, 1257-1258.
43. Ibid.
44. Thucydides, II, 38.
45. Rostovtzeff (1963), 267.
46. Petronius, 82-83.
47. Cicero, *De Officiis*, lines 150-151.
48. Seneca, *Epistles*, 27: 5-6.
49. See Finley (1974).
50. Murray (1951), Dodds (1951), and Popper (1962).

CHAPTER FOUR

1. Quoted in Eisenstein, (1980), 651.
2. Eisenstein (1980), 113; Steinberg (1974), 16ff.; Febvre (1976), Chapter 3.
3. Febvre (1984), 10-11; Eisenstein (1980), 6, 11-16, 32, 66-74.
4. Boorstin (1983), 485.
5. Eisenstein (1980), 170ff., 296.
6. Goldschmidt (1943), 98.
7. Burckhardt, (1958), 254.

8.   Hooykaas (1972), 112.
9.   Boorstin (1983), 349-50.
10. Popkin (1964).
11. Bacon (1623), (1951), 468.
12. Ibid., 488-489.

CHAPTER FIVE

1.   Whitehead (1954), 16.
2.   Eisenstein (1980), Chapter VII.
3.   Sarton (1957), 55-62, 137-138, 175-178.
4.   Hall (1957), 30.
5.   Dijksterhuis (1961), 167.
6.   Eisenstein (1980), 277-288; also see Yates (1972).
7.   Quoted in Eisenstein (1980), 475.
8.   Quoted in Haydn (1960), 269.
9.   Quoted in Eisenstein (1980), 472.
10. Ibid., 476.
11. Popper (1963), 46.
12. Boorstin (1983), 357.
13. Rossi (1970), 48.
14. Ibid., 71.
15. Ibid.,72.
16. Eisenstein (1980), 109-110.
17. Ibid., 464.
18. Thiel (1957), 181.
19. Kuhn (1959), Chapter V.
20. Quoted in Thiel (1957), 85.
21. Russell, quoted in Eisenstein (1980), 630-631.
22. Thiel (1957), 181.
23. Quoted in Boorstin (1983), 311.
24. Hooykaas (1972), 136.
25. Quoted in Boorstin (1983), 302.
26. Eisenstein (1980), 18, 627.
27. Ibid., 631.
28. Sarton (1957), 90.
29. Eisenstein (1980), 630.
30. Kuhn (1959), 224.
31. Langford (1971), 61.
32. Koestler (1968), 448.
33. Galileo, (1957), 169.
34. Ibid., 177.
35. Ibid., 186.
36. Ibid., 206.
37. Ibid.
38. Ibid., 195.
39. Koestler (1968), 437; Langford (1971), Chapter III.

40. Galileo (1957), 218.
41. Quoted in Langford (1971), 92.
42. Galileo (1632), 27-37, 101, 464.
43. Popper (1961).
44. For the latest irrational explanation of these two matters, see Thomas Kuhn, *The structure of Scientific Revolutions*; also see Popper's criticisms in *The Growth of Scientific Knowledge*, edited by Imre Lakatos and Alan Musgrave.
45. Eisenstein (1980), 667-668.
46. Santillana (1955), 326.

CHAPTER SIX

1. Oakeshott (1975), 186-187.
2. Gierke (1958), 92.
3. Ullman (1961), 33.
4. Printed in Marty (1959), 111.
5. Oakeshott (1975), 211.
6. Burke (1969), 2.
7. Kelley (1970), 112.
8. Erasmus, *Way of Reaching True Theology*, quoted in Burke (1969), 60.
9. Harbison (1959), 93.
10. Ozment (1980). 155-181.
11. Gilmore (1962), 38.
12. Carlyle, Vol. IV, 201, n. 1.
13. Tierney (1964), 132.
14. Sabine (1950), 270.
15. Hirsch (1967), 128-129; Febvre (1984), 249; Steinberg (1974), Chapter III.
16. Cipolla (1969), 52ff.; Ozment (1980), 201.
17. Goldschmidt (1943), 11-12, 77, 84.
18. Lund (1971), 136; Ozment (1980), 155; Elton (1972), 186.
19. Ross and McLaughlin (1958), 405.
20. Burke (1969), 11, 55; Butterfield (1981), 187-188; Boorstin (1983), 576-577.
21. Harbison (1959), 47.
22. Berman (1983), 600-601.
23. Ullman (1961), 102.
24. Gilmore (1962), 175.
25. Spitz and Lyman (1965), 197.
26. Eisenstein (1980), 310, 375.
27. Quoted in D'Entreves (1951), 34.
28. Berman (1983), 206.
29. Aquinas, *Summa Theologica*, Part I of Second Part, Question 95, Article 2.
30. Ibid.
31. Burke (1969), 32-33.
32. Gilmore (1961), 13.
33. Berman (1983), 32.
34. D'Entreves (1951), 68-69.
35. Ullman (1961), Part III.

36. Oakeshott (1975), 215-218.
37. Steinberg (1974), Chapter IV.
38. Hillerbrand (1970), 90.
39. Quoted in Ross and McLaughlin (1958), 83.
40. Harbison (1959), 100.
41. Steinberg (1974), 123.
42. Quoted in Ross and McLaughlin (1958), 83.
43. Hillerbrand (1970), 103.
44. Hughes (1957), 71.
45. Eisenstein (1980), 329-367.
46. Ibid., 336-338.
47. Ibid., 415.
48. Ibid., 356, 366.
49. Quoted in Popkin (1964), 2.
50. Oakeshott (1975), 225.
51. Neither Germany nor Italy became states until centuries later, even though both countries had many printing presses. The reason for this, I think, is that in both countries, small feudal domains had already come under secular control before the arrival of printing. The advent of the printing press simply helped these secular rulers solidify and strengthen the existing arrangements of the many small, contentious realms within both of these countries.
52. Bennett (1983), 38.
53. Elton (1972), 174-210.
54. Allen (1957), 275-285.
55. Machiavelli, *The Prince* (1532), Chapter XVII.
56. Thomas Elyot, *The Boke named the Governor* (1576).
57. Rice (1970), 96
58. Elton (1953), 266.
59. Elton (1978), 68-86.
60. Bodin, *Six Books of the Republic* (1576).
61. Maitland (1901), 210.
62. Hogue (1981), 181.
63. Berman (1983).
64. Thomas (1979), 223.
65. McIlwain (1947), 94-95; see also Judson (1964), Chapter I, esp. 19-22.
66. Siebert (1965), 130-132, 140.
67. Cantor (1967), 18, 198.
68. Sabine (1950), 477-478.
69. Quoted in Fink (1945), 1.
70. Quoted in Fink (1945), 61.
71. Sabine (1950), 496-508, and Fink (1945), Chapter 13.
72. Wormuth (1949), 69; Viles (1967), 48-49.
73. Judson (1964), 258; Hayek (1960), 169, 210; Wormuth (1949), 64.
74. Andrews (1963), 13.
75. Cantor (1967), 441; Andrews (1963), 40-43.

CHAPTER SEVEN

1. Heilbroner (1962), Chapter III.
2. Lopez (1971), 48-49.
3. Pirenne (1946), 106.
4. Braudel (1984), 94-112, 419.
5. Marx, Capital (1867), XXVI.
6. Quoted in Tuchman (1978), 37.
7. Lerner (1968).
8. Lerner (1968), 13.
9. Cipolla (1976), 215; and Tuchman (1978), Chapter V.
10. Bloch (1966), 113.
11. Quoted in Tuchman (1978), 37.
12. Penrose (1952), 241.
13. Ibid., 18-19.
14. Boorstin (1983), 271; Brown (1979), 155.
15. Eisenstein (1980), 193.
16. Penrose (1952), 241.
17. Mukerji (1983), Chapter 3.
18. Boorstin (1983), 267.
19. Penrose (1952), 290.
20. Boorstin (1983), 268.
21. Wilford (1981), 27, 69-70.
22. Mukerji (1983), 92.
23. Penrose (1952), 277.
24. Febvre and Martin (1984), 182.
25. Penrose (1952), 261; Brown (1979), 164.
26. Smith (1776) (1952), 271.
27. Bloch (1964), 126 ff.
28. Cipolla (1976), 198, 268.
29. Menninger (1969), 322ff.
30. Hirsch (1967), 3.
31. Menninger (1969), 327.
32. Eisenstein (1983), 382.
33. Menninger (1969), 426-427.
34. DeRoover (1974), 139.
35. Sombart (1908), Vol II, Part I, 118.
36. Weber (1946), 17.
37. Robertson (1973), Chapter I; Samuelson (1961), Chapter II.
38. Weber (1978), 92-93.
39. Ibid., 96.
40. Lander (1977), 36.
41. Sombart (1915), 127.
42. DeRoover (1974), 174.
43. Menninger (1969), 334, 428.
44. Taylor (1956), 179.
45. Sombart (1915), 128.
46. Wright (1935), 162-167.

47. Weber (1976), 22.
48. Clough (1959), 99.
49. Eisenstein (1980), 554.
50. Cipolla (1969), 185; Kranzberg and Pursell (1967), 150.
51. Wright (1935), 565-566.
52. Weber (1984), 164-173.
53. Smith (1776) (1952), 3.
54. De Roover (1974), 120.
55. Menninger (1969), 427.
56. Quoted in Tawney (1954), 29.
57. Ibid., 28.
58. Ibid., 28.
59. Michelman (1983), 168.
60. Tawney (1954), 38-40.
61. Nelson (1969), Chapter I.
62. Ibid., 74-75.
63. Heckscher (1973), II, 288-289,
64. Quoted in Robertson (1973), Appendix.
65. Quoted in Heckscher (1935), II, 116.
66. Quoted in Coleman (1969), 122.
67. Ibid., 136.
68. Packard (1927), 49.
69. Day (1947), 96.
70. Heckscher (1935), I, 171.
71. Smith (1776) (1952), 287.

CONCLUSION

1.   See Perkinson, *Getting Better: Television and Moral Progress* (1991).
2.   See Perkinson, *No Safety in Numbers: How the computer quantified everything and made people risk-aversive* (1995).

Bibliography

SPEECH

Annals of the New York Academy of Sciences. *Origins and Evolution of Speech*, Vol. 280, 1976.

Ashen, Ruth Nanda. *Language: An Enquiry into Its Meaning and Function* (New York: Harper & Brothers, 1957).

Bartley, W. W., III. "Wittgenstein and Homosexuality." *Salamagundi* (1982); Nos. 58-59: 179 ff.

Bickerton, Derek K. *Roots of Language* (Ann Arbor, Mich.: Karoma Publishers, 1987).

Braidwood, Robert J. *Prehistoric Man,* 8th ed. (Glencoe, Ill.: Scott Foresman, 1975).

Bronowski, Jacob. "Human and Animal Language," in *To Honor Roman Jacobson: Essays on the Occasion of his Seventieth Birthday*, Vol. I (The Hague: Mouton, 1967).

Bronowski, Jacob. "Language, Name, and Concept." *Science* (1970); 168: 669-673.

Bronowski, Jacob. *The Ascent of Man* (Boston: Little, Brown & Co., 1973).

Brunner, Jerome. "How to Do Things with Words," in Doris Aronson and Robert W. Rieber (eds.), *Psycholinguistic Research: Implications and Applications* (Hillsdale, N.J.: Lawrence Erlbaum Associates, 1979).

Buhler, Karl. *Sprachtheorie: die Darstellungsfunction der Sprache*, 2nd ed. (Stuttgart: Gustav Fischer, 1965).

Campbell, Joseph. *The Masks of God: Primitive Mythology* (New York: The Viking Press, 1959).

Cassirer, Ernst. *Language and Myth* (New York: Dover Publications, 1946).

Childe, Gordon. *What Happened in History? (*Hammondsworth: Penguin Books, 1948).

Clark, Grahame. *World Prehistory: A New Outline* (Cambridge, U.K.: Cambridge University Press, 1969).

Cohen, Yehudi A., ed. *Man in Adaptation: The Biosocial Background* (Chicago: Aldine, 1968).

Colum, Padraic. *Myths of the World* (New York: Grosset & Dunlap, 1969).

Crombie, Donald. "The Group System of Man and Paedomorphosis," *Current Anthropology* (1971); 12 (2): 147-169.

Dahrendorf, Ralf. *Life Chances* (Chicago: University of Chicago Press, 1979).

Diamond, Stanley, ed. *Culture in History* (New York: Columbia University Press, 1960).

Eccles, John C. *The Human Psyche* (New York: Springer International, 1980).

Farb, Peter. *Word Play* (New York; Bantam Books, 1975).

Farb, Peter. *Humankind* (New York: Bantam Books, 1980).

Firth, J. R. *The Tongues of Men and Speech* (London: Oxford University Press, 1964).

Fontenruse, John. *The Ritual Theory of Myth* (Berkeley: University of California Press, 1971).

Frankfort, Henri. *Kinship and the Gods* (Chicago: University of Chicago Press, 1978).

Frankfort, Henri, H.A. Frankfurt, John A. Wilson, Thorkild Jacobsen, and William A. Irwin. *The Intellectual Adventure of Ancient Man* (Chicago: University of Chicago Press, 1977).

Gombrich, Ernst. *The Sense of Order* (New York: Cornell University Press, 1969).

Goody, Jack. *The Domestication of the Savage Mind* (Cambridge, U.K.: Cambridge University Press, 1977).

Gregory, Richard L. *Mind in Science: A History of Explanations in Psychology and Physics* (Cambridge, U.K.: Cambridge University Press, 1981).

Hewes, Gordon. "Abridged Bibliography on the Origin of Language," in Roger W. Westcott, eds., *Language Origins* (Silver Springs, Md.: Linstock Press, 1974).

Hewes, Gordon. *Language Origins: A Bibliography* (The Hague: Mouton, 1975).

Hill, Jane H. "On the Evolutionary Foundations of Language." *American Anthropologist* (1972); 74 (3): 308-317.

Hockett, Charles F. "The Origins of Speech." *Scientific American* (1960); 203: 88-96.

Hockett, Charles F. *Man's Place in Nature* (New York: McGraw-Hill, 1973).

Innis, Harold A. *The Bias of Communication* (Toronto: University of Toronto Press, 1982).

James, E. O. *The Ancient Gods* (New York: G. P. Putnam's Sons, 1960).

Jaynes, Julian. "The Evolution of Language in the Late Pleistocene." *Annals of the New York Academy of Sciences*, Vol 280, 1976.

Jaynes, Julian. *The Origin of Consciousness in the Breakdown of the Bicameral Mind* (Boston: Houghton-Mifflin Co., 1976).

Leakey, Richard E., and Roger Lewin. *People of the Lake* (New York: Avon, 1979).

Lee, R. B., and Irven Devore, eds. *Man the Hunter* (Chicago: Aldine, 1971).

LeGros Clark, W. E. *History of the Primates* (Chicago: University of Chicago Press, 1963).

Levi-Strauss, Claude. *The Elementary Structures of Kinship* (Boston: Beacon Press, 1969).

Levi-Strauss, Claude. *Structural Anthropology* (New York: Basic Books, 1973).

Levy, Gertrude R. *The Gate of Horn: A Study of the Religious Thought of the Stone Age* (London: Faber and Faber, 1963).

Lieberman, Philip. *On the Origins of Language* (New York: Macmillan, 1975).

Lieberman, Philip, and Edmund Crellin. "On the Speech of Neanderthal Man." *Linguistic Inquiry* (1971); 11 (2): 203-222.

Lieberman, Philip, Edmund Crellin, and Dennis H. Klatt. "Phonetic Ability and Related Anatomy of the New born and Adult Human, Neanderthal Man and the Chimpanzee." *American Anthropologist* (1972); 74 (3): 287-307.

Marshack, Alexander. *The Roots of Civilization* (New York: McGraw-Hill, 1972).

McNairn, Barbara. *The Method and Theory of V. Gordon Childe* (Edinburgh: Edinburgh University Press, 1980).

Moscovici, Serge. *Society against Nature: The Emergence of Human Societies* (Atlantic Highlands, N.J.: Humanities Press, 1976).

Mournin, G. "Language Communication, Chimpanzees." *Current Anthropology* (1976); 17: 1-21.

Oppenheim, A. Leo. *Ancient Mesopotamia* (Chicago: University of Chicago Press, 1964).

Pfeiffer, John E. *The Creative Explosion* (New York: Harper & Row, 1982).

Pfeiffer, John E. *The Emergence of Man* (New York: Harper & Row, 1972).

Popper, Karl. *Objective Knowledge* (London: Oxford Press, 1972).

Premack, David, and Ann James Premack. *The Mind of an Ape* (New York: W. W. Norton, 1983).

Redfield, Robert. *The Primitive World and Its Transformations* (Ithaca, N.Y.: Cornell University Press, 1953).

Revesz, Geza. *The Origins and Prehistory of Language* (Westport, Conn.: Greenwood Press, 1970).

Rosenstock-Huessy, Eugen. *The Origins of Speech* (Warwick, Conn.: Argo Books, 1981).

Sagan, Carl. *The Dragons of Eden* (New York: Random House, 1977).

Schlipp, Paul A., ed. *The Philosophy of Karl Popper* (LaSalle, Ill.: Open Court, 1974).

Schrier, A. A., and F. Stollnitz, eds. *Behavior of Non-Human Primates* (New York: Academic Press, 1971).

Sebock, Thomas, ed. *How Animals Communicate* (Bloomington, Ind.: Indiana University Press, 1971).

Smith, Ron. *Mythologies of the World: A Guide to Sources* (Urbana, Ill.: National Council of Teachers of English, 1981).

Stamm, James H. *Inquires into the Origin of Language: The Fate of a Question* (New York: Harper & Row, 1976).

Swadesh, Morris. *The Origin and Diversification of Language* (Chicago: Aldine-Atherton Press, 1971).

Ucko, Peter J., Ruth Tringham, and C. W. Dimbleby, eds. *Man, Settlement and Urbanism* (London: Duckworth, 1972).

Vygotsky, L. S. *Thought and Language* (Cambridge, Mass.: Harvard University Press, 1962).

Westcott, Roger W., ed. *Language Origins* (Silver Springs, Md.: Linstock Press, 1974).

Wiener, Norbert. *Cybernetics* (New York: The MIT Press and John Wiley & Sons, Inc., 1961).

Wilson, John A. *The Culture of Ancient Egypt* (Chicago: University of Chicago Press, 1963).

Wittfogel, Karl A. *Oriental Despotism* (New Haven, Conn.: Yale University Press, 1957).

Young, J. Z. *An Introduction to the Study of Man* (Oxford, U.K.: Clarendon Press, 1971).

WRITING

Aaboe, Asger. *Episodes from the Early History of Mathematics* (New York: Random House, 1964).

Adams, Robert. *The Evolution of Urban Society* (Chicago: Aldine, 1966).

Adams, Robert. *Heartland of Cities* (Chicago: University of Chicago Press, 1984).

Adkins, A. W. H. *From the Many to the One* (Ithaca, N.Y.: Cornell University Press, 1970).

Adkins, A. W. H. *Moral Values and Political Behavior in Ancient Greec* (London: Chatto & Windus, 1972).

Aristotle. *Constitution of Athens,* translated by Kurt von Fritz and Ernst Kapp (New York: Hafner Publishing Co., 1950).

Austin, M. M., and P. Vidal-Naquet. *Economic and Social History of Ancient Greece* (London: B. T. Batsford, 1977).

Boorstin, Daniel. *The Discoverers* (New York: Random House, 1983).

Burn, Andrew. *The World of Hesiod* (New York: Dutton, 1937).

Burn, Andrew. *The Pelican History of Greece* (New York: Penguin Books, 1982).

Butterfield, Herbert. *The Origins of History* (New York: Basic Books, 1981).

Carney. T. F. *The Economics of Antiquity* (Lawrence, Kan.: The Coronado Press, 1973).

Chamoux, François. *The Civilization of Greece* (New York: Simon & Schuster, 1965).

Chiera, Edward. *They Wrote on Clay* (Chicago: University of Chicago Press, 1966).

Childe, V. Gordon. *Man Makes Himself* (New York: New American Library, 1951).

Clark, Grahame. *World Prehistory: A New Outline* (Cambridge, U.K.: Cambridge University Press, 1969).

Colum, Padraic. *Myths of the World* (New York: Grosset & Dunlap, 1969).

Contenau, Georges. *Everyday Life in Babylon and Assyria* (London: Edward Arnold, 1964).

Daniel, Glynn. *The First Civilizations, the Archaeology of their Origin* (New York: Thomas Y. Crowell Company, 1968).

Dantzig, Tobias. *Number: The Language of Science* (Garden City, N.Y.: Doubleday, 1956).

Davisson, William I., and James E. Harper. *European Economic History*, Vol. I (New York: Appleton-Century Crofts, 1972).

De Camp, L. Sprague. *The Ancient Engineers* (New York: Ballantine Books, 1974).

de Coulanges, Fustel. *The Ancient City* (1864) (Garden City, N.Y.: Doubleday, 1955).

De Romilly, Jacqueline. *Magic and Rhetoric in Ancient Greece* (Cambridge, Mass.: Harvard University Press, 1975).

de Solla Price, Derek J. *Science Since Babylon* (New Haven, Conn.: Yale University Press, 1961).

Diringer, David. *The Alphabet: A Key to the History of Mankind* (New York: Funk & Wagnalls, 1968).

Disch, Robert, ed. *The Future of Literacy* (Englewood Cliffs, N.J.: Prentice-Hall, 1973).

Dodds, Eric R. *The Ancient Concept of Progress* (Oxford, U.K.: Oxford University Press, 1951).

Dodds, Eric R. *The Greeks and the Irrational* (Berkeley: University of California Press, 1951).

Durant, Will. *The Life of Greece* (New York: Simon & Schuster, 1939).

Ehrenberg, Victor. *The Greek State* (London: Methuen, 1969).

Eliade, Mircea. *Patterns in Comparative Religion* (New York: New American Library, 1974).

Fairservice, Walter A., Jr. *The Threshold of Civilization* (New York: Charles Scribner's Sons, 1975).

Farb, Peter. *Humankind* (New York: Bantam Books, 1980).

Finley, M. I. *The Ancient Economy* (Berkeley: University of California Press, 1974).

Finley, M. I. *The World of Odysseus* (New York: Penguin, 1979).

Finley, M. I. *Economy and Society in Ancient Greece* (New York: The Viking Press, 1982).

Finley, M. I. *Politics in the Ancient World* (Cambridge, U.K.: Cambridge University Press, 1983).

Finnegan, Ruth. *Oral Poetry* (Cambridge, U.K.: Cambridge University Press, 1977).

Frankfort, Henri, and H. A., John Wilson, Thorkild Jacobsen, and William A. Irwin. *The Intellectual Adventure of Ancient Man* (Chicago: University of Chicago Press, 1946).

French, Alfred. *The Growth of the Athenian Economy* (London: Routledge, Kegan, Paul, 1964).

Frisch, Hartvig. *Might and Right in Antiquity* (New York: Hafner Publishing Co., 1949).

Gelb, I. J. *A Study of Writing* (Chicago: University of Chicago Press, 1963).

Gernet, Louis. *The Anthropology of Ancient Greece* (Baltimore, Md.: The Johns Hopkins Press, 1981).

Golden, James L., *et al. The Rhetoric of Western Thought* (Dubuque, Iowa: Kendall-Hunt, 1978).

Goody, Jack, ed. *Literacy in Traditional Societies* (Cambridge, U.K.: Cambridge University Press, 1969)

Gordon, Cyrus. *The Common Background of Greek and Hebrew Civilizations* (New York: Basic Books, 1968).

Guthrie, W. K. C. *A History of Greek Philosophy, Vol. I* (Cambridge, U.K.: Cambridge University Press, 1967).

Guthrie, W. K. C. *The Sophists* (Cambridge, U.K.: Cambridge University Press, 1971).

Haas, W., ed. *Writing Without Letters* (Manchester, U.K.: Manchester University Press, 1976).

Harris, Marvin. *Cannibals and Kings* (New York: Vintage Books, 1978).

Harris, Roy. *The Origin of Writing* (LaSalle, Ill.: Open Court, 1986).

Havelock, Eric A. *Origins of Western Literacy* (Toronto: The Ontario Institute for Studies in Education, 1976).

Havelock, Eric A., and Jackson P. Hershbell. *Communication Arts in the Ancient World* (New York: Hastings House, 1978).

Havelock, Eric A. *The Greek Concept of Justice* (Cambridge, Mass.: Harvard University Press, 1978).

Havelock, Eric A. *The Literate Revolution in Greece and Its Cultural Consequences* (Princeton: Princeton University Press, 1982).

Havelock, Eric A. *Preface to Plato* (Cambridge, Mass.: Harvard University Press, 1982).

Hawkes, Jacquetta. *Prehistory* (New York: New American Library, 1965).

Hesiod. *Theogony* (Indianapolis, Ind.: Bobbs-Merrill Co., 1953).

Hesiod. *Works and Days* (Indianapolis, Ind.: Bobbs-Merrill Co., 1951).

Hooper, Finley. *Greek Realities* (Detroit, Mich.: Wayne State University Press, 1978).

Hyland, Drew A. *The Origins of Philosophy* (New York: Putnam's Sons, 1973).

Iserlin, B. S. J. "The Earliest Alphabetic Writing," *The Cambridge Ancient History*, 2nd ed., Vol. 3, Pt. 1, pp. 794-818 (Cambridge, U.K.: Cambridge University Press, 1982).

Jaacobsen, Thorkild. *Toward the Image of Tammuz and other Essays on Mesopotamian History and Culture* (Cambridge, Mass.: Harvard University Press, 1970).

Jaeger, Werner. *The Theology of the Early Greek Philosophers* (Oxford, U.K.: Oxford University Press, 1947).

Jaeger, Werner. *Paideia Vol. I* (New York: Oxford University Press, 1965).

Jeffery, L. H. "Greek Alphabetic Writing," *The Cambridge Ancient History*, 2nd ed., Vol. 3, Pt. 1, pp. 819-833 (Cambridge, U.K.: Cambridge University Press, 1982).

Kirk, G. S. *Myth: Its Meaning and Function* (Cambridge, U.K.: Cambridge University Press, 1979).

Kirk, G. S., and J. E. Raven. *The Presocratic Philosophers* (Cambridge, U.K.: Cambridge University Press, 1962).

Kraeling, Carl H., and Robert M. Adams, eds. *City Invincible* (Chicago: University of Chicago Press, 1960).

Kramer, Samuel N. *Sumerian Mythology* (Philadelphia: University of Pennsylvania Press, 1972).

Linforth, Ivan M. *Solon the Athenian* (Berkeley: University of California Press, 1919).

Logan, Robert. *The Alphabet Effect* (New York: William Morrow & Co., 1986).

Marshack, Alexander. *The Roots of Civilization* (New York: McGraw-Hill, 1972).

Murray, Gilbert. *Five Stages of Greek Religion* (Garden City, N.Y.: Doubleday, 1951).

Murray, Oswyn. *Early Greece* (Atlantic Highlands, N.J.: Humanities Press, 1980).

Oates, David and Joan. *The Rise of Civilization* (New York: Phaidon Press, 1976).

Ogg, Oscar. *The 26 Letters* (New York: Thomas Y. Crowell, Co., 1948).

Ong, Walter J. *Orality and Literacy* (New York: Methuen, 1982).

Oppenheim, A. Leo. *Ancient Mesopotamia* (Chicago: University of Chicago Press, 1964).

Oppenheim, A. Leo. "The Position of the Intellectual in Mesopotamian Society." *Daedelus* (1975); 4 (2): 37-46.

Ostwald, Martin. *Nomos and the Beginnings of the Athenian Democracy* (Oxford, U.K.: Oxford University Press, 1969).

Oxenham, John. *Literacy: Writing, Reading and Social Organization* (London: Routledge and Kegan Paul, 1980).

Pattison, Robert. *On Literacy* (New York: Oxford University Press, 1982).

Petronius. *The Satyricon,* translated by William Arrowsmith (New York: New American Library, 1959).

Pfeiffer, John E. *The Creative Explosion* (New York: Harper & Row, 1982).

Phillips, Patricia. *The Prehistory of Europe* (Bloomington, Ind.: Indiana University Press, 1980).

Polanyi, Karl. *Trade and Market in Early Empires* (Glencoe, Ill.: The Free Press, 1957).

Popper, Karl, *The Open Society and Its Enemies,*Volume I (London: Routledge and Kegan Paul, 1962).

Roebuck, Carl. *The World of Ancient Times* (New York: Charles Scribner's Sons, 1966).

Rosenstock-Huessy, Eugen. *The Origin of Speech* (Warwick, Conn.: Argo Books, 1981).

Rostovtzeff, M. *Greece* (New York: Oxford University Press, 1963).

Sabloff, Jeremy A., and C. C. Lamberg-Karlovsky, eds. *Ancient Civilization and Trade* (Albuquerque: University of New Mexico Press, 1975).

Schmandt-Besserat, Denise. "The Earliest Precursor of Writing." *Scientific American* (June 1978): 50-59.

Senner, Wayne M., ed. *The Origins of Writing* (Lincoln: University of Nebraska Press, 1989).

Smith, David E., and Sekuthiel Ginsburg. *Numbers and Numerals* (Washington, D.C.: The National Council of Teachers of Mathematics, 1937).

Solmsen, Friedrich. *Hesiod and Aeschylus* (Ithaca, N.Y.: Cornell University Press, 1949).

Solmsen, Friedrich. *Intellectual Experiments of the Greek Enlightenment* (Princeton, N.J.: Princeton University Press, 1975).

Starr, Chester G. *The Economic and Social Growth of Early Greece: 800-500 B.C.* (New York: Oxford University Press, 1977).

Thomas, Hugh. *A History of the World* (New York: Oxford University Press, 1977).

Thomson, George. *Studies in Ancient Greek Society* (London: Lawrence & Wishart, 1955).

Ullman, B. L. *Ancient Writing and Its Influence* (New York: Cooper Square Publishers, 1963).

Ure, P. W. *The Origin of Tyranny* (Cambridge, U.K.: Cambridge University Press, 1922).

Vernant, Jean-Pierre. *Myth and Society in Ancient Greece* (Atlantic Highlands, N.J.: Humanities Press, 1980).

Vernant, Jean-Pierre. *The Origins of Greek Thought* (Ithaca, N.Y.: Cornell University Press, 1982).

Webster, T. B. L. *From Mycenae to Homer* (London: Methuen, 1958).

Zimmern, Alfred. *The Greek Commonwealth* (New York: Oxford University Press, 1961).

PRINTING

Albion, Robert G., ed. *Exploration and Discovery* (New York: Macmillan, 1965).

Alighieri, Dante. *On World Government* (*De Monarchia*) (1317) (New York: The Liberal Arts Press, 1957).

Allen, J. W. *A History of Political Thought in the Sixteenth Century* (London: Methuen, 1957).

Andrews, William G. *Constitutions and Constitutionalism* (Princeton, N.J.: Van Nostrand Co., 1963).

Ashley, Maurice. *England in the Seventeenth Century* (London; Penguin Books, 1952).

Aston, Trevor. *Crisis in Europe: 1560-1660* (Garden City, N.Y.: Doubleday, 1967).

Bacon, Francis. *The New Atlantis* (1624) (London: Oxford University Press, 1951).

Bainton, Ronald H. *Here I Stand: A Life of Martin Luther* (Boston: Beacon Press, 1956).

Bennett, H. S. *English Books and Readers 1475 to 1557* (Cambridge, U.K.: Cambridge University Press, 1983).

Berman, Harold J. *Law and Revolution* (Cambridge, Mass.: Harvard University Press, 1983).

Bloch, Mark. *Feudal Society* (Chicago: University of Chicago Press, 1964).

Bloch, Mark. *French Rural History* (Berkeley: University of California Press, 1966).

Boorstin, Daniel. *The Discoverers* (New York: Random House, 1983).

Braudel, Fernand. *The Structures of Everyday Life* (New York: Harper & Row, 1981).

Braudel, Fernand. *The Wheels of Commerce* (New York: Harper & Row, 1982).

Braudel, Fernand. *The Perspectives of the World* (New York: Harper & Row, 1984).

Brown, Lloyd A. *The Story of Maps* (New York: Dover, 1979).

Burckhardt, Jacob. *The Civilization of Renaissance Italy* (New York: Harper & Row, 1958).

Burke, Peter. *The Renaissance Sense of the Past* (New York: St. Martin's Press, 1969).

Burrell, Sidney, ed. *The Role of Religion in Modern History* (New York: Macmillan, 1964).

Butterfield, Herbert. *The Origins of Modern Science* (New York: The Free Press, 1965).

Butterfield, Herbert. *The Origins of History* (New York: Basic Books, 1981).

Cantor, Norman F. *The English* (New York: Simon & Schuster, 1967).

Carlyle, Robert W. *A History of Medieval Political Theory in the West* 6 Volumes (London: W. Blackwood & Sons, 1907-1936).

Chaytor, H. J. *From Script to Print* (New York: October House, 1967).

Chabod, Federico. *Machiavelli and the Renaissance* (New York: Harper, 1965).

Cipolla, Carlo M. *Before the Industrial Revolution* (New York: W. W. Norton Co., 1976).

Cipolla, Carlo M. *Clocks and Culture* (New York: W. W. Norton Co., 1977).

Cipolla, Carlo M. *Literacy and Development in the West* (New York: Penguin, 1969).

Clough, Shepard B. *The Economic Development of Western Civilization* (New York: McGraw-Hill, 1959).

Coleman, D. C., ed. *Revisions in Mercantilism* (London: Methuen, 1969).

Davis, Natalie S. *Society and Culture in Early Modern France* (Stanford, Calif.: Stanford University Press, 1975).

Day, Clive. *Economic Development in Europe* (New York: Macmillan, 1947).

D'Entreves, Alexander Passerin. *The Medieval Contribution to Political Thought* (Oxford, U.K.: Oxford University Press, 1939).

D'Entreves, Alexander Passerin. *Natural Law* (London: Hutchinson's Library, 1951).

D'Entreves, Alexander Passerin. *The Notion of the State* (Oxford, U.K.: Oxford University Press, 1967).

De Roover, Raymond. *Business, Banking and Economic Thought in Late Medieval and Early Modern Europe* (Chicago: University of Chicago Press, 1974).

Dickens, A. G. *The Age of Humanism and Reformation* (Englewood Cliffs, N.J.: Prentice-Hall, 1972).

Dijksterhuis, E. J. *The Mechanization of the World Picture* (New York: Oxford University Press, 1961).

Dobb, Maurice. *Capitalist Entrepreneurial Social Progress* (London: George Routledge & Sons, 1925).

Dreyer, J. L. E. *A History of Astronomy* (New York: Dover, 1963).

Earle, Peter, ed. *Essays in Economic History, 1500-1800* (Oxford, U.K.: Clarendon Press, 1974).

Eisenstein, Elizabeth L. *The Printing Press as an Agent of Change* (New York: Cambridge University Press, 1980).

Eisenstein, Elizabeth L. *The Printing Revolution in Early Modern Europe* (New York: Cambridge University Press, 1983).

Elias, Norbert. *State Forming and Civilization* (Oxford, U.K.: Basil Blackwell, 1982).

Elton, G. R. *The Tudor Revolution in Government* (Cambridge, U.K.: Cambridge University Press, 1953).

Elton, G. R. *Policy and Police* (Cambridge, U.K.: Cambridge University Press, 1972).

Elton, G. R. "Sessional Printing of Statutes, 1484-1547," in Eric Ives and R. Knecht, eds. *Wealth and Power in Tudor England* (London: Athlone Press, 1978).

Elyot, Sir Thomas. *The Boke Named the Governor* (1531) (London: Dent, 1962).

Erasmus, Desiderus. *In Praise of Folly* (1516) (Princeton, N.J.: Princeton University Press, 1941).

Erasmus, Desiderus. *Julius Exclusus* (1517) (Bloomington, Ind.: Indiana University Press, 1968).

Febvre, Lucien, and Henri-Jean Martin. *The Coming of the Book* (London: Verso Editions, 1984).

Ferguson, Wallace K., *The Renaissance* (New York: Harper & Row, 1962).

Figgis, John N. *From Gerson to Grotius* (Cambridge, U.K.: Cambridge University Press, 1916).

Fink, Zera S. *The Classical Republicans* (Evanston, Ill.: Northwestern University Press, 1945).

Foucault, Michael. *The Order of Things* (New York: Random House, 1970).

Franklin, Julian H. *Jean Bodin and the Rise of Absolutist Theory* (Cambridge, U.K.: Cambridge University Press, 1973).

Friedrich, Carl J. *Constitutional Government and Democracy* (Waltham, Mass.: Blaisdell Publishing Co., 1968).

Galilei, Galileo. *Dialogue Concerning the Two Chief World Systems* (1632) (Berkeley: University of California Press, 1967).

Galilei, Galileo. *Discourses and Opinions of Galileo*, translated by Stillman Drake (Garden City, N.Y.: Doubleday, 1957).

Garin, Eugenio. *Italian Humanism* (Oxford, U.K.: Basil Blackwell, 1965).

Gierke, Otto. *Political Theories of the Middle Ages* (Boston: Beacon Press, 1958).

Gilmore, Myron P. *Argument From Roman Law in Political Thought, 1200-1600* (Cambridge, Mass.: Harvard University Press, 1961).

Gilmore, Myron P. *The World of Humanism* (New York: Harper & Row, 1962).

Gimpel, Jean. *The Medieval Machine* (New York: Penguin Books, 1977).

Goldschmidt, E. P. *Medieval Texts and Their First Appearance in Print* (London: N. P., 1943).

Gouch, G. P. *Political Thought in England* (London: Oxford University Press, 1916 [1915]).

Gouldner, Alvin W. *The Dialectic of Ideology and Technology* (New York: Oxford University Press, 1976).

Green, Robert W. *Protestantism and Capitalism* (Boston: D. C. Heath, 1959).

Hall, A. Rupert. *The Scientific Revolution, 1500-1800* (Boston: Houghton-Mifflin, 1957).

Harbison, E. Harris. *The Christian Scholar in the Age of Reformation* (New York: Charles Scribner's Sons, 1959).

Havighurst, Alfred F., ed. *The Pirenne Thesis* (Boston: D. C. Heath, 1958).

Haydn, Hiram, *The Counter Renaissance* (Gloucester, Mass.: P. Smith, 1960).

Hayek, F.A., *The Constitution of Liberty* (London: Routledge and Kegan Paul, 1960).

Heckscher E. F. *Mercantilism*, 2 Volumes (London: G. Allen and Unwin, 1935).

Heer, Friedrich. *The Intellectual History of Europe*, 2 Volumes (Garden City, N.Y.: Doubleday, 1968).

Heilbroner, Robert L. *The Worldly Philosophers* (New York: Simon & Schuster, 1961).

Heilbroner, Robert L. *The Making of Economic Society* (Englewood Cliffs, N.J.: Prentice-Hall, 1962).

Hill, Christopher. *The Century of Revolution, 1603-1714* (New York: W. W. Norton and Co., 1966).

Hillerbrand, Hans J. *Erasmus and His Age* (New York: Harper & Row, 1970).

Hirsch, Rudolph. *Printing, Selling and Reading, 1450-1500* (Wiesbaden: Otto Harrassowitz, 1967).

Hogue, Arthur R. *Origins of the Common Law* (Indianapolis, Ind.: Liberty Press, 1981).

Hooykaas, Reijer. *Religion and the Rise of Modern Science* (London: Chatto and Windus, 1972).

Hughes, Philip. *A Popular History of the Reformation* (Garden City, N.Y.: Doubleday, 1957).

Johnson, Jerah, and William Percy. *The Age of Recovery* (Ithaca, N.Y.: Cornell University Press, 1970).

Judson, Margaret A. *The Crisis of the Constitution* (New York: Octagon Books, 1964).

Kelley, Donald R. *Foundations of Modern Scholarship* (New York: Columbia University Press, 1970).

Koenigsberger, H. G., and George L. Mosse. *Europe in the Sixteenth Century* (London: Longmans, 1968).

Koestler, Arthur. *The Sleepwalkers* (London: Hutchinson, 1968).

Kramer, Stella. *The English Craft Guilds* (New York: Columbia University Press, 1927).

Kransberg, Melvin, and Carol Pursell, eds. *Technology in Western Civilization* (New York: Oxford University Press, 1967).

Kristeller, Paul Oskar. *Renaissance Thought* (New York: Harper & Row, 1955).

Kuhn, Thomas S. *The Copernican Revolution* (New York: Random House, 1959).

Kuhn, Thomas S. *The Structure of Scientific Revolutions* (Chicago: University of Chicago Press, 1970).

Lakatos, Imre, and Alan Musgrave, eds. *Criticism and the Growth of Knowledge* (Cambridge, U.K.: Cambridge University Press, 1970).

Lander, J. R. *Conflict and Stability in Fifteenth Century England* (London: Hutchinson &

Co., 1977).

Langford, Jerome. *Galileo, Science and the Church* (Ann Arbor: University of Michigan Press, 1971).

Lerner, Robert. *The Age of Adversity* (Ithaca, N.Y.: Cornell University Press, 1968).

Lindsay, A. D. *The Modern Democratic State* (New York: Oxford University Press, 1962).

Littleton, A. C., and B. S. Yarney. *Studies in the History of Accounting* (Homewood, Ill.: Richard Irwin, 1956).

Lopez, Robert. *The Commercial Revolution of the Middle Ages* (Englewood Cliffs, N.J.: Prentice-Hall, 1971).

Losee, John. *A Historical Introduction to the Philosophy of Science* (New York: Oxford University Press, 1980).

Lubasz, Heinz. *The Development of the Modern State* (New York: Macmillan, 1964).

Lund, Eric. *A History of European Ideas* (Reading, Mass.: Addison-Wesley, 1971).

Machiavelli, Niccolò. *The Prince* (1532) (New York: Appleton-Century-Crofts, 1947).

Maitland, Frederick W. *English Law and the Renaissance* (Cambridge, U.K.: Cambridge University Press, 1901).

Maitland, Frederick W. *The Constitutional History of England (1908)* (Cambridge, U.K.: Cambridge University Press, 1979).

Marsak, Leonard. *The Rise of Science in Relation to Society* (New York: Macmillan, 1964).

Marty, Martin E. *A Short History of Christianity* (New York: Meridian Books, 1959).

Mazzeo, Joseph. *Renaissance and Reformation* (New York: Pantheon Books, 1965).

McIlwain, Charles H. *Constitutionalism: Ancient and Modern* (Ithaca, N.Y.: Cornell University Press, 1947).

McLuhan, Marshal. *The Gutenberg Galaxy* (New York: Signet Books, 1969).

Menninger, Karl. *Numbers, Words and Number Symbols* (Cambridge, Mass.: M.I.T. Press, 1969).

Metraux, Guy S., and François Crouzet. *The Evolution of Science* (New York: Mentor Books, 1963).

Michelman, Irving S. *The Roots of Capitalism in Western Civilization* (New York: Frederick Fell, 1983).

Moore, Barrington, Jr. *Social Origins of Dictatorship and Democracy* (Boston: Beacon Press, 1967).

Moran, James. *Printing Presses: History and Development* (Berkeley: University of California Press, 1973).

Morral, John B. *Political Thought in Medieval Times* (Toronto: University of Toronto Press, 1980).

Mukerji, Chandra. *From Graven Images* (New York: Columbia University Press, 1983).

Mumford, Lewis. *The Story of Utopias* (New York: Boni & Liveright, 1922).

Mumford, Lewis. *Technics and Civilization* (New York: Harcourt Brace and World, 1963).

Nef, John U. *Cultural Foundations of Industrial Civilization* (New York: Harper & Row, 1960).

Nelson, Benjamin. *The Idea of Usury* (Chicago: University of Chicago Press, 1969).

Oakeshott, Michael. *On Human Conduct* (Oxford, U.K.: Clarendon Press, 1975).

Ozment, Stephen. *The Age of Reform: 1250-1550* (New Haven, Conn.: Yale University Press, 1980).

Packard, Lawrence B. *The Commercial Revolution* (New York: Henry Holt and Co., 1927).

Parry, J. H. *The Establishment of European Hegemony: 1423-1715* (New York: Harper & Row, 1961).

Penrose, Boies. *Travel and Discovery in the Renaissance* (Cambridge, Mass.: Harvard University Press, 1952).

Perkinson, Henry J. *Getting Better: Television and Moral Progress* (New Brunswick, N.J.: Transaction Publishers, 1991).

Perkinson, Henry J. *No Safety in Numbers: How the Computer Quantified Everything and Made People Risk-Aversive* (Cresskill, N.J.: Hampton Press, 1995).

Pirenne, Henri. *Economic and Social History of Medieval Europe* (New York: Harcourt, Brace and Co., 1946).

Poggi, Gianfranco. *The Development of the Modern State* (Stanford, Calif.: Stanford University Press, 1978).

Polanyi, Karl. *The Great Transformation* (Boston: Beacon Press, 1957).

Pollard, Sidney. *The Idea of Progress* (New York: Penguin Books, 1971).

Popkin, Richard H. *The History of Scepticism from Erasmus to Descartes* (Assen, Netherlands: Koninklijke Van Gorcum, 1964).

Popper, Karl. *The Logic of Scientific Discovery* (New York: Science Editions, 1961).

Popper, Karl. *Conjectures and Refutations* (London: Routledge and Kegan Paul, 1963).

Postman, Neil. *Amusing Ourselves to Death* (New York: Viking, 1985).

Reynolds, Robert L. *Europe Emerges* (Madison: University of Wisconsin Press, 1961).

Rice, Eugene F., Jr. *The Foundations of Early Modern Europe: 1460-1559* (New York: W. W. Norton, 1970).

Robertson, H. M. *Aspects of the Rise of Economic Individualism* (1933) (Clifton, N.J.: Augustus Kelley, 1973).

Rosenberg, Nathan, and L. E. Birdzell, Jr. *How the West Grew Rich* (New York: Basic Books, 1986).

Ross, James B., and Mary M. Mclaughlin, eds. *The Portable Renaissance Reader* (New York: The Viking Press, 1958).

Rossi, Paolo. *Philosophy, Technology and the Arts in the Early Modern Era* (New York: Harper & Row, 1970).

Sabine, George H. *A History of Political Theory* (New York: Henry Holt & Co., 1950).

Samuelson, Kurt. *Religion and Economic Action* (London: W. Heinemann, 1961).

Santillana, Georgio de. *The Crime of Galileo* (Chicago: University of Chicago Press, 1955).

Sarton, George. *Six Wings: Men of Science of the Renaissance* (Bloomington: Indiana University Press, 1957).

Scoville, Warren C., and J. Clayburn La Force, eds. *The Middle Ages and the Renaissance* (Lexington, Mass.: D. C, Heath, 1969).

Scoville, Warren C., and J. Clayburn La Force, eds. *The Sixteenth and Seventeenth Centuries* (Lexington, Mass.: D. C. Heath, 1969).

Seagle, William. *The Quest for Law* (New York: Alfred A. Knopf, 1941).

Siebert, Fredrick S. *Freedom of the Press in England, 1476-1776* (Urbana, Ill.: University of Illinois Press, 1965).

Slavin, Arthur, ed. *The New Monarchies and Representative Assemblies* (Boston: D. C. Heath, 1964).

Small, Christopher. *The Printed Word* (Aberdeen, Scotland: Aberdeen University Press, 1982).

Smalley, Beryl, ed. *Trends in Medieval Political Thought* (New York: Barnes & Noble, 1965).

Smith, Adam. *An Inquiry into the Nature and Causes of the Wealth of Nations* (1776), Great Books of the Western World, Vol 39 (Chicago: The Encyclopedia Britannica, 1952).

Smith, Preserved. *A History of Modern Culture* (New York: Henry Holt & Co., 1930).

Sombart, Werner. *Modern Capitalism* (London: T. Fisher Unwin, 1908).

Sombart, Werner. *The Quintessence of Capitalism* (London: T. Fisher Unwin, 1915).

Spitz, Lewis W., and Richard W. Lyman, eds. *Major Crises in Western Civilization* (New York: Harcourt, Brace and World, 1965).

Steinberg, S. H. *Five Hundred Years of Printing* (New York: Penguin, 1974)

Stone, Laurence. *The Crisis of the Aristocracy* (New York: Oxford University Press, 1967).

Strauss, Leo. *Liberalism, Ancient and Modern* (New York: Basic Books, 1968).

Strayer, Joseph R. *On the Medieval Origins of the Modern State* (Princeton, N.J.: Princeton University Press, 1970).

Sweezy, Paul. *The Transition from Feudalism to Capitalism* (London: Unwin Brothers, 1978).

Swetz, Frank J. *Capitalism and Arithmetic* (LaSalle, Ill.: Open Court, 1987).

Taylor, R. Emmett. "Luca Pacioli," in A. C. Littleton, and B. S. Yarney, eds. *Studies in the History of Accounting* (Homewood, Ill.: Richard Irwin, 1956), 175-184.

Tawney, R. H. *Religion and the Rise of Capitalism* (New York: New American Library, 1954).

Thiel, Rudolph. *And There Was Light* (New York: Mentor Books, 1957).

Thomas, Hugh. *A History of the World* (New York: Harper & Row, 1979).

Tierney, Brian. *The Crisis of Church and State: 1050-1300* (Englewood, N.J.: Prentice-Hall, 1964).

Tilley, Charles, ed. *The Formation of National States in Western Europe* (Princeton, N.J.: Princeton University Press, 1975).

Tuchman, Barbara W. *A Distant Mirror* (New York: Ballantine Books, 1978).

Tuma, Elias H. *European Economic History* (New York: Harper & Row, 1971).

Tuveson, Ernest Lee. *Millenium and Utopia* (New York: Harper & Row, 1964).

Ullman, Walter. *Principles of Government and Politics in the Middle Ages* (New York: Barnes and Noble, 1961).

Vile, M. J. C. *Constitutionalism and the Separation of Powers* (Oxford, U.K.: Clarendon Press, 1967).

Vindograff, Paul. *Roman Law in Medieval Europe* (Oxford, U.K.: Oxford University Press, 1961).

Wallenstein, Immanuel. *The Modern World System* (New York: W. W. Norton & Co., 1984).

Watzlawick, Paul. *The Invented Reality* (New York: W. W. Norton & Co., 1984).

Weber, Max. "Professional Ethics," in Hans Gerth and C. Wright Mills, eds. *From Max Weber: Essays in Sociology,* (New York: Oxford University Press, 1946).

Weber, Max. *The Protestant Ethic and the Spirit of Capitalism* (New York: Charles Scribner's Sons, 1976).

Weber, Max. *Economy and Society* Volume I (Berkeley: University of California Press, 1978).

Weber, Max. *General Economic History* (New Brunswick, N.J.: Transaction Books, 1984).

Whitehead, Alfred N. *Science and the Modern World* (New York: Mentor Books, 1954).

Wilford, John Noble. *The Mapmakers* (New York: Alfred A. Knopf, 1981).

Williams, Raymond. *Keywords* (New York: Oxford University Press, 1985).

Wormuth, Francis D. *The Origins of Modern Constitutionalism* (New York: Harper & Row, 1949).

Wright, Louis B. *Middle Class Culture in Elizabethan England* (Chapel Hill, N.C.: University of North Carolina Press, 1935).

Yates, Frances. *The Rosicrucian Enlightment* (London: Routledge and Kegan Paul, 1972).
Zagorin, Perez. *Rebels and Rulers, 1500-1660* (Cambridge, U.K.: Cambridge University Press, 1982).

Index

About the Author

HENRY J. PERKINSON is a Professor in the Department of Culture and Commu-nication, New York University. He has written extensively on educational history and educational theory, including *Learning From Our Mistakes* (Greenwood, 1984). He has also published *Getting Better: Television and Moral Progress* (1991).

ISBN 0-89789-431-6

EAN

9 780897 894319

90000>

HARDCOVER BAR CODE